OKRs

T0292811

for
dummies®
A Wiley Brand

OKRs

by Paul R. Niven

OKRs For Dummies®

Published by: **John Wiley & Sons, Inc.,** 111 River Street, Hoboken, NJ 07030-5774, www.wiley.com

Copyright © 2023 by John Wiley & Sons, Inc., Hoboken, New Jersey

Published simultaneously in Canada

For general information on our other products and services, please contact our Customer Care Department within the U.S. at 877-762-2974, outside the U.S. at 317-572-3993, or fax 317-572-4002. For technical support, please visit https://hub.wiley.com/community/support/dummies.

Wiley publishes in a variety of print and electronic formats and by print-on-demand. Some material included with standard print versions of this book may not be included in e-books or in print-on-demand. If this book refers to media such as a CD or DVD that is not included in the version you purchased, you may download this material at http://booksupport.wiley.com. For more information about Wiley products, visit www.wiley.com.

Library of Congress Control Number: 2023941244

ISBN 978-1-394-18348-7 (pbk); ISBN 978-1-394-18350-0 (ebk); ISBN 978-1-394-18349-4 (ebk)

SKY10050765_071123

Contents at a Glance

Table of Contents

Introduction

Hi, I'm Paul, and it's my pleasure (really, I love this stuff) to serve as your guide to the brilliant world of objectives and key results, which I abbreviate as OKRs throughout the book.

I have no idea when you're reading this. It could be during an economic boom time with job growth accelerating, the stock market escalating to record highs and, to quote Herbert Hoover, a chicken in every pot (apologies to vegans). Or perhaps you've picked up this book in an anxious period of economic turmoil, with corporate profits plummeting, layoffs dominating the headlines, and nothing but instant ramen noodles in every pot (apologies to anyone who eats).

Although I can't predict the economic conditions that exist as you peruse these pages, one thing I can be sure of is that, regardless of the circumstances you're currently facing, staying committed to what matters most to execute your organization's strategy will be of paramount importance to you, your employees, and those you serve. To help you with that commitment, you have no better tool than OKRs to drive focus, alignment, and engagement.

Tools are powerful things when used with proper care and guidance. A chainsaw is a tool, but you wouldn't want to be in the vicinity of someone with no training wielding one in your backyard ("I'm pretty sure I can reach that branch . . . aaaah!!") Although poorly implemented OKRs are unlikely to end in catastrophe, if you don't develop the program with care, it can drain significant human and financial resources. A poor OKRs implementation can also deprive you of a critical differentiator in any economic environment: the laser-like focus on those things, and only those things, that will catapult your organization to the next level.

I wrote this book so that you don't squander that opportunity. *OKRs For Dummies* is your definitive guide on how to design and implement a successful and sustainable OKRs program, one that will provide lasting benefits in the form of intense focus, enhanced engagement, and top-to-bottom alignment.

About This Book

OKRs have become an immensely popular framework, relied on by organizations of all types and sizes, all around the globe, to effectively execute their strategies. There are many reasons for the system's rise to prominence, a primary one being its relative simplicity. When it comes to OKRs, you don't need a magnifying glass to follow the arrows, boxes, and concentric circles that make up some of today's elaborate and overly complex management solutions. OKRs contain just two concepts: objectives (what you aspire to do) and key results (how you'll demonstrate achieving that objective). But *simple* doesn't mean *simplistic*. Numerous potential pitfalls and challenges lurk about, ready, willing, and very able to stall your OKRs progress to a halt. That's why you need this book.

As with any popular management system, you'll find no shortage of OKRs advice floating around — some of it valuable, much of it questionable, and a portion of it downright wrong. I've been working in this field for close to three decades and have chronicled in these pages the lessons learned from working with hundreds of organizations of every conceivable industry, size, and location. Throughout these pages, I map the entire OKRs journey for you to ensure that regardless of whether this is your first attempt at implementing OKRs, or you've tried and struggled with the system in the past, you can find the right information at the right time to maximize your use of the OKRs framework.

To make the content as accessible as possible, I've divided the book into five parts.

>> **Part 1: Introducing OKRs:** In this part, I'll share the power of goal setting, provide a brief but illuminating peek into the history of OKRs, and give you an overview of the basics. Because a number of "wannabe" systems may be vying for your attention, I also compare OKRs with other frameworks and demonstrate the many benefits OKRs have to offer.

>> **Part 2: Preparing to create OKRs:** Whether you're sprinting from the starting line in a Formula 1 auto race, starting a new project at work, or embarking on OKRs, getting off to a good start is vital. The chapters of this part equip you with everything you need to begin your OKR effort on the right foot. You see how determining your "why" for OKRs is the very first thing you should do, outline critical OKRs roles for people within your organization to play, receive guidance on where and when to create OKRs, and discover insights on the raw materials used to develop OKRs.

>> **Part 3: Creating OKRs:** Let the games begin! This part of the book is devoted to providing you with all the tools, tips, and techniques (and maybe even some other things that start with *t*) that you need to create a powerful set of OKRs. This part begins with why training is critical to the success of OKRs and then walks you step by step through the process of creating OKRs, including

formulas, characteristics, and insider tips to write powerful OKRs. You'll probably have a few questions along the way, so I end this part with a set of frequently asked questions on OKRs.

>> **Part 4: Managing with OKRs:** You're not going to let all that hard work of creating OKRs go to waste, are you? Not a chance! In this part of the book, I pass along the information you need to ensure that you don't "set and forget" your OKRs. You discover how to run OKRs review meetings that maximize learning, learn how to score your OKRs, and find tips and advice on how to ensure that OKRs become ingrained in the culture of your organization.

>> **Part 5: The Part of Tens:** If you're looking for some quick inspiration, this is the place to go. The chapters in this part offer my top ten lists on common questions about OKRs that you're likely to field from your team, must-do items to ensure OKRs success, and tips for creating dynamic and impactful OKRs.

Foolish Assumptions

In writing this book, I'm assuming that you're a human being who cares enough to not simply go to ChatGPT or any other AI tool and type "Give me OKRs for my business." Or maybe you tried that and it didn't yield the results you were looking for, which led you to this book. If so, welcome!

I'm also assuming that you're implementing OKRs for an organization of some type, whether a for-profit company or a nonprofit or government organization. However, having said that, the advice in these pages can, for the most part, apply to individuals and even families.

Icons Used in This Book

Throughout the book, you find icons in the margins that highlight certain types of valuable information. Following are the icons you'll encounter, along with a brief description of each:

TIP

The Tip icon marks tips and shortcuts that you can use to make OKRs easier. They're practical in nature and include specific steps you can take to improve the OKRs process.

REMEMBER

The Remember icon marks ideas or information to always keep in mind.

WARNING

The Warning icon tells you to watch out! It marks important information that may save you headaches when planning for, creating, and managing with OKRs.

Beyond the Book

In addition to the abundance of information and guidance related to OKRs that this book provides, you get access to even more help and information online at Dummies.com. Check out this book's online Cheat Sheet by going to www.dummies.com and entering *OKRs For Dummies Cheat Sheet* in the search box.

Where to Go from Here

Where to go from here very much depends on where you are on your own OKRs journey, and of course your personal reading style. Whether I'm reading a novel, business book, or shampoo label, I'm the type of person who likes to read from end to end in sequential order. But not everyone is like that, and like all *For Dummies* books, this book is designed for you to be able to jump to the sections that are immediately relevant to you.

If your organization is new to OKRs, I recommend that you do read the chapters in order, because they guide you chronologically through the process. You may be tempted to skip over early chapters that cover topics such as the "why" of OKRs, or determining key OKRs roles, and get to the meat of writing objectives and key results, but you'll be better served in the long run if you take the time to understand and aptly apply all the principles covered in the early part of the book.

If you're reading this book because you've attempted OKRs in your organization but hit some hurdles, you may want to dive into specific chapters that address your pain points. But reading from the beginning can help to ensure that you don't make the same mistakes twice, and will therefore pay considerable dividends in the end. Whatever you choose, I hope you enjoy the book, and I would love to hear from you. You can reach me at paul@okrstraining.com. Good luck, and have fun!

1

Introducing OKRs

Objectives and key results (OKRs) is a powerful goal-setting and strategy-execution framework embraced by organizations of all types and sizes the world over. Its wide applicability and proven effectiveness are two of the many attractions of the system.

In this part, you discover the value of goal setting and dip briefly into stories of the people who brought the OKRs framework to life. You find out the core components of the OKRs system and compare it with other goal-setting tools. This part also details the many benefits OKRs have to offer an organization, including focus, alignment, engagement, accountability, visionary thinking, and the management of growth.

Chapter 1

Achieving Goals with OKRs

You've probably set many goals in your life. In fact, setting ambitious goals is a hallmark of the human experience. As a species, humans are ardent strivers. Whether the goal is to conquer space, cure debilitating diseases, or perform five push-ups every morning, people are constantly working toward desired results. In many ways, the pursuit of goals gives life meaning and purpose through the articulation of what you want, the planning to meet it, the execution of that plan, and, ultimately, the very rewarding experience of achieving your goals.

Organizations are avid goal setters as well, and OKRs is the framework of choice for successful goal setting around the globe in every possible type of organization: startups, nonprofits, government agencies at all levels, small- and medium-sized enterprises, and Fortune 500 conglomerates. *OKRs* stands for Objectives and Key Results, a simple and proven system for translating your aspirations into reality. OKRs provide the structure necessary to create goals that are crystal clear and will keep you laser-focused on concentrating your efforts on what matters most to deliver the outcomes you want.

This chapter introduces the OKRs framework in broad strokes. I talk about the value of goal setting, examine the components of OKRs, and briefly compare the OKRs approach to other goal-setting systems you may be familiar with.

OKRs Are a Goal-Setting System

As noted previously, humans are avid goal setters, constantly striving to improve our performance regardless of the field or endeavor we choose. Perhaps you have experience in setting goals in some of these domains:

>> **Family:** Partner, children, extended relations

>> **Physical:** Health, fitness, and wellbeing

>> **Work:** Career, volunteering

>> **Spiritual:** Religious or other spiritual affiliations

>> **Relationships:** With friends or others

>> **Hobbies:** Interests beyond work

Some of my goal-setting memories bring me a few chuckles, such as my goal of winning a "Best Screenplay" Academy Award after taking one screenwriting class. I even pictured Steven Spielberg having the honor of bestowing the Oscar on me. Hey, the more specific a goal the better, right? I talk a lot more about the value of specific goals in this book.

Your company probably has goals related to sales, customer satisfaction, retaining the best people, and a host of other elements designed to propel you past your competition. Whether people have their companies or themselves in mind, there is little doubt that setting goals is a very healthy and positive activity, one that everyone should pursue with rigor. Problems occur, however, in how people go about writing and constructing those goals. That's where many people, whether crafting goals for companies or themselves, get stopped in their tracks almost instantly.

It's common, for instance, to write goals that are vague and nebulous: "Get more fit." "Be the best company in our industry." They sound good — and few would argue with the merits of either of those examples — but the quality that specifically marks real success is missing from both. A number of other pitfalls loom out there in the goal world as well, such as

>> Setting unrealistic goals that you have no genuine chance to achieve

>> Having too many goals at one time

>> Failing to account for any assistance you'll require from others in achieving your goals

WARNING

Goal setting is perceived by most people to be a relatively easy notion, one that requires little in the way of preparation or study. I return to this topic throughout the book, but for now, just be aware that in order to effectively implement OKRs in your organization, you need to change the way people think about the process of goal setting.

Despite the potential challenges, goal setting is one of the most powerful things you can do in your organization (and your life). You just need a better, more reliable system, and that's where OKRs come in.

Sounds good, huh? Maybe if I'd have known about OKRs back when I was practicing that Oscar speech, I'd actually be clutching a gold statue now. The good news for me and you is that it's never too late to succeed, so go ahead and get started!

Seeing the Value in Goal Setting

The title of this section makes it sound as if I'm trying to convince you that goal setting has something to offer. But maybe you're already convinced and are a believer in the power of setting ambitious goals, with a lifetime of experience to back up that claim. If so, great — we have that in common. On the other hand, perhaps you do need to be convinced of goal setting's value. You may be reading this book because your boss placed a bulk order, handing out a copy to every manager in the company with strict orders to read it, and over the weekend no less. Maybe you came up in the school of hard knocks and don't believe in the woo-woo world of setting goals. Well, I've got news for you: Goal setting, especially with the use of OKRs, really works, and I'm going to win you over to this idea, I promise.

Back in 1968, when the Beatles song "Hey Jude" was dominating the airwaves, a little-known professor from the University of Maryland named Edwin Locke published a blockbuster article that would revolutionize the field of goal setting. "Toward a Theory of Task Motivation and Incentives," based on Locke's pioneering research, showed that setting goals led to higher performance in a wide range of domains. Whether it concerned office workers toiling in smoke-infested offices (it was the 1960s, remember), loggers felling timber in northern British Columbia, or truckers rolling along the blacktop, Locke demonstrated that setting goals improved performance in a statistically significant fashion. It wasn't uncommon, for example, to see performance gains of more than 200 percent! Forget free love and flower children; the real revolution of the 1960s was goal setting.

Locke went on to collaborate with a professor from the University of Toronto named Gary Latham. Together they conducted hundreds of studies on goal setting and reviewed hundreds more, all culminating in their 1990 magnum opus,

A Theory of Goal Setting & Task Performance. Although it's not a page turner a là Dan Brown or Agatha Christie, it's a revelation. Locke and Latham demonstrated unequivocally that setting goals led to improved results, and as an added bonus, working toward a goal boosted motivation.

Locke and Latham made clear that certain types of goals are better than others. Specific and challenging (but not too challenging) goals were critical to improved performance. Both of these characteristics (specificity and challenge) are vital to OKRs, as you discover in the chapters ahead. Speaking of OKRs, I think I've kept you waiting long enough, so let me know introduce the star of our show, "Objectives and Key Results."

FROM MBOs TO OKRs – THE PEOPLE AND IDEAS WHO BROUGHT OKRs TO LIFE

OKRs are not a business fad, but are based on, and have since improved upon, a number of common-sense, historically proven business principles. Here's a brief sketch of some major players in bringing the OKRs framework to where it is today:

Peter Drucker: Considered by many to be the greatest management thinker of the 20th century, Peter Drucker was a true management rock star and writer of more than 30 ground-breaking books. In his 1954 title *The Practice of Management,* he introduced the concept of Management by Objectives, or MBOs. Very briefly, the idea was that all employees need objectives that spell out what contributions are expected of them and their teams. Drucker tied the idea of having objectives to the company's strategy (goals of the business) and said they should be cross-functional in nature when necessary. Drucker had a huge and influential megaphone, and companies from coast to coast began creating MBOs.

Andy Grove: As CEO of Intel from 1987 to 1998, Andy Grove was behind much of the growth of Intel, leading the company from manufacturing memory chips to being the globe's foremost supplier of microprocessors. Grove had a keen interest in management and recognized the potential benefits of a well-constructed and implemented version of Drucker's MBO system. Grove boiled it all down to just two questions to be answered: 1) Where do I want to go (the objective); and 2) How will I pace myself to see if I am getting there? He eventually called the answer to the second question your *key result.* So when we use the acronym OKRs today, we owe it to Grove. Thank you, Andy!

Grove also experimented with the cadence of settings goals: Out were annual goals, and in were quarterly and sometimes even monthly objectives. Fast feedback and agility were critical in staying ahead of the competition, so OKRs had to be consistent with that goal. Grove also believed that the concept of stretch was vital with OKRs.

John Doerr: Doerr was a partner at the Silicon Valley venture capital firm Kleiner Perkins Caulfield & Byers when they made crafty bets on a number of startups destined to become household names. Ever heard of a little outfit called Amazon? Kleiner Perkins netted a tidy billion-dollar return on their investment of 8 million dollars. Doerr also worked at Intel in the early 1970s and was introduced to OKRs in a course conducted by Andy Grove. The framework became a key tool in Doerr's toolkit for working with entrepreneurs and their companies, including the company of our final two names. Doerr's popular book *Measure What Matters* offers a number of inspirational stories on the use OKRs from the likes of Bono and Bill Gates that you can use to demonstrate the power of OKRs. That book doesn't provide step-by-step guidance on creating OKRs (hence the need for this book).

Larry Page and Sergey Brin: These are the creators of Google. Like many startups that eventually rose to global prominence, they started humbly, in that most Silicon Valley of ways, in a garage. However, they were fortunate enough to move early board meetings to a much more sophisticated location — a small office above an ice cream shop in downtown Palo Alto. There, John Doerr introduced the duo to OKRs, and Google decided to use the system from day one. Brin, Page, and subsequent leaders have consistently pointed to the system as a guiding force in the company's never-ending upward trajectory.

Examining the Components of OKRs

The heading of this section sounds cold and clinical, but the fact of the matter is that goal setting, especially using OKRs, can be . . . wait for it . . . *fun.* As Locke and Latham (see the previous section) made clear, goal setting improves motivation, and who doesn't like the feeling of being motivated to pursue something you care about?

More good news is that OKRs is a terminology-light framework. The framework involves just three terms: *objectives, key,* and *results.* Actually, it's three words and a conjunction. Yes, I looked it up; "and" is a conjunction. But really it's just two terms: *objectives* and *key results,* more commonly referred to as OKRs. In the upcoming section, I define these terms and look at an example.

REMEMBER

Terminology matters in any kind of change initiative, including OKRs. You may find that some people will abbreviate the acronym to OKR, omitting the *s.* There is no agreed-upon acronym, but in this book I use the plural OKRs and suggest that you do the same. However, what's most important is that whatever acronym you choose, you use it consistently throughout your organization.

Defining an "objective"

An *objective* is a statement of a broad, qualitative goal designed to propel the organization forward in a desired direction. There are a few things to unpack in that simple definition. The first is the word *qualitative*. This word points to the fact that objectives are aspirational statements and don't include numbers. (As you find out shortly, numbers are the domain of the key results.)

The second word to put under the microscope is *organization*. You can, and most likely will, create OKRs at multiple levels of your organization: the company-level; business unit; department team; and so on. Thus, the word *organization* in the definition is meant to be generic.

Finally, the last part of the definition notes propelling the organization forward in a desired direction. This is the essence of an objective, which, to keep things nice and simple, asks, "What do we want to do?"

Writing a basic objective

Now comes one of the hardest tasks I faced in writing this book: providing the very first example of an objective. Why was it so difficult? Because no matter what field or industry I draw on, there is a risk that some people will think, "Oh, so OKRs are for only those types of companies." Or, "Well, that doesn't apply to me." Oy! Always remember that you can use OKRs anywhere and everywhere, from writing pop songs to ending malaria. So don't read too much into the following example.

Say that your company has a mobile app that has been crashing lately, much to users' chagrin. That's a strategic problem, and OKRs are very well-suited to help you overcome strategic challenges. So here's a possible objective:

Reduce mobile app crashes in order to increase user satisfaction.

Ta-da! You've just had your first exposure to an actual OKR-style objective. Exciting, isn't it? (Surely it's one of those "remember where you were moments" as you soak this in.) This example objective is a relatively simple statement, but it is composed of three parts that all effective objectives have in common:

>> **It starts with a verb.** By its very nature, an objective is action oriented, so you always want to begin one with a verb.

Your verb choice will depend on the objective you're striving toward, but every word matters in the objective, and the verb you choose sets the stage for the rest of the statement.

- **The verb is followed by a description of what you want to do.** In this case, you want to reduce mobile app crashes. Now, a lot of people would stop right there. "Reduce mobile app crashes" sounds like a worthy objective. But, and this is one of the most important *but*s in this entire book, there is a third component to a well-written objective, and that is . . .

- **The "in order to" or "so that."** This final part captures the business impact of the first two components of the objective. Why is it important to reduce mobile app crashes? Because you believe that it will lead to increased user satisfaction. That final component is the most important, because it makes clear the strategic relevance of the objective: why it matters. I'll bet you could stop reading right now and quickly brainstorm a dozen things you'd like to get done in the next few months. Doing that is relatively easy, but when you add that third component of *why* the objective is strategically important now, you quickly recognize what really matters, and which objectives are the critical ones to pursue.

TIP

Share this formula for writing an objective with your team:

Verb + what you want to do + in order to / so that (business impact)

Some people bristle at formulas and a paint-by-number approach to objective creation, but goal setting is not a natural muscle for most people. They need all the help they can get in writing effective OKRs, especially in the beginning. Providing a formula or template simply gives people a leg up on the task without inhibiting their creativity in any way. After all, the formula doesn't dictate what verb to use, or why their objective is important. It simply provides a path for creating objectives that will be technically sound and add value.

Defining a key result

Now you can turn your attention to key results. A *key result* is a quantitative statement that measures the achievement of a given objective. The key results answer the question, "How will you know you've achieved the objective?" Of course, the most important word in the definition of "key result" is *quantitative*. A key result should consist of raw numbers, dollar amounts, percentages, or even dates, which you will use in the case of milestone key results.

Writing key results

In the earlier "Writing a basic objective" section, the example objective was "Reduce mobile app crashes in order to increase user satisfaction." Now you have to decide what set of key results will demonstrate the achievement of that objective. You may want to try these:

1. Study app crashes and determine the three most common causes by May 15th.

2. Develop fixes and update the app by June 1st.

3. Decrease the number of mobile app crashes from 5 to 1.

4. Increase app store rating from 4.2 to 4.8.

A question I get frequently is, "How many key results should we have for each objective?" Although there is no absolute right or wrong answer to the question, a good rule of thumb (as rules of thumb go) is three to five. But beyond the number, you should think in terms of telling a story with your key results. By that I mean that the key results should work together in a coordinated way to demonstrate the success of the objective.

Continuing with the example objective, if you're going to reduce mobile app crashes, you first need to find out why the app is crashing by determining the common causes. That topic provides a good opening "chapter" in your story of success for this objective. This key result is a *milestone*, which is binary – either you achieve it or you don't. Milestones are like hurdles that you need to get over in order to measure the ultimate business impact outlined in the objective.

REMEMBER

A milestone key result always includes a date — how quickly you believe you can achieve the milestone without sacrificing quality.

After studying the reasons for the crashes, your next key result is devoted to developing fixes and updating the app. Think again of your story: First you study the causes, and then you develop fixes. This, too, is a milestone key result.

Now things get interesting. Your third key result measures the reduction of mobile app crashes from five to one. This is a *metric key result* because it has numbers. This key result also slots nicely into your story. You've studied the crashes, applied a fix, and your hypothesis is that by doing so, you'll see a reduction in app crashes.

REMEMBER

Hypothesis is a critical word in the context of OKRs, and in measurement in general. Whenever you measure anything, you're making your best guess that it is related to your desired outcome.

The final key result, "Increase app store rating from 4.2 to 4.8," is also a metric, again because it has numbers. It also holds the distinction of being the most important of the example's key results because it directly measures the business impact of increasing users' satisfaction that was identified in the objective. Therefore, it's a great and logical ending to a strategic story.

I strongly encourage you to use the story concept when constructing your set of key results. Begin with the end in mind by identifying your business impact key result and then work backward, asking what drives, or leads to, that key result. Doing so will help you craft a comprehensive and cohesive set of key results.

Well, that pretty much sums up OKRs. It has been a pleasure serving as your guide; I hope you enjoyed reading the book, and please do leave a review on Amazon . . . Hold on. Wait a minute — there is definitely a lot more to say about OKRs. It's a framework that is — cliché alert — simple but not simplistic. But hey, I can't give away all the secrets in Chapter 1.

Read on to get the whole fun and exciting story of how to make OKRs work for your organization.

Comparing OKRs to Other Goal-Setting Systems

OKRs aren't the only game in town when it comes to organizational goal-setting frameworks. Over the years, a host of systems have been applied by companies anxious to reap the benefits of setting and meeting audacious goals. Some are still used today; many have faded into the history books; and still others have disappeared without a trace. In the sections that follow, I compare and contrast OKRs to some of the more popular frameworks you may have used in the past, or indeed may be using now. Spoiler alert: I show you how OKRs tops them all.

OKRs versus SMART goals

If you'll pardon the mixed metaphors, I want to jump right into the deep end and address the elephant in the room: aren't OKRs just another way of writing SMART goals? On the surface, this may seem to be the case, but in reality, no, not at all. The acronym SMART, and the associated method of goal setting, can be attributed to a 1981 paper by consultant George T. Doran. In the years since that time, SMART goals have maintained a consistent popularity in management circles. Typically, the letters stand for Specific, Measurable, Attainable, Relevant, and Time-bound. I say "typically" because over the years, various definitions have been applied to some of the SMART letters. For example, the R can represent results-based, realistic, or reasonable. That's one of the troubles with SMART: Nobody is exactly sure what it stands for.

At first glance, a well-written OKR seems to have much in common with a SMART goal. For example, in OKRs, both objectives and key results must be specific in order to drive the actions necessary for achievement. Each of the other elements of SMART are always present with OKRs as well. But to say that a SMART goal is the same as an OKR is off base. SMART goals — and this is an important distinction — don't include accompanying objectives, so there is no context for the goal; you don't know why you're pursuing it.

Another significant difference between the two is one of scope. SMART is a stand-alone idea that has no accompanying structure. In the end, that makes it more a helpful rule of thumb than a rigorous strategy-execution system. OKRs, on the other hand, include a set of underlying management practices that are absent from SMART goals. Robust OKRs systems are governed by a carefully crafted management review cadence, one that recognizes the operating reality of the organization and constantly challenges the status quo by focusing on stretch targets.

OKRs versus KPIs

KPI stands for *Key Performance Indicator*. The term is very popular (you'll even find a *For Dummies* book on the topic), but unfortunately, it is not used in a consistent manner across all organizations, which can lead to confusion. Generally, however, most organizations use KPIs to monitor operational performance: elements that must be measured quickly and frequently. For example, it's very common for an organization to monitor the "uptime" of its core systems. KPIs such as uptime tend to last forever and don't change. You always want to monitor how available your core systems are to your users. OKRs, on the other hand, focus on demonstrating business value and strategic impact. OKRs will change in recognition of your strategy and core challenges.

You can — and most organizations will — use both KPIs and OKRs. Anything tactical requiring frequent monitoring will be the basis of a KPI, whereas more strategic endeavors will require OKRs. Table 1-1 outlines some of the other differences between the two systems.

OKRs versus 4DX

4DX stands for "The 4 Disciplines of Execution." As with SMART goals, OKRs and 4DX share a number of elements. Both demand a focus on what truly matters for organizational success — the Wildly Important Goal, or WIG, in 4DX, and the Objective and Key Results in OKRs. Both systems suggest the use of both lag and lead measures (key results, in OKRs parlance). A method of easily grasping progress is also a shared characteristic. Finally, both frameworks posit that regular reviews are crucial to progress, momentum, and execution.

TABLE 1-1   ## Comparing and Contrasting OKRs and KPIs

Distinguishing Factor	OKRs	KPIs
Purpose	Strategic – focus, alignment, engagement, visionary thinking	Tactical – evaluation of business activities
Duration	Typically quarterly or by trimesters	Annual with frequent updates
Defined in the context of an objective	Yes, by definition	No
Focused on maintenance, health metrics	Rarely	Often
Intended to increase alignment among teams	Often	Rarely
Linked to incentive compensation	Rarely	Often
Originates "bottoms up" from teams and individuals	Often	Rarely
Change frequently	Yes (by selected cadence)	No

The biggest difference between the two systems is cadence. When you set a WIG, you do so for the entire year; for example, a WIG may be "Increase revenue from $20 million to $40 million by December 31st." For that WIG, you create lag and lead measures that you monitor throughout the year. OKRs may also be set annually, but they are also (commonly) set quarterly or by trimester. Although the annual OKRs will not change during the year, the quarterly OKRs are adjusted to reflect the strategic context faced by the organization. I believe that these strategic adjustments are an advantage of the OKRs method. Most pundits would agree (and statistics confirm) that competition in virtually all industries is rapidly increasing, which has the tendency to reduce the usable life of a strategy. Things can change so quickly nowadays that what seemed like yesterday's urgent priorities are no longer on our radar today. OKRs, with their focus on a shorter cadence, allow organizations to rapidly respond to changes in their environment, making strategy execution (and strategy itself) more dynamic, agile, and emergent.

OKRs versus BSC

The Balanced Scorecard (BSC) is a performance management and strategy execution framework developed by Robert Kaplan and David Norton in the early 1990s. I have extensive experience with the system; a company I worked with at the time was an early adopter of the BSC and used it to great success.

The BSC challenges organizations to create objectives and measures in four distinct, yet related, perspectives of performance:

>> **Financial:** This realm typically encompasses growth, profitability, asset utilization, and shareholder value.

>> **Customer:** The focus here is on acquiring, satisfying, and retaining targeted customers with a unique value proposition.

>> **Internal processes:** These are the activities and processes that drive value for customers and may include operations, innovation, manufacturing, branding, and more.

>> **Employee learning and growth:** This area includes intangibles such as employee knowledge and culture that drive results.

As with the other systems discussed previously, OKRs and the BSC share some common DNA. Both include objectives accompanied by measurements, called *key results* in the OKRs framework. There are two significant differences between the systems.

The first difference is cadence. As with 4DX, most BSC practitioners will set annual objectives and measures. This is a potential shortcoming with BSC because it introduces the possibility of an insidious enemy of good measurement: the set-it-and-forget-it mentality. Objectives and measures that seemed inspiring and exciting in January have lost their luster and are disregarded by October. In contrast to BSC objectives and measurements, OKRs are created more frequently throughout the year, providing agility and allowing for flexibility based on your strategic circumstances.

Another possible pitfall of the BSC is the necessity of employing the four-perspective model throughout the organization. For lower-level teams in a company, those perspectives can become more difficult to populate with meaningful objectives and measures because such teams often focus on a small and discrete set of outcomes. For these groups, creating objectives and measures in all four perspectives can sometimes degrade to a tick-the-box exercise in which they put forward items with very little actual value in terms of moving the business forward.

Conversely, you create OKRs by determining what's most strategically important right now. It could be a customer challenge, a supply-chain opportunity, or a recruiting drive. You have no need to create excess objectives and measures. Rather, the focus is on what's important right now, allowing teams to isolate and execute effectively.

Chapter **2**

The Benefits of OKRs

I n Chapter 1, I joke that this book may have been given to you by your boss with the strict "suggestion" that you read it right away, even though you're not a believer in the power of goals. But required reading from the boss is without a doubt a real thing, as I've heard from countless clients over the years. Here's a typical exchange:

> Me: How did you hear about OKRs?

> Prospective client: Our CEO made us . . . (awkward pause) . . . we all read a book about OKRs . . .

If you've read the first chapter, I hope you now recognize the value OKRs can bring to your organization, but you're probably still a bit concerned about the costs of implementing the program. After all, you and your team are swamped already with fires to fight, pressing issues to deal with, figuring out who left the week-old tuna sandwich in the fridge, and a million other problems. Why take on something else now? The answer is simple: because OKRs offer a number of significant and proven benefits to both you and your organization.

In this chapter, I pull back the curtain on some of those many benefits, both for your company overall and for your associates. You discover how OKRs can help you crack the code of executing strategy, why OKRs drive passion and commitment from your teams, and how the system provides what may be the most important attribute of success for any modern organization: unrelenting focus.

REMEMBER

OKRs can be considered a change initiative, and selling the need for any change program is critical to its eventual success. Use the benefits in this chapter to help craft your change story.

Overcoming Common Organizational Challenges with OKRs

A mountain of evidence supports the idea that we all think we're different, and in most cases better, than the average person. One of my favorite illustrations of this is the fact that three-quarters of people say they're better than average drivers. Men in particular hold this view, with a full eight of ten noting their superiority. Spending five minutes on any road in the world will disprove that statistic. And, of course, mathematically we can't all be better than average, but that doesn't stop us from thinking that we, the royal *we*, are different. So it goes with organizations. I've lost count of how many times I've been told by a company executive, within the first five minutes of meeting them, how different they are.

It's partially true that, when it comes to the organizational world, plenty of differences exist — in industry types, locations, cultures, and the list goes on and on. But after 25-plus years in the trenches of consulting, I've learned there is more that unites us as organizations than divides us. In the following sections, I outline three challenges that all organizations face (yes, even your different, above-average company):

>> Executing your strategy

>> Sustaining growth

>> Dealing with disruption

Read on for details on these challenges and how OKRs can help overcome each one.

Acknowledging the difficulty of executing strategy

Would you like some proof that executing strategy is a problem most organizations struggle with and need help in overcoming? How's this: The book *Execution*, by Ram Charan and Larry Bossidy, spent 150 weeks on the *New York Times* bestseller list in the early 2010s. Execution has always been an enormous challenge for organizations. If Bossidy and Charan had been around in 1450 and were able to convince Gutenberg to have their ideas be the first thing churning out of his printing press, they probably would have had a hit on their hands even way back then.

The problem of putting your strategy into play continues today. In one recent survey, more than 400 global executives chose execution as the biggest challenge facing leaders around the world — and they had more than 80 potential challenges to choose from!

Before I talk about why execution is so difficult, I want to back up and consider a more fundamental question: What do the numbers say? In other words, what percentage of organizations actually do effectively execute their strategy? What's your guess? Whatever you said, it was probably too high. Estimates of execution vary, but on the high end, just 25 to 35 percent seem able to turn their strategy into reality. At the low end of estimates, the figure is a dismal ten percent. Given the practically incalculable number of hours organizations spend crafting strategy, that's a lot of value being left on the table.

The two main causes of execution failure

Execution is one of those hard-to-get-your-arms-around problems because in reality, any number of things can derail it, from a poorly crafted strategy itself to organizational inertia to executive politics and game playing, all of which can lead to misaligned people and projects. There are, however, two fundamental issues that appear to consistently disrupt execution efforts: 1) lack of strategic understanding, and 2) an inability or unwillingness to measure the execution of the strategy. Fortunately, OKRs can help with both.

A frequent cause of execution unraveling is the simple fact that many people in the organization don't understand the company's strategy, and I think you'd agree that it's pretty difficult to execute something you don't understand. Here are some statistics to back up these assertions:

>> Just 55 percent of middle managers can name even one of their company's top five priorities (see "Why Strategy Execution Unravels — and What to Do About it," by Donald Sull et al., Harvard Business Review, March 2015).

>> Sixty-seven percent of employees don't understand their role when new initiatives are launched (see "The 5 Pillars of Strategy Execution" at https://www.gartner.com/smarterwithgartner/the-five-pillars-of-strategy-execution).

>> Eighty percent of senior executives say their strategy isn't well understood (see *Strategy That Works,* by Paul Leinwand and Cesare R. Mainardi, 2016).

>> Seventy-four percent of managers say that the rotting tuna sandwich left in the fridge is the biggest strategic problem they face.

Okay, I made that last one up, but if we really did conduct a poll, who knows?

Effective OKRs should align with your company's strategy and, therefore, a prerequisite of the process is ensuring that you've clearly and consistently communicated your strategy from top to bottom. Only then can you expect teams to create aligned OKRs that signal their unique contribution. For many companies, the creation of strategy is a "black box" type of activity, shrouded in mystery, conducted by a privileged few, and rarely communicated beyond the C-Suite.

OKRs demand that the strategy be explained and made as explicit as possible so that companies can use their strategy as the raw material to create OKRs. This effort goes beyond producing a few glitzy PowerPoint slides to flash across a giant screen for ten seconds at your next Town Hall. It means having real conversations, helping people understand the company's overall strategy, and allowing them to determine their role in its execution.

Your organization will be rewarded with focused OKRs that help you overcome the feeble execution numbers I presented earlier if it does the following:

>> Takes the time and effort to share their strategy

>> Stays open to the tough questions it may engender

>> Provides the guiding rationale for its existence

TIP

Don't just have executives read bullets on a PowerPoint slide to share your strategy with employees. Whether in person or virtually, break your teams into small groups and challenge them to poke holes in the strategy you've created, contemplate competitors' responses, and outline how they can contribute.

Measurement is crucial

A second culprit in the battle of execution is the inability or unwillingness of most organizations to effectively measure the distinct elements of their strategy. A robust strategic plan frequently outlines the products and services you intend to sell, the value proposition you're putting forth to your target markets, unique competencies your people possess, and more. All these encompass a hypothesis — your best guess based on available information of what it will take to succeed in your competitive arena.

Next you have to test those assumptions through measurement, and many companies fail to do so. Rather than track customer engagement, innovation, the effectiveness of new selling channels, and a host of other attributes of their strategy they fall back on the same tired metrics that tend to be almost exclusively financial in nature.

"You can't manage what you can't measure" is a wise adage I heard early in my career. If you don't measure the elements of your strategy, you're unable to make course corrections, adjust on the fly, and shift directions based on what's happening in the world. Instead, you're stuck reading out the same boring financial statement every month, quarter, or year. As noted previously, effective OKRs, which are basically measures of success, are always derived from the strategy of the organization. Thus, by embarking on an OKRs program, you're instantly combating one of the deadliest forms of execution failure.

A commitment to measuring the elements of your strategy allows your organization to

>> Make course corrections

>> Adjust on the fly

>> Shift directions based on what's happening in the world

Recognizing the challenge of sustaining growth

In the section "Acknowledging the difficulty of executing strategy," earlier in this chapter, I talk about some of the elements comprising most strategic plans: products and services you'll focus on selling; the value proposition you're putting forth to your target markets; unique competencies possessed by your people; and more. Let me introduce another item often featured in strategies: growth. In what will probably be the least surprising and most obvious statistic I cite in this entire book, an estimated 90 percent of strategic plans have some reference to growth. Again, such references aren't surprising because every organization in the world, from Tesla to Google to the neighborhood kids' lemonade stand, wants to grow. It's pretty much an unquestioned imperative of organizational life: grow or die.

But here's the thing: Growing revenue and profits year over year is hard, and getting harder all the time. Of course, there are people who study these exciting facts of organizational life, and in one such study of 4,793 companies (I love the specificity of that number of companies!), the researchers found that just eight percent grew their revenues by at least five percent year after year, and fewer still consistently grew their profits (see "How the Growth Outliers Do It," by Rita Gunther McGrath, *Harvard Business Review*, 2012). I hope the kids running the lemonade stand have a backup plan.

So is it a lack of opportunities that inhibits growth? Not according to most senior executives, who see opportunities in their home markets as well as abroad. The world is shrinking, after all, and commerce is truly a global game.

What tends to snare growth comes down to two broad categories:

» Internal factors

» A steady stream of enticing opportunities

The slow drip of internal issues

When I speak of internal factors that stifle growth, I'm talking about issues that arise within the four walls of the organization, some of which can grow slowly and then suddenly turn into enormous problems, sort of like that leak you're ignoring in your shower faucet. Trust me, as one speaking from wet and ultimately expensive experience: You need to get a wrench and fix it now.

The organizational equivalent of a slow drip can sometimes take the form of a changing culture. When you're a scrappy startup or small business, you're up for throwing caution to the wind and taking risks that may or may not pay off, but as the company grows and the stakes get higher, it's a lot more difficult to roll the dice on chancy experiments. Before you know it, your creative and innovative culture has transformed into a stifling bureaucracy, where three signatures are required for a bulk order of paper towels from Costco.

But growth-oriented companies do experiment and innovate; that's how they stay one step ahead of their competition.

Opportunities! So many opportunities!

The other broad category of challenge that many organizations face as they grow is a never-ending stream of exciting opportunities that present themselves with consistent regularity. I see this with my own business. As OKRs have gained prominence as a proven goal-setting and execution framework, more and more offers get dangled in front of me: podcasts, partnerships, promotions, and lots of other enticing opportunities, even some that don't start with the letter p.

Opportunities are great; the challenge is in separating the signal from the noise and determining which opportunities align with your core purpose and strategy. In other words, the challenge is to maintain your focus on what matters most. Enter OKRs, a system specifically designed to help you do the following:

» Stay the course

» Avoid distractions

» Emphasize what matters most, right now

OKRs are not meant to help you keep track of your mundane, business-as-usual activities; rather, they help you frame your desired future by steadying your aim on what will deliver the biggest bang for your strategic buck.

REMEMBER

Even if you're fortunate enough to be in a high-growth industry and are currently riding a wave of growth in your company, things can change quickly and dramatically. Monitor both the hard (financial) indicators and the soft stuff (such as cultural transformations) to keep the pedal down on growth.

Working with the threat of disruption

A disruption is a break or interruption in the normal course of some activity, and although it sounds like a negative, in our personal lives it can be a blessing. Have you ever tried to undergo a major change, perhaps by ending a toxic relationship, making a major career pivot, or changing your diet in the hopes of improving your health and longevity? These are difficult endeavors, for sure, and we need all the help we can get in achieving them. Surprisingly perhaps, disruption can help. Psychologists found in one study that people who moved homes — a major disruption for most of us — were almost three times as likely to be successful at making a major change (see *How to Change*, by Katy Milkman). It's something to keep in mind as you're scrolling Zillow or Realtor.com: The change may do you good.

In the business world, however, disruption is one of those words that strikes fear in the hearts of executives, who tend to favor the status quo whenever possible. The corporate version of disruption is represented by the process in which a smaller company, often with fewer resources, moves upmarket to challenge larger, incumbent businesses, frequently employing better technology and a lower cost structure. Hesitant to stop the gravy train of higher profit margins, the larger companies are often slow to react, thereby upping the odds that they will be disrupted.

Disruption is a trendy concept these days (think: Uber turning the taxi industry upside down, even though it has been around forever). The transistor radio, introduced in the 1950s, shook up the radio market that was previously dominated by large, expensive systems considered to be pieces of furniture in the homes of people who had the time and money to lounge and listen. In the future, 3D printing will likely disrupt the market for shipping goods around the world because manufacturers can now custom fabricate and print parts on-site.

Using OKRs doesn't completely safeguard your industry from being a disruption target, but the thoughtful use of an OKRs program can ensure that you remain vigilant to the clues that would indicate disruption may be on the horizon. "Program" is the key word in the previous sentence. In this case, it refers to OKRs in a broader sense, beyond the critical function of strategic measurement.

TIP

Organizations that excel with OKRs make the framework the centerpiece of an operating model, one that treats every OKRs cycle as a mini strategic planning exercise in which you scan your environment looking for trends and signals of change. You can then use those signposts to create OKRs that inoculate you from the possible effects of disruptive actors in your space.

Understanding How Your People Will Benefit from OKRs

Avoiding the perils of disruption while fueling growth and driving execution are all wonderful benefits you can achieve with OKRs, but what about your people, the ones making the sales calls, inventing your next breakthrough product, answering customer inquiries, and all the rest. What's in it for them?

As it turns out, plenty! OKRs help the people in your organization

>> Focus on what matters most

>> Maintain alignment with the organization's goals, no matter their level

>> Feel more engaged

>> Increase their sense of accountability

>> Nurture visionary thinking

>> Avoid confusion because they can easily understand and use the system

The cherry on top is that your benefits are twofold: OKRs not only drive employee success, engagement, and motivation, but in turn provide dividends to your company as well. There is a lot to unpack here, as the saying goes, so read on to flesh out this list of benefits to the people who comprise your organization.

Focusing on what matters most

No self-respecting business book author would ever complete a manuscript without at least one Abraham Lincoln story to illustrate a key point. So, I'm anteing up right now with an Honest Abe tale that shines a brilliant light on the topic of focus.

As told by Ryan Holiday in his book *Stillness Is the Key,* early in the American Civil War, Lincoln was besieged by his generals with competing plans for how to secure victory in the bloody internecine battle of the States. Confusion reigned and hope was in short supply. Most felt the war could be won only by enormous battles in the nation's biggest cities like Richmond, New Orleans, and maybe even Washington, D.C., itself. Lincoln considered the counsel of these battle-scarred veterans and then laid out a map across a large table and pointed decisively to Vicksburg, Mississippi, a fortified town high on the bluffs of the Mississippi river.

Although the city was held by rebel troops, Lincoln realized that Vicksburg not only held control of the mighty Mississippi but also connected other bodies of water, as well as rail lines that supplied Confederate armies throughout the South. "Vicksburg is the key," he told the room of assembled generals, and he turned out to be right. It took a number of years, but Lincoln's focus on Vicksburg ultimately split the South in two and gained the North control of the Mississippi River. Every important victory from that point forward was made possible by Vicksburg. That's the power of focus.

Fortunately for most of us, the stakes at work aren't life and death, but that doesn't mean that focus isn't critical in our day-to-day lives as well. One thing we all have in common with the dilemma faced by President Lincoln is an avalanche of choices: how to spend each day; what projects to work on; where to place your attention. You may think, "Well, if I just work hard, work fast, I can get it all done." Unfortunately, you can't; there simply aren't enough hours in the day. I read recently that the average professional in America has in excess of 40 hours of unfinished work on their desk at any given moment.

OKRs help you cut through the fog, the vortex, the whirlwind — pick your metaphor — by forcing you to identify what matters most right now in order to demonstrate your contribution to the organization's success. As you discover later in the book, with OKRs, less is more, meaning that you isolate the critical areas you need to focus on to succeed.

REMEMBER
OKRs aren't a glorified billboard upon which you showcase everything you've been hired to do. On the contrary, the system is designed to help you think strategically, like President Lincoln, about the few things that deliver the biggest impact.

Aligning from top to bottom and beyond

In my training workshops with clients, I often show a picture of a boat, helmed by a team rowing in perfect harmony as they glide seemingly effortlessly across a sparkling lake. It's a fairly heavy-handed and obvious metaphor to introduce the topic I'm about to discuss, but it's always effective. I ask the group, "Is your organization like this? Are all your 'oars' in the water at the same time?" In 25-plus years of consulting, only once have I had a group say, "Yes, that's us. We enjoy perfect alignment." At which point they got up, joined hands, sang *Kumbaya*, and proceeded outdoors to roast marshmallows on an impromptu firepit in the parking lot.

No, sadly, that corporate fairy tale is not true. Not once in my experience has a group agreed that the picture is a fair representation of their situation.

Alignment is perhaps the most prized, yet most elusive, state dreamed of by corporate executives and employees alike. No one wants to work at cross-purposes, having your efforts undermined whether unintentionally or maliciously by another group, and seeing execution thwarted as a result. Misalignment is a form of friction that every organization would be happy to do without, and OKRs can go a long way in eliminating this toxin from your corporate veins. The system achieves this little miracle in two ways: by promoting both vertical and horizontal alignment.

Vertical alignment represents the process through which all OKRs are vetted in the context of the company's overall strategy. Basically, it forces the question: Will the OKR, if achieved, help the company move one step closer to the execution of its strategy?

Horizontal alignment refers to the process of identifying and managing mutual dependencies between different departments or teams, with one team relying on the support or collaboration of another team to achieve its own OKRs. This type of alignment emphasizes the coordination and cooperation required across departments to promote collective success.

Thinking vertically

As I emphasize earlier in the chapter, OKRs aren't a dumping ground to catalog every activity a team undertakes. Instead, they challenge you to determine the most important thing, or small number of things, you can be working on right now to mark your contribution to success. As teams draft OKRs and share them with leadership through a standard review process, the conversation naturally shifts to the strategic relevance of what they've created. These dialogs are powerful opportunities to gauge understanding of strategy (remember how little of that understanding exists) and ensure that all teams write OKRs that, when aggregated collectively across the company, will drive execution of strategy.

TIP

When creating OKRs, whether you use a software system, Google Sheets, Excel, or the back of a napkin, be sure to include fields for teams to identify alignment, both vertical and horizontal. For vertical alignment, you should clearly communicate how the chosen OKR aligns with the organization's overall goals. For horizontal alignment, it's important to identify any dependencies on other departments necessary to achieve your OKR.

The silo scourge

What's the nastiest, most flinch-inducing word you can use at your next company meeting, one sure to get the rapid attention of even the most checked-out member of your team? To find it, you'll have to go a lot farther in the alphabet than you may expect, but when you get to *s*, you can stop. The word is *silo*. Companies hate silos and have been waging war with them, often with little to show for their efforts, for as long as organizational entities have existed.

I'm sure you don't need to be reminded of what a silo is, but in case your company actually does sing *Kumbaya* and roast marshmallows in the parking lot in joyous celebration of your harmony, I'll go ahead and define the term. Silos represent groups or teams with specific expertise that are separated by department, location, or specialty. They often unwittingly pursue department goals rather than contribute to overall company aspirations.

Silos have always been a problem, but the long shadow cast by their negative impact has grown in recent decades as cross-functional work has become increasingly critical in achieving overall ends. It's a simple fact: Work in modern organizations relies on the coordination of teams. Think, for example, of Sales and Marketing, or Product and Engineering. OKRs can't eliminate silos with one swipe of a magic wand, but when a certain practice is followed with rigor and discipline, the framework can significantly reduce the problem.

Rooting out dependencies

The simple practice I refer to in the previous sentence is identifying and managing dependencies. As teams create OKRs, in addition to identifying the vertical alignment discussed previously, they must determine whose help in the organization they need to achieve the OKR, and what specific form that help needs to take.

That's the identification part. Next, the team creating OKRs meets with the dependent team and clearly articulates the assistance they require, making their request as specific as possible: the number of hours required, the tasks necessary for completion of the OKR, and so on. Clarifying these issues fosters a dialog among the teams, and one of two things can happen:

>> The dependent team can agree to provide the requested assistance, in which case the two teams have a shared OKR.

>> The dependent team may suggest that given their current responsibilities, they just don't have the bandwidth to provide the help needed.

In the latter case, the issue is escalated to leadership, whose job it is to sort things out and decide what will take place. Perhaps the dependent team will be forced to provide the requested assistance, or their own OKRs will be determined to be of sufficient importance that they aren't required to play ball with the other team. Either way, transparency is increased, priority and resource allocation decisions have been made, and overall alignment is enhanced.

Increasing engagement

Immediately stop daydreaming, sharpen your focus, and prepare to be invigorated. Do I have your attention? Apparently *invigorated, sharp,* and *immediately* are attention-grabbing words, and I'm hoping to take hold of your full cognitive capacity because I know you could be tempted to skim this section, or skip it entirely. Employee engagement seems to be a squishy concept at best, one far removed from actual business success, and what could it possibly have to do with OKRs, right?

First, I want to put to bed the notion that engagement doesn't align with overall success. One study of more than 750 companies found that one of the most effective levers you can pull to increase total shareholder return is to invest in employee engagement. Now do I have your attention?

Next, to wrestle with the "squishy" problem, what is engagement, anyway? Well, what it's not is simply employee satisfaction or happiness. Droves of people attest to being satisfied and relatively happy in their jobs, but that's a far cry from being engaged. When I work with clients and ask them to describe the concept of employee engagement, here are some of the words and phrases frequently offered:

Committed	Passionate
Proactive	Connected
Risk-taking	Caring

Interestingly, that list of suggestions is consistent across industries, geographies, and cultures, and correctly taps into the spirit of engagement, which is best represented as an emotional commitment to the company and its customers. Engaged employees really do go the extra mile in seeing things through for the ultimate benefit of their colleagues and, eventually, the firm's customers.

The Gallup organization has been surveying employees globally for decades and thus has millions of data points to string together when creating aggregate engagement data, which sadly is not overly positive. Although the numbers swing gently from year to year, overall they're quite stubborn:

>> About 20 percent of the global workforce are highly engaged

>> Some 50 to 60 percent are in the vast middle

>> About 20 percent are actively disengaged

That last cohort is the dangerous one for productivity and morale. Researchers estimate that disengaged employees cost the U.S. economy (for example) about 500 billion dollars in lost productivity annually. Apparently, checked-out employees are more interested in doom-scrolling Twitter and checking their Instagram feeds on the company's dime than in taking care of customers.

My flag is firmly planted in the Theory Y notion of human motivation, which suggests that most people are internally motivated and, at their core, want to engage through a meaningful contribution — not just collect a paycheck. Surveys consistently back that point up, with a majority of employees, especially younger groups, voicing their desire to make a difference in their work.

Ah, the best laid plans. We're all bright-eyed and bushy-tailed when we start our careers, or join a new company, but over time, like an '83 Chevy left outside for too many winters, we corrode. But in most cases, it's not our core values that let us down.

Employees who don't understand the company's strategy and don't see how they fit in can quickly become disillusioned, confused over priorities, and skeptical about their opportunities to contribute. These issues can drive a lack of focus in their work, which can be compounded by alignment problems across the enterprise. Before long, a once-bright, ambitious, about-to-set-the-world-on-fire employee has decided that sleepwalking through the workday is a better idea. What a waste.

As teams create OKRs and share them with leadership, a conversation ensues on strategy and the strategic relevance of chosen OKRs. These conversations offer tremendous potential to drive employee engagement through, yes, engaging your associates in the process. Writing an effective OKR relies heavily on understanding the company's strategy, and thus every OKR drafting session provides an opportunity to assess peoples' knowledge of the strategy, their commitment to it, and their belief that they can contribute. The best leaders grasp the reins of this opportunity, fostering a two-way dialogue, answering questions, filling in knowledge gaps, and encouraging teams and individuals to showcase their piece of the puzzle that is strategy execution.

REMEMBER

Employee engagement doesn't benefit only individual employees. By increasing engagement, you're likely to also boost profitability, lower turnover, and increase total shareholder return.

Driving accountability with strategic knowledge

A common response that prospective clients provide to the question "Why are you creating OKRs?" is to enhance what they see as flagging accountability in their organization. Leaders want people to accept responsibility and embrace the notion of "the buck stops here." But for employees, accountability can be a scary concept, associated as it is with the notion of ultimate responsibility for a designated process, project, or metric, over which they may not possess complete control. No one wants to own something that they ultimately can't influence. Hence the constant push and pull of applying accountability in most organizations.

The OKRs system embraces accountability through the designation of owners of every key result created. Occasionally you'll have more than one owner, but in most cases, a single individual is responsible and accountable for the achievement of the key result.

Being the accountable one certainly doesn't mean that the person is stranded on an island, alone, just them against the world, toiling to see the key result through to completion. They have allies in their fight, the most prominent ally being the gift of strategic knowledge gained through the process of developing the OKR. As mentioned previously, OKRs are best created through interactive, open dialogs about the company's strategy and the team or individual's role in bringing it to fruition.

Accountability is also fostered in the OKR world by utilizing a robust check-in procedure throughout the period. As the days tick past, it's vital to meet frequently and discuss progress on the OKR. In these meetings, candid discussions of the efforts being made to advance on the OKR often bring resource issues to the surface, which takes a significant bite out of the "I can't control the outcome" problem.

REMEMBER
Regular check-ins ensure that teams are considering every element of what it will take to succeed with the OKR, and if outside assistance is required in some form to bridge the control gap, and that assistance is possible, it's given and accountability is enhanced.

Rising to the next level through visionary thinking

Earlier in the chapter, I squeezed in my required Abraham Lincoln story, and now I'm hitting the daily double of must-have historical mentions with a Steve Jobs quote, and this is only Chapter 2! One of the Apple co-founder's most oft-repeated lines is this: "We're here to put a dent in the universe. Otherwise, why else even be here?" Did you know that the actual quote is somewhat longer and the original source is a 1985 *Playboy* magazine article? But I digress. Regardless of the specific wording and where Jobs said it, the dent in the universe image struck a chord, and you'll hear it reverberating through the halls of companies from Silicon Valley to Wall Street to this day.

Jobs wasn't preaching small, incremental improvements or minor updates to standard business operating procedures. He implored his teams to think in an audaciously grandiose fashion in order to create breakthrough products and services that their customers may not even know they needed or wanted.

Thinking of this order demands creativity, innovation, experimentation, and a healthy dose of chutzpah. But when the stars align, payoffs are truly astronomical in scope. OKRs can serve as the fuel for this inspirational level of thinking by diverting focus from the mundane, day-to-day, business-as-usual activities that tend to occupy us most of the time to the goals that fire our universe-denting missile into space.

I'm sure the previous sentence sounds hyperbolic, but it didn't just sprout from my overly active imagination or some creative genius at Hallmark. No, it's science, remember? My goal-setting heroes, Locke and Latham (introduced in Chapter 1), proved through hundreds of field experiments across a wide spectrum of domains that visionary goals improve results. People with "hard" goals often outperformed those with easy-to-achieve goals by a factor of 250 percent. So go ahead, dream big. OKRs can take you anywhere you want to go.

Working within a system that is easy to understand and use

The single biggest benefit of OKRs may be the ease with which they can be understood and used when implemented with rigor and discipline. And do we ever need some simplicity in the organizational world right now! I sometimes wonder if a secret society of business pundits and gurus gets together in some clandestine location — maybe Bond-villain style inside a volcano — to dream up new systems. The more convoluted, complicated, and incomprehensible they are, the better, and the more likely a desperate CEO will be to plunk down six- and seven-figure fees to attempt to implement them, no questions asked. You know what I'm talking about: frameworks and systems with diagrams that defy geometric and grammatical logic, the kind you need a business Sherpa to interpret for you.

A business solution doesn't need to be that way, though. A simple, well-implemented framework — yes, OKRs — will pay off handsomely in employee understanding and buy-in, which will inevitably drive faster execution and outsized results at the organizational level. I doubt that the secret society of gurus will admit me to their evil lair anytime soon, but maybe if I start creating non-sensical acronyms, they'll nominate me for membership. With that in mind, here's one that outlines how and why OKRs are easy to understand and use. Here goes; it's DECK:

>> *D is for distilling.* OKRs distill the meaning of goal-setting to its core components: The *objective* describes what you want to do, and the set of accompanying *key results* demonstrate achievement of that objective. Nothing more; nothing less.

>> *E is for empathy.* We, the humble purveyors of OKRs among whose ranks I count myself, feel your pain. I'm a business owner, too, and the last thing I want is byzantine systems with seven steps for this and eight steps for that, which lead me to scratching my head wondering what I'm doing and whether my company is any closer to achieving its goals. So on behalf of everyone who coaches, facilitates, and trains in this field, we're keeping it real for you.

>> *C is for clarity.* There are just a few essential characteristics of an effective OKR, which I cover in detail in Chapters 8 and 9. Stick to those and you'll be writing rock-solid OKRs in no time.

>> *K is for Ka-Boom!* That's the feeling you're going to have, or maybe the jubilant cry you're going to sing forth, when you experience your first aha moment using OKRs. I can't say for sure when it will happen, because every organization is different, but I can say for sure that if you follow the tips in this book, it will happen. Maybe as you're crafting OKRs, you'll feel a thrill as you recognize that you've created something that truly aligns with, and contributes to, the company's strategy. Or perhaps during an OKRs retrospective, when you analyze your results as a team, you'll discover a hidden assumption that may unlock the key to future success. *Ka-Boom!*

Your story is waiting to be written.

2

Preparing to Create OKRs

Investing time in preparing to create your OKRs will help to ensure that you set a solid foundation for the success of your implementation. It will also greatly increase the chances that you'll reach desired outcomes for the program.

In this part, you discover the critical elements involved in writing OKRs. You find out why determining your unique rationale for implementing OKRs is vital to success, and discern the key roles people play in maximizing that success. You also see how to determine where and when to create OKRs, and delve into the raw materials of OKRs: mission, vision, and strategy.

Chapter 3

First Things First: Identify Why You Are Creating OKRs

I have a lot of management heroes, and among them is the late Stephen Covey, author of the mega bestselling book *The 7 Habits of Highly Effective People*. Covey penned a number of other books during his career, including one called *First Things First*, in which he tells the story of the big rocks. Essentially it goes like this: Imagine you have a glass jar that you're trying to fill with rocks, pebbles, and sand. How can you fit them all into the jar? Starting with the fine-grain sand will fill the bottom of the jar and leave no room for the rocks and pebbles, so that approach is out. If you put the pebbles in first, you may have room for the sand, but forget about squeezing the rocks in. It turns out that the only way to get everything into the jar is to start by putting the big rocks in, followed by the pebbles, and then finally pouring in the sand to fill the spaces in between.

Covey used this simple parable to illustrate a critical principle everyone should follow: Begin with the most important things — the big rocks — whether in your day, your week, or your life. When it comes to OKRs, the big rock, the really big rock (think: a trailer-sized boulder), is the answer to this question: Why are you creating OKRs, and why now? In Chapter 2, I mention that most leaders, when giving me an overview of their company, quickly tell me how "different" they are. But here's what all these executives, managers, team leaders, and individual contributors have very much in common: how busy they are and how fast things are moving.

I'd love to tell you that OKRs are a slam-dunk, walk-in-the-park, easy-to-implement system, but OKRs involve change, and the path of change is never easy or straightforward. During your implementation, you'll sometimes find that progress isn't quite what you hoped for, and momentum can vanish faster than a gambler's lucky streak. These are the moments when you need a rallying cry, and that motivational yelp comes in the form of your "Why OKRs" mantra. This chapter shows you why you must clearly identify why you want to start the process of adopting the OKRs system in your organization. But first, it's helpful to know how *not* to start your OKRs journey. After that, the chapter takes you on a deep dive for help answering the "why OKRs" question, ensuring that you have a response that fires up your team, from top to bottom.

REMEMBER

The only constant is change, and falling behind is not an option. When things are traveling at warp speed and everyone has more plates spinning than Erich Brenn on the Ed Sullivan Show (if you're unders 60, you'll probably need to look him up, so here you go: https://www.youtube.com/watch?v=Zhoos1oY404), the most valuable resource you and your colleagues possess is attention, and it's a closely guarded resource at that. If you want, or dare I say expect, your employees to commit what is likely their most precious asset, you must share with them the big rock of why the investment is valuable for both them and the company.

Knowing How *Not* to Kick Off Your OKRs Journey

When I started my consulting career, I was often greeted by clients with a slightly suspicious look as they extended their hand and said, "You're younger than we expected." That's code for "Does this guy really know what he's doing?" These days, when a client executive introduces me to their team, it's a different tune altogether. "We hired Paul because he's written seven books on this topic and worked with hundreds of companies over the last couple of decades. We just hope our workshops don't interfere with his nap schedule." No, that last part about the naps isn't true . . . yet. The point is, I've been doing this work for a long time, and my antenna for picking up signals — whether positive or negative — is highly tuned. When meeting a new client, I can usually tell early on whether

>> They have a strong chance of thriving with OKRs.

>> The endeavor is going to be a painful slog grinding to an inevitable failure.

>> The effort will never get off the ground at all.

Certain red flags have been waved in my face over the years, the type that will — please excuse the mixed metaphors — put you behind the eight ball right from the start. In this section, I describe two particularly poor choices for starting your OKRs journey, both of which I've experienced a number of times over the years. It's not impossible to rebound from these less-than-auspicious beginnings, but as you'll see later in the chapter, you can take much more beneficial first steps than these to kick off your OKRs implementation.

It's not just me who believes that getting off to a strong start is important. More than 2,000 years ago, Plato noted that "[t]he beginning is the most important part of the work." It doesn't matter whether you're an ancient Greek philosopher or a 21st-century leader; you have only one chance to make a great first impression.

Avoid having your administrative assistant call consultants

Every time my company receives an inquiry from a potential new client, it triggers a little dopamine hit. It's always interesting and exciting to open an email from a prospect. Questions abound: Where are they from? What industry are they in? What prompted them to reach out and learn more about our services? But that little rush evaporates in an instant when the inquiry reads something like this:

"Hi, I'm Ashley, the CEO's admin assistant. He asked me to reach out to companies like yours because we're interested in implementing OKRs. Can you please send me a list of your services and prices."

I'm not taking shots at Ashley here. She (and just as often it's a Jim or Justin) is just doing her job, following up on her boss's wishes. I am, however, suggesting that this is a less-than-ideal way to start the OKRs process. Every organization will require a customized cocktail of services in order to reach their specific goals. You're not buying a t-shirt online here, folks. When selecting a partner, if your only basis for the choice is a bare menu of prices and services, you're depriving yourself of the value that comes from a true partnership between provider and your company. And, frankly, it demonstrates a lack of commitment on the prospect's part if they can't even summon the interest to hold a conversation with potential providers.

What to do instead

If you want help in implementing OKRs, here are three things any CEO or leader should do when selecting a potential consulting partner:

>> **Conduct research on the topic.** Know what you're buying! And, backing up from that, here's something even more basic: Know *why* you're buying. What is the specific business reason you have for reaching out to a consulting partner now? What is the problem you're trying to solve with OKRs? I say more about this later in the chapter, in "Getting to Your 'Why' for Creating OKRs," but only by answering these questions can you make an informed choice based on what the market has to offer.

>> **Go beyond the sticker.** Don't ever select a partner solely on the lowest price. In the rarest of occasions, you'll get lucky and find a firm whose low prices are not representative of a lack of skill or experience. But for the most part, the old axiom fits: You get what you pay for. Deep subject-matter expertise, relevant experience, and cultural fit are the true yardsticks for a healthy relationship between client and provider. Sometimes you'll pay a bit more for those aspects, but the rewards far outweigh the incremental hit to your P & L.

>> **Assign the work to a decision-maker.** Never have an administrative assistant or other person with no decision-making power conduct calls with your potential partner. Chapter 1, page 1 of any book on change management will tell you that senior executive support is the make-or-break ingredient in any initiative. That commitment starts from the day you decide to reach out for some external help. Whenever possible, do it yourself to demonstrate to everyone your personal dedication to selecting the right partner for your specific needs.

Chapter 13 covers the topic of using consultants in much more detail.

TIP

If you're a CEO, you simply may not have the bandwidth to lead the OKRs program on a day-to-day basis, including the initial screening of potential partners. It's okay to delegate, but ensure that you choose someone relatively senior who possesses decision-making rights.

Don't embark on a change effort lightly

If, when I ask a leader: "Why are you implementing OKRs, and why now?" they answer, "Well, I read a bestseller about OKRs, and it seemed to make sense," I know we may have a problem. That's because readers may come away with the impression that the OKRs framework is simple to implement. Although the framework is easy to understand, as discussed in the previous chapter, actual implementation can always prove challenging.

But no book, including the one you're holding in your hand, can do the work of harnessing the power of OKRs for you. Having a book's message resonate with you should not be the primary reason for embarking on any organizational change effort.

What to do instead

I don't have to tell you how difficult it is to make change happen. Without a compelling justification as to why the change is necessary, already overburdened employees will either tune it out or wait it out. Every change, including OKRs, must begin with a well-conceived and crisply delivered answer to the questions "why?" and "why now?" CEOs who have witnessed the downsides of change know this truth well, which is why, in a recent study of 2,724 change leaders conducted by the consulting firm McKinsey (see *Beyond Performance 2.0*, by Scott Keller and Bill Schaninger), 62 percent said that "[c]ommunicating a compelling vision to motivate and inspire" was the most important leadership behavior during a change program.

Getting to Your "Why" for Creating OKRs

The first section of this chapter suggests what *not* to do when starting an OKRs process. Now it's time to look at what you must do when launching OKRs. First, share a powerful and meaningful change story with your teams. To do so, you must go above and beyond trite, tired, and oft-repeated lines such as "We need to work together more effectively" (everyone knows that already) or "We need to bring more value to the market" (not exactly goosebump inducing).

A better approach is to weave a broader narrative that outlines any or all of the following:

>> How excelling in OKRs allows you to get closer to customers, offering solutions to their problems

>> How OKRs, with their focus on transparency, will help bring teams closer together, improving your working environment

>> How OKRs allow everyone the chance to demonstrate their contribution to overall success

Just as there are innumerable ways to plot a novel or film, choices abound when crafting your organization's change story.

Determining your unique reason for implementing OKRs

To offer a persuasive change story to share with your teams, you need to identify the compelling and legitimate reasons for launching an OKRs initiative. In this section, I describe a number of possible motives for moving to the OKRs world, but you shouldn't consider them a buffet from which to choose at random. Instead, contemplate each in the context of your own company, discuss them with your team, and determine what resonates, and why. At the end of the day, or more aptly, at the beginning of OKRs, the system must solve a specific business issue or a combination of issues specific to you.

The need for awareness and execution of strategy

According to researchers, if you were to ask a hundred people in your company to name one of your top-three goals, about 85 would come up with something pulled from the ether that is not even in the ballpark of what leaders had previously presented. OKRs can correct that problem because a prerequisite for developing OKRs is an understanding of strategy that drives a conversation culminating in the depiction of how your teams contribute. OKRs drive the communication and recognition of strategy in an organization.

A way to manage fast growth

This is a high-class problem, but a problem nonetheless. Companies riding a rocket ship of growth face a number of challenges, chief among them keeping everyone focused on what truly matters, and why. Growth is almost always accompanied by a multitude of opportunities, and determining what fits and what doesn't is imperative in maintaining your upward trajectory. OKRs go above and beyond the day-to-day activities, forcing you to select the truly strategy-executing, value-adding, and other hyphenated adjectives that keep you focused on riding high.

The need to correct misalignment

If you were to step back and take a critical and objective view of your company, would the image of a bunch of six-year-olds playing soccer come to mind? It's the organized chaos of a jumble of tots scrambling this way and that, turf flying, and the ball occasionally inching forward in a performance that doesn't exactly match the precision of *Swan Lake*. Although things usually aren't as extreme (fortunately) at most organizations, alignment issues are front and center, with siloed teams working in blissful ignorance of what's happening down the hall. The process of identifying and managing dependencies when creating OKRs can stunt the growth of silos by quickly spotlighting opportunities for teams to come together, using shared OKRs to drive results.

A method for keeping the right focus

Focus as a rationale for OKRs underpins all those discussed in the preceding sections, and it will most likely be among the first things you think of when reflecting on the challenges you face. It's little wonder that remaining focused presents challenges. Here's an example of the information explosion people have been exposed to in the last four decades: In 1986, the bombardment of information that came at everyone through television, radio, and reading added up to about 40 newspapers' worth of information — a day! By 2007, the amount had skyrocketed to 174 newspapers' worth of information per day. Given the speed and pace of change, attention spans globally are shrinking dramatically. As a result of this lowered attention span, it's becoming harder every day to determine what really matters. But this area is where OKRs shine. The OKRs process, when conducted with a disciplined approach, forces recognition of what truly makes a difference in driving the company forward.

TIP

Everyone has blind spots, and sometimes the real challenges your organization faces aren't immediately apparent to well-insulated executives accustomed to hearing nothing but good news. When considering the challenges prompting you to implements OKRs, canvass your entire organization for input (or a sample, if yours is an extremely large enterprise) to unearth a variety of opinions.

Knowing your why is crucial

One of my favorite books in college was *A Theory of Cognitive Dissonance*, by Leon Festinger. Cognitive dissonance suggests that people have a psychological need to align their actions with their beliefs, eliminating any inconsistencies or dissonance between them. Festinger said it's difficult to behave in a different way if the behavior is inconsistent with your view of the world. Festinger didn't have OKRs in mind when postulating his theory, of course, but it definitely applies. When implementing OKRs, you're asking people to act in a different way than they may be accustomed to by using a new form of goal-setting system. If they don't believe in that system, Festinger's theory predicts that they won't go along, which means that your effort is dead or on life support before you even get started.

If, however, people believe in the change, they are more inclined to alter their own behavior and support it. Therefore, it's critical at the outset of your work with OKRs to clearly outline your why — your change story. Take every opportunity and use every medium available to share that story with your entire organization. Town Halls, Slack channels, carrier pigeons — use whatever tool you have available to get the message across to every single team member. Give employees the opportunity to fully understand and ultimately embrace the journey you're about to go on together.

REMEMBER

Research consistently shows that the most important leadership behavior during a change initiative like OKRs is communicating a compelling vision to motivate and inspire people to make the change.

See the sidebar "Memo from a CEO: Why We're Adopting OKRs" for an example of a company-wide communication from the CEO of a client I worked with. To ensure confidentiality, I've altered it slightly and redacted the company's name. Keep in mind this is just one piece of their overall communication and training plan around OKRs.

I hope this chapter has convinced you that taking the time to carefully consider your reason for implementing OKRs is a gift that truly keeps on giving. Crafting a vivid and inspiring change narrative will ensure that your entire team, from the C-Suite to the front line, are united in purpose as you start down this exciting path together.

MEMO FROM A CEO: WHY WE'RE ADOPTING OKRs

This has been a year of change for the global economy, the markets we service, and, therefore, *OurCompany* and its affiliated and subsidiary companies. When going through so much change, it's easy to embrace the things that you know and feel comfortable with, making a new initiative like OKRs (Objective and Key Results) challenging to embrace. As such, I think it's important to understand why *OurCompany* is embracing an OKR culture and why I believe it is now even more important than ever to ensure alignment of the broader *OurCompanhy* organization.

OurCompany is a collection of businesses that have come together over a number of years. We are fortunate to have great business segments and segment leadership; however, we are also challenged with transitioning from several business lines to one unified company where Strategy Execution, Leadership, and Continuous Performance work in tandem. Although this is a worthy goal, it is not an easy transition.

Creating transparency, alignment, and accountability between our overall business strategy, each business line, and the teams doing the work has proven to be difficult to manage. Although we all want transparency, how much is too much and how often is too often can be difficult to tell.

As I researched how contemporary companies make connections between strategy and execution, I found many companies that express a real passion for Objectives and Key Results, or OKRs (even companies like Google have utilized OKRs to go grow from start-up to industry leader). As I learned more about this powerful framework, I began to get excited about the possibilities it presents for *OurCompany*.

As I shared with many of you, I believe it is critically important for us to operate as one *OurCompany* to achieve shared outcomes and ensure that we can best serve our stake-holders. At times we have struggled to do this without a clear methodology to connect shared objectives to deliverables and outcomes. OKRs provide us with tried-and-true methods to establish cross-functional Objectives, commit to outcomes and deliverables (via Key Results) and share them with the teams that are critical to making it all work together.

I recognize that *OurCompany* is going through a lot of transition, and that this new framework represents a change that will take commitment and support from everyone, especially our Senior Leadership Team. What I need from you is to keep an open mind through this journey, share your thoughts with your leadership team, and apply this framework in your business.

Together we will transform the industry by changing operating paradigms and creating more efficient, liquid, transparent, and resilient markets.

Chapter **4**

Filling Vital OKRs Roles within the Organization

D o you have a favorite holiday movie? A perennial favorite in the United States is *National Lampoon's Christmas Vacation*, which celebrates the mis- adventures of Clark W. Griswold. An iconic scene in the movie features the transformation of Clark's money-grubbing boss, Mr. Shirley, as he reinstates the bonus that Clark was desperately depending on. A contrite Mr. Shirley, who had previously promised to withhold bonuses, realizes the error of his miserly ways and notes earnestly, "It's people that matter." Good for you, Frank Shirley.

Although you can choose among many sophisticated OKRs software tools to serve as a powerful ally, along with an army of skilled and talented consultants, the dif- ference between success, mediocrity, or failure in your OKRs implementation will come down to the people you have involved in leading your OKRs implementation. Despite the worry that artificial intelligence will one day usurp us all, there will never be a technological substitute for the talents, knowledge, and passion of peo- ple in bringing the promise of OKRs to life.

Eventually, depending on how far in the organization you deploy OKRs, every employee will be involved in the process and have the chance to express their con- tribution, but to ensure that your implementation is on solid footing from day one, your organization must fill three roles: executive sponsor, OKRs champion, and OKRs ambassadors. In this chapter, I describe the inner workings of each role, give you pointers on how to select the right people, and explain why each is a must-have if you hope to get the most from OKRs.

Securing an Executive Sponsor: A Critical Component

When I'm interviewed by prospective clients to lead them through an OKRs process, they all tend to ask a number of questions, such as "How long does it take?" "How much does it cost?" and, apropos to this chapter, "Who needs to be involved?" Those are among the greatest hits of OKRs questions that come up every time, but maybe a quarter of organizations also tee up with this provocative query: "Have you ever had any implementations that failed?"

The short answer is, yes, a few, and here's one that illustrates the imperative of having executive sponsorship. Hired by the chief of staff to lead a full-scale implementation for a financial services company, I couldn't, despite my many efforts, secure a conversation with the CEO until after the ink on the contract was already dry. Still, he seemed to listen thoughtfully when we did get to have that conversation.

But then his rally-the-troops speech during our first session in front of the executive team was a rambling mess, with little connection to OKRs (which he kept pronouncing "orks" when he did mention it). Eventually he turned the session over to me to lead, but 15 minutes into the first exercise, he exploded in frustration and forcefully disparaged the goings-on. Clearly, he had not read my proposal or glanced at a single page of the materials on OKRs, nor had he communicated effectively with his chief of staff concerning the expectations for the engagement. Needless to say, this company's implementation was over before the mid-morning coffee was wheeled into the room.

Fortunately, that is my only true consulting disaster, but it's one that I've never forgotten. Seared into my brain forever was the absolute imperative of confirming that executive sponsorship exists for an OKRs engagement. Of course, I could broaden that last statement to note that executive sponsorship is critical for any type of change effort you're undertaking.

REMEMBER

Without executive sponsorship, you have virtually no chance of generating and maintaining the effort necessary to institute the change and incorporate it into your culture.

In the following sections, I explore this vital topic, examining what, exactly, sponsorship is, the responsibilities that accompany it, and what it looks like in action.

Understanding Executive Sponsorship and Why It's Important

In Chapter 3, I noted the disturbing trend of diminishing human attention spans, and the impact that is having on our work lives as our thoughts bounce from one shiny attention-grabbing object to the next, never really committing our full cognitive capacity to anything that doesn't generate a "like" or "retweet." Attention is without doubt a scarce resource, and like any valuable commodity, it has to be guarded diligently and directed where it will produce the most impact. With so much being blasted at us every moment of every day that decision — where to place our attention — is getting harder all the time, but one rule stands above all others in providing guidance to this challenge:

> Everyone watches what the boss watches.

It's as simple as that. If something is important to the CEO, it immediately has my attention, and I'm committed to focusing my attention on it. Thus if you, as an executive, expect your teams to fall in line and use OKRs to full advantage, you must first demonstrate your personal commitment to the effort.

If you're an organizational leader thinking of adopting OKRs, carefully consider your capacity and desire to fulfill the following core obligations before committing to an OKRs rollout:

>> Possess an understanding of OKRs

>> Be able to define success and communicate the need for OKRs

>> Champion the use of OKRs at the senior leadership level

>> Approve funding for the OKRs initiative

>> Work with other leadership to develop a playbook

>> Be the final decision-maker

Keep reading for more details about each of these core responsibilities of the executive sponsor.

Possessing knowledge of OKRs

You can't effectively sponsor something you don't understand.

This truth makes OKRs research the first stop on your sponsorship journey. I've actually had clients over the years tell me their executives are too busy to attend OKR fundamentals training. I could wrap my entire body in that red flag. Executive sponsors must go beyond a casual knowledge of OKRs by

>> Understanding the methodology's history

>> Taking the time to learn how to write technically sound OKRs

>> Determining exactly how OKRs fit with their company's overall goal-setting system

>> Carefully plotting out an implementation path

Defining success and why you believe in OKRs

I devoted an entire chapter (Chapter 3) to this topic, so if you skipped over it, you may want to flip back and give it a read. Business books and business book authors are often accused of being repetitive, so I don't devote paragraphs to the "why OKRs" decision here; suffice to say that you need your own reason for embracing OKRs, and it can't be "Because Google did it."

Championing the use of OKRs at the senior leadership level

This item in the core obligation list could be in the running for the Captain Obvious element of sponsorship. You can't just talk the talk; you need to walk the walk, which means employing OKRs to gauge execution and drive the leadership meeting agenda. If you preach OKRs to your employees but then meet with your team and discuss nothing but the most recent financial statements, you're sending the message that OKRs really don't matter. This element is more difficult than it appears because it forces a change in what can be long-established meeting agendas and rhythms that have become calcified over time and resistant to attempts at change.

Approving funding for the initiative

Yes, there is a financial cost to OKRs, but in true sales fashion, let me rephrase that: An *investment* is required. If you choose to hire a consulting partner, doing so will of course entail fees. The use of OKRs software, which is a logical and beneficial choice for many organizations, will also cost you some money. And, finally, you'll need an OKRs champion and a cadre of ambassadors to ensure the smooth operation of your OKRs initiative, all of which will translate to diverting people, at least temporarily, from their current roles — another potential cost of the system.

REMEMBER

Fees and costs are very much a relative thing. Supplying ramen noodles to your exhausted staff may be considered an extravagant treat if you're a startup with five people, whereas Fortune 50 companies may be accustomed to seven-figure engagements with the McKinseys of the world. Regardless of where you are on that spectrum, you must be willing to make the applicable investments in OKRs if you hope to gain the full benefits offered by the system.

Determining your OKRs "playbook" with the champion and executive team

Consider your OKRs "playbook" to be your customized user's manual for OKRs at your organization. This document lays out the rules of the road for OKR use and provides the following information:

>> Who will create OKRs

>> How often to review the OKRs

>> What scoring mechanism to use

>> How to manage alignment

TIP

You may need to include a host of other elements relating to your implementation in your playbook as well. Some of these elements may change over time, but it's important to put a stake in the ground at the outset so that your teams know what you expect of them when you task them with using OKRs.

Serving as a final point of escalation on OKRs issues

This responsibility plays out primarily in making decisions relating to cross-functional OKRs. Say that Team A has created an OKR and identified a dependency on Team B. In other words, Team A can't achieve the OKR without Team B's assistance. The two teams have talked things over, and as much as Team B understands and would like to help, they determine that they just don't have the capacity to provide the requested assistance.

At this point, the decision about Team B's involvement is escalated, and for certain high-profile and important OKRs, it may even go all the way up to the CEO, who will be the final arbiter on whether Team B will be required to assist Team A. In any situation of this nature, not everyone is likely to be pleased with the outcome, but if leadership communicates the decision with honesty and candor and relates it to the overall strategy of the organization, everyone will understand, and knowledge of strategy will be enhanced.

So if you thought that reading a book or getting a few pointers from a CEO friend who uses OKRs was all it takes to be an effective sponsor, be aware that it's a significant responsibility, one that represents the very foundation of success for an OKRs program.

I'm not the only person who sees executive sponsorship as a key component of success. Participants in one survey were asked to rank people in an organization based on how important they are to the success of a change program, and a whopping 70 percent chose the most senior leader as number one (see *Beyond Performance 2.0*, by Scott Keller and Bill Schaninger).

Everyone watches what the boss watches. If OKRs aren't important to the CEO, they won't be important to anyone else.

Seeing sponsorship in action

Earlier in the chapter, I share a recollection of one of the worst days of my consulting career, so it's only fitting that I balance it with one of my favorite work-related memories: a dramatic story of executive sponsorship in action. Using the word *dramatic* to represent a concept like executive sponsorship may seem over the top, but for me, it was a real movie moment that illustrates the commitment of an effective executive sponsor. So I'm going to present it in equally cinematic fashion.

To set the scene: In a hotel meeting room, long bars of golden late-afternoon sun stream through the windows across a u-shaped table. Twelve executives are assembled, some sitting upright, some slumping, others casting long glances at the many flip-chart pages taped to the walls. The usual flotsam and jetsam of a day's meeting cover the table: coffee cups, muffin wrappers, balled-up paper, and an assortment of laptops, phones, and tablets. It has been a long day, and everyone is justifiably fatigued from the effort of creating the company's first set of organizational OKRs. The consultant, Paul, turns over a fresh page of flip-chart paper.

Paul, writing on the flip chart, says "We've made some great progress today! Let's take one more look at these OKRs to make sure we're happy with them." Hearing something behind him, Paul turns to see Tom, a tech VP in the company who is restlessly tapping his pen against the table. After a moment or two, Tom raises his hand. "Yes, Tom?" Paul nods to him. Tom drops his hand to the table with an audible thud and says: "Can you let me know when we're going to be done here? I have real work to do."

Twelve sets of eyes turn to focus on Paul. How will he react? This is a nightmare scenario — a VP questioning the very essence of the work they're doing. Paul takes a deep breath and is about to speak when the CEO, Jason, rises from his chair, shoves it back, walks directly to Tom, and hovers over him.

"We're here today crafting the OKRs that we'll use for the next year to gauge the execution of our new strategy," Jason says. "The OKRs that we'll then share with every member of this organization so that they can create their own OKRs, and we can finally get the alignment we've all said has been lacking around here for years." Locking his eyes with Tom's, the CEO says, "If you don't think this is the most important place you can be right now, then I don't think you belong at this table."

Everyone is silent as the CEO strides back to his chair. A message has been delivered.

Talk about a drop-the-mic moment. Jason made it abundantly clear to everyone in the room that day that OKRs were a central piece of the organization's future, and anyone who didn't buy into that vision shouldn't be there. Organizational grapevines being what they are, it wasn't long before that story had reached every office, cube, and foosball table of the company, quickly becoming part of corporate lore. Well, surprise, surprise, that implementation went on to be one of the most successful I've ever had the privilege of being part of, and I'm convinced the seeds of that success were planted in that meeting room.

REMEMBER

You certainly don't need to look for an opportunity to pounce on a skeptical subordinate in order to display executive sponsorship. there are many less dramatic actions you can take. For example, adhering to the responsibilities I outline in the earlier section, "Understanding executive sponsorship," is a great way to demonstrate your commitment to OKRs.

TIP

Don't keep your sponsorship a secret. Use every chance you get to communicate the value of OKRs, and your belief in the system, whether at Town Halls, via internal emails, or through your company blog.

Gaining executive sponsorship

Thus far, this chapter has provided a lot of sponsorship tips aimed directly at the CEO or senior executives, but what if you're not the CEO? Perhaps you're a director, or a manager who's excited about the prospect of what OKRs have to offer the organization but who lacks the decision-making power to make it happen. What should you do?

Fortunately, you can pursue a number of angles to try bringing executives around to the notion of OKRs. Here are a few tips to consider:

>> **Educate your executives.** I noted previously how important it is for executives to understand OKRs — how to write them, how to integrate them into the fabric of the company, and so on — so the first arrow in your quiver should be knowledge transfer. This transfer can take many forms, including books like the one you're reading right now, YouTube videos on the subject, case studies from other organizations, or any of the countless articles on OKRs circulating on the web. The undeniable power of peer pressure can be a real ally here, so if you can find evidence of OKR success at organizations your senior executive admires, by all means share that information enthusiastically.

>> **Link OKRs to a challenge you face:** If yours is an organization operating here on planet Earth in the early 21st century, it's safe to say that you face one or two of the following challenges:

- Competition is tougher than it's ever been.

- Global economies never seem to remain stable for any length of time.

- The pace of change is constantly accelerating.

These macro elements apply to just about every organization in existence. Meanwhile, within your own four walls, you no doubt have to confront your company's unique set of problems, whether they relate to alignment, focus, or a clinging to the status quo.

You know that OKRs are particularly well-suited to help you battle the challenges you face, so take it upon yourself to prepare a presentation for your leadership in which you document how OKRs can supply the means to overcome that challenge. When they see how OKRs prove to be your best defense in future-proofing your company, they're likely to jump aboard.

>> **Pilot OKRs in your own unit:** You may not have the power to authorize a full-scale rollout of OKRs across your enterprise, but you most likely have the means to use OKRs in your own team, department, or unit. If that's the case, do it! After you show the effects of OKRs, in terms of visionary thinking, alignment, and focus, word will spread quickly, and before long the C-Suite will be aware of what you're up to and be anxious to spread your success across the company.

TIP

I think back frequently to the CEO mentioned in the opening of the chapter, the one who clearly didn't understand the value of OKRs. What a missed opportunity for that organization. That CEO had a wonderful chance to dominate their market but was held back by a few pressing issues that I'm confident a robust OKRs implementation could have surmounted. Instead, that organization's OKR journey was over in less time than it takes to get a good haircut because of a CEO who failed at the one job no CEO can afford to take lightly: sponsorship.

WARNING

The fastest way to show employees you're not serious about OKRs is to have a CEO who doesn't actively sponsor the rollout in words and actions.

Choosing Your OKRs Champion: A Vital Role for OKRs success

Like many people, I love having plants in my house — orchids, ornamental palms, lucky bamboos — to add a refreshing splash of color and literally breathe life into any room they're placed in. But there's a problem: I'm not the most reliable waterer of said plants, and were it not for my uber-dependable wife's caretaking of our leafy friends, they'd be ready for the compost bin before you know it. Plants need care and attention to thrive and bring vitality to our lives, and the same can be said of OKRs.

Unfortunately, you can't simply announce the launch of OKRs, send out a crudely prepared template for people to complete, and expect to be on the cover of *Fortune* the next month. Like that peace lily on your mantle, OKRs require nurturing to grow and prosper.

In the "Securing an Executive Sponsor" section, earlier in this chapter, I outline the importance of an executive sponsor in getting the program off the ground and sustaining it throughout its development. However, an executive sponsor alone is not enough. Given their endless duties — you know, that pesky running-the-company thing — they simply don't have the bandwidth to actually manage the OKRs process. For that, you need someone to act as the philosophical and logistical heart and soul of the OKRs implementation, and that person is the OKRs champion.

"What does it take to succeed with OKRs?" is a question I've heard hundreds of times over the years, and being the good fence-sitting consultant that I am, I often reply with the tried-and-true "It depends." Which is true: It depends on many factors, but for my money, maybe the single biggest differentiator of OKRs success is having a dynamic, committed OKRs champion in your organization. In this section, I examine this champion role and tell you why it's critical to your success.

Understanding the role of an OKRs champion

One meaning of the word *champion* refers to fighting or arguing for a cause. *Fight* and *argue* sound a bit aggressive, but essentially that's what your OKRs champion will do: promote and defend the cause of OKRs throughout the organization. The champion is your on-the-ground OKRs leader in the organization, the one who, if this were a sports team, would wear the oversized *C* on their jersey.

Your executive sponsor provides air cover for OKRs, supplies the inspiration, and, when necessary, rallies the troops behind your guiding rationale, but it's the champion who gets things done and ensures that your rollout is on the right track. Champions wear many hats in keeping the OKR flame lighted throughout your implementation. Put your feet up and settle in to absorb the following lengthy list of some of the many duties resting on the shoulders of your champion:

>> **Works with the executive sponsor and leadership team to determine the OKRs playbook:** As described earlier in the chapter, the playbook is your customized user's manual for employing OKRs. The champion works side by side with your executive team in crafting this document, and the champion's input is especially critical because they represent the entire the organization.

>> **Serves as in-house subject-matter expert for OKRs:** Put simply, the champion should know more about the theory and practice of OKRs than any other person in your company. They'll be required to read the books and articles, attend webinars, and network with other OKRs users in order to bolster their knowledge on the subject, ensuring that there is virtually no question for which they don't have an answer.

>> **Leads in-house OKRs training programs:** There is no better way to learn something than to teach it. Building on the knowledge referred to in the preceding bullet, your champion will lead OKRs training sessions across the company. They may not do this from day one; if you use a consultant to assist you, the consultant will most likely provide initial training, with your champion attending and gradually conducting more of the session on their own. (Chapter 13 looks at the benefits of using an OKRs consultant.)

>> **Acts as lead administrator for OKRs software (if applicable):** Software can be a terrific enabler of OKRs success, but it must be employed thoughtfully to maximize the benefits. If you decide to use software for OKRs (see Chapter 12 for more in OKRs software), the champion will serve as lead administrator and must know the system inside and out.

>> **Leads the development of OKRs communications:** Many organizations have communications experts, graphic designers, and other creative resources to lean on to craft OKRs-related messages. If you have such resources, that's a bonus, but those teams can't work in isolation. The

champion must be with them to ensure that your OKRs messaging is on point to your brand (such as why you're implementing OKRs), inviting of questions, and always informative.

It goes without saying that the person filling the role of leading communications about OKRs needs to be a skilled communicator. But even so, they need to be vigilant about *what* they're communicating. See the "Anyone want some toast?" sidebar for a cautionary tale, albeit not related to OKRs, about the price you pay for being a poor communicator, even when you think you've nailed it.

ANYONE WANT SOME TOAST?

I'm a big believer in filling out the cards left in hotel rooms that allow you to order your breakfast in advance by checking what you'd like and hanging the card outside your door. It's efficient, but on one occasion, I may have gone a little overboard in my desire to communicate effectively.

I usually skip regular choices and instead fill out the "Special Requests" section at the bottom. This time, to draw the staff's attention to this choice, I drew a bold square around the blank lines in that section, and to really reinforce my order, I decided to number my selections. My aim was to leave no room for interpretation.

I wrote in bold and legible capital letters: "1. Orange Juice. 2. Coffee. 3. Half-grapefruit" (the latter because at least half the time, they bring grapefruit juice, so I hoped to set it apart from the drinks). Finally, I wrote, "4. Whole wheat toast." I ticked the "6:45 to 7:00" box, circled it for extra attention, and hung the card on my door. "Nothing left to chance," I thought as I tucked myself into bed.

The next morning I awoke at 6 a.m. and confirmed that the room service breakfast card had been retrieved. At 6:52 a.m., a sharp knock on my door announced room service. Right on schedule!

The bubbly young server greeted me enthusiastically and bounded into my room with tray in hand, placing it on the coffee table as requested. Expecting a bill at that point, I was surprised when she said she just had to get my other trays. (Trays? Plural?) She soon delivered two more heaping trays, and in all, I received one glass of orange juice, two cups of coffee, three half-grapefruits, and four orders of toast. An order of toast is two slices, each cut in half, so my order amounted to 16 pieces. The toast was piled so high that the cover teetered above the stack.

Perhaps to this day, employees at that hotel still tell the tale of the legendary man in room 324 who eats 16 pieces of toast for breakfast. Moral of the story: Communication is crucial, but must be done with care.

>> **Facilitates OKRs ambassador meetings:** As you find out in the final section of this chapter, effective ambassadors can sow buy-in and support for OKRs across your company, and to fulfill that role, they need to convene regularly to share best practices, challenges, concerns, and so on. The champion creates the agenda and facilitates these meetings.

>> **Manages the OKRs budget:** The executive sponsor sets and approves the budget, but after the process is in motion, it's the champion who dons the green eyeshades and monitors the dollars and cents being spent on the program.

>> **Tracks progress against overall plan:** With your playbook in place, you have a plan for action, and the champion takes primary responsibility to ensure that the plan is on track — keeping tabs on everything from who is creating OKRs and when, to whether your software system is performing as per expectations, to monitoring the timely performance of OKRs retrospectives.

>> **Ensures the initial alignment of OKRs:** Driving cross-functional collaboration is essential, but as I note elsewhere, it doesn't just magically happen. Horizontal alignment has to be orchestrated, and the initial conductor is your champion. The champion ensures that teams who should be working together are in fact united in OKR matrimony and that the resulting OKRs are driving the desired alignment.

>> **Serves as initial escalation point for OKRs issues:** Before issues bubble all the way up to the CEO's desk, the champion steps in to provide assistance to any teams who haven't amicably agreed to work together on a shared OKR. This role is a natural offshoot of the previous bullet on ensuring alignment.

>> **Researches and provides input to executives on potential OKRs linkages, such as performance reviews and incentive compensation:** At some point, you'll need to decide whether OKRs will impact the performance review and rating process, or if you'll be a pioneer/maverick and link incentive compensation to OKRs. These decisions have significant consequences, so getting them right in view of your unique circumstances is essential. Your champion will require deep knowledge of your current processes, and will then conduct extensive research on the possible linkages, examining case studies and networking with other organizations that have been down those roads in order to provide appropriate advice to your leadership.

I cover a lot of ground in this section because recognizing the responsibilities of your champion, and committing to selecting the right person, are foundational to realizing the benefits of OKRs. I know it took a while to read, but trust me, writing it was a lot of work as well, and now I'm feeling a little peckish, so I think I'll get a snack. For some reason, I feel like toast.

Picking the perfect OKRs champion

It probably won't come as a surprise to you that I love books and reading, digging into everything from noir fiction to biographies to history, and of course everyone's favorite, business books. To keep an eye out for new volumes that might interest me, I subscribe to the *New York Review of Books*, which, as the name implies, provides thorough and detailed reviews on books of every conceivable topic. One of my guilty pleasures, after I've read the scholarly articles, of course, is going to the last page, which contains, among other advertisements, personal ads. As you may surmise, these aren't super racy or salacious entries (we're talking NYRB subscribers, after all), but they do adhere to many of the tropes you find in personals, with lots of references to sandy beaches, late-night cocktails, and, always, Italy.

Imagine that your organization is looking for the perfect OKRs champion to helm your rollout. What might a personal ad searching for that certain someone look like? How about something like this:

> Are you a middle manager or above, ideally at the director level, in your organization? Are you a great communicator, someone who can influence others with spellbinding oratorical skills and fluent writing? Do you have that special talent of always winning people's hearts and minds, whatever it is you're advocating for?

> Are you organized and able to track multiple things at one time, never letting the whirlwind of the daily grind prevent you from focusing your eyes on the prize? Do those same eyes never lose sight of the details that matter? Are you enthusiastic, and excited to share your passion with others?

> Do you want to grow in the organization and be seen as a coach and mentor to others? Can you think outside the box, coming up with innovative solutions to complex problems? Are you willing to spend up to 50 percent of your time driving this implementation? If the answer is yes to all these questions, we'd love to meet you.

Okay, so there's nothing in this ad about moonswept beaches, moseying through antique shops on rainy Saturday afternoons, or artisanal cheese making, but if you're casting your net for a great OKRs champion and know someone who ticks all the boxes above, go and recruit them right now. I mean *right now*, because they are hard to come by.

If it just so happens that the person likes everything you have to say but is a bit reluctant because of the 50-percent time commitment in the ad, let them know that it's a high-end estimate; that obligation will likely be necessary only at the very outset of your implementation, when everything is ramping up simultaneously. When your process is on more stable ground (two or three cycles in), their commitment will probably max out at about 25 percent of their time.

TIP

An employee who has been designated as "high potential" or a "rising star" can make an excellent OKRs champion. The varied nature of the role, which encompasses strategy, communication, and goal setting, will provide more opportunities for the high achiever to learn more about multiple facets of the business and expand their growth curve.

Grasping why the champion is critical to OKRs success

The OKRs framework attracts a lot of fans because of its perceived simplicity, and indeed the lightweight nature of the system is an enormous advantage. However, it has a lot of moving parts to coordinate in order to deliver as promised. Goal setting is, of course, a primary element of OKRs, but you have to consider change management as well, along with strategy, cross-functional alignment, linkages to other processes such as performance reviews and compensation, and the cultural context in which all this is taking place. So . . . not as easy as it may first appear.

Someone has to keep these balls in the air, ensuring that your implementation is proceeding as planned with execution, alignment, and focus sharpening with each successive period you use OKRs. The champion is your master juggler in this three-ring circus of OKRs deployment — planning, communicating, pondering, and generally ensuring that you sustain the momentum necessary to ingrain OKRs into your culture.

In many ways, the champion is the "face" of the program, and that's a not-to-be-overlooked ingredient of successfully implementing any change: the recognition from everyone across the company that someone is masterminding this journey and has their best interests at heart.

I've worked on hundreds of OKRs implementations in my time as a consultant, and when I scan that panorama, what always comes to mind first are the great champions I've had the pleasure to collaborate with. Every outstanding champion has always been one move ahead in the chess game that is OKRs. While the implementation is still in its infancy, they've looked ahead, anticipating the questions employees will have, the best way to score and review OKRs, or what roadblocks they may encounter in attempting to drive alignment. The talented champions I've known have been in full control of the process, guiding it every step of the way and transforming the promise of OKRs into reality.

REMEMBER

The champion is the logistical and philosophical heart of the OKRs process, without whom success in driving OKRs will be much more difficult.

Bringing OKRs Ambassadors On Board

A common myth regarding the Sistine Chapel in the Vatican holds that Michelangelo alone painted the masterpiece, when in fact he had a team of several assistants who did everything from purchasing pigments to constructing the scaffolding upon which Michelangelo lay when creating his masterwork. And the great master is, of course, not alone in this regard; virtually nothing in this world is created through the lone efforts of a single person. Although my name appears on the cover, many other people helped to bring this book to fruition: my wife, who is always the first reader of everything I write and offers invaluable suggestions; the *Dummies* editorial team, who have guided me through every step of the process; and the countless colleagues with whom I've discussed portions of the book before and during its creation.

"It takes a village" may be one of the most apt expressions in the English language because most endeavors benefit from the contribution of many hands.

OKRs are certainly no exception. As important as the executive sponsor and champion are to your implementation, they're not enough to make the process take hold across your company. To ensure that OKRs form deep roots in the company and are embraced at all levels, you need to enlist one last group: your ambassadors.

No, I'm not referring to the people with the cushy jobs in foreign countries — the ones who spend millions of taxpayer dollars redecorating worn-out old mansions to hold tea parties with other stuffed-shirt dignitaries. Those are definitely not the type of ambassadors I'm referring to in this context. Our OKRs ambassadors are crucial representatives of the OKRs movement within your company, a cadre of enthusiastic supporters who prove vital in assisting OKRs to go beyond flavor of the month and blossom into a framework deeply ingrained in your culture. In the next section, I examine the responsibilities of ambassadors, how to select them, and how to maximize their potential for outsized impact.

Understanding the Role of an OKRs Ambassador

Few things are more stressful than the first day at a new job. Meeting with your co-workers can be nerve-wracking while also figuring out the technology platforms and trying not to inadvertently violate any cultural norms before anyone even knows your name. Like me, you've probably had your share of good first days and not-so-good first days and can clearly recall both. My best first-day experience took place early in my career. I was greeted warmly at the door that morning by a member of the team I'd be working with, who then shepherded me through those inaugural hours, introducing me to people within and outside our group, providing a helpful tutorial on the preferred tech tools I'd be using, showing me where everything was kept, and even providing a little gossip to get me hooked into the company grapevine.

In a nutshell, the person who helped me that day made things easy, and that's what an OKRs ambassador can do for teams using OKRs in your organization. Ambassadors smooth the way for your implementation by providing essential services that teams will need in order to internalize and prosper with OKRs. I use the plural "ambassadors" because, unlike the one-person champion role, you'll have multiple ambassadors throughout your organization.

The actual number of ambassadors will depend on your initial rollout. If you start with a phased approach consisting of, say, ten teams, you want one ambassador per team. If, however, yours is a large organization and you're involving the entire company from day one, 20 to 30 ambassadors should suffice, again depending on how many employees you have. Regardless of the number, the core responsibilities are the same. Here are the five core tasks of an OKRs ambassador:

>> Serve as an OKR expert and evangelist

>> Coach teams through creating OKRs

>> Help teams distinguish OKRs from business as usual

>> Serve as the point of contact

>> Be the liaison between groups

I delve further into these roles in the following sections.

Serving as internal OKR expert and evangelist of the system

Ambassadors don't require the expertise of the OKRs champion, but simply knowing what OKRs stands for won't cut it, either. They must be equipped with the skills to write and spot technically sound OKRs, understand how alignment will be facilitated using OKRs, and identify potential roadblocks to the widespread adoption of the system. Ambassadors use their enhanced training to not only coach others (as I explain shortly) but also communicate the benefits of OKRs and drive support from their assigned teams.

Coaching teams on creating and reviewing OKRs

Coaching is an ideal role for the ambassadors because they should know their teams' operations, challenges, and opportunities better than any external consultant or facilitator. They can use that knowledge to ensure that their teams write OKRs that clearly demonstrate their contribution to overall strategy execution. During the quarter (assuming you use quarterly OKRs), the ambassadors check in regularly to gauge progress. Finally, at the end of the quarter, your ambassadors will help to facilitate OKRs retrospectives that focus on not only the numerical results but also what employees have learned that can lead to even better outcomes going forward.

Helping teams distinguish between business-as-usual work and OKRs

The role of distinguishing OKRs from business-as-usual work relates to the previous item on coaching but merits its own mention. Many teams, when first introduced to the concept of OKRs, can grasp the system's potential value and intellectually know that OKRs are designed to encourage audacious thinking, but they reflexively write OKRs that simply describe their business-as-usual day jobs.

For example — and this isn't meant to pick on Human Resources (HR) — but a business-as-usual responsibility of most HR teams is administering benefits. However, benefit administration shouldn't be an OKR for HR because it never changes. The ambassador will step in when a team creates a business-as-usual OKR, challenging the team to move beyond the day to day and think bigger, more experimentally, and grander.

Acting as a point of contact for all things OKR-related for their area

As the designated subject matter expert on OKRs, the ambassador is the go-to source for information on OKRs, whether that means fielding questions on technical aspects, helping with overall implementation planning, or (and this will happen), explaining why anyone should pay attention to OKRs in the first place. If the ambassador is unable to answer the question, they escalate it to the champion.

Serving as liaison with other ambassadors and the champion

The liaison role may be the breakthrough superpower that a strong group of ambassadors can provide to your organization because they have insider knowledge of how the implementation is actually playing out on the ground. Your cadre of ambassadors should assemble at least quarterly to provide updates on what's working well in their region of OKR-land, what challenges are arising, and generally what people are saying about the system.

If one group, for instance, is seeing strong results from aspirational, technically sound OKRs, that's the best-practice pixie dust you want to spread to every other team using the framework. Conversely, if you're receiving consistent reports of challenges, such as difficulties with entering OKRs into whatever system you've decided to use, that is valuable information that you need to act upon immediately.

I mention in the opening of this section that one of the stress-inducing possibilities of a first day on the job is violating office norms before you're even aware of them. The great first day I described, with all the helpful hints provided and advice offered, didn't prevent me from falling into that trap. My previous company had supplied snacks free of charge to all employees, and our communal fridges were always nicely outfitted with a wide assortment of calorie bombs. So, at my new company, I made the assumption that a similar policy was in place, and on my second day on the job, I helped myself to a chocolate doughnut from the fridge in our kitchen. Big mistake. A hair-raising cry of "Who took my doughnut!" soon rang through the hallways, and, realizing my error, I scooped up and disposed of any remaining crumbs faster than an F1 driver takes the straights at Monte Carlo. (I'm admitting this for the first time, so if it was your doughnut I pilfered, you have my sincere apology.)

Outlining the Profile of an OKRs Ambassador

Every organization has people with outsized influence and stature beyond their place on the org chart. Call them influencers, cultural brokers, or connectors, they're the ones other folks to go when they need information, have a problem, or require advice on working with another person or team. You're probably thinking of a few people like that right now; if so, they may be ideal candidates for the role of an OKRs ambassador.

Beyond some technical attributes that I address in a moment, ambassadors require well-honed interpersonal skills to communicate the why and how of OKRs to their charges, as well as to share information on your process with the larger group of ambassadors. If, for some reason, individual names of potential candidates aren't popping into your head, ask around in the teams that will be creating OKRs: Who do people seek out for help and information? When you start hearing the same names repeatedly, you're on your way to filling your ambassador roster.

Experience with measurement systems, ideally OKRs, isn't a prerequisite for success as an ambassador, but it's a definite plus. Any past familiarity will lessen your upfront training burden as well as burnish the ambassador's credibility because team members will recognize that this won't be their ambassador's first goal-setting rodeo. Many people appreciate being guided by competent hands.

One caveat to keep in mind, however, is that "experience with OKRs" is a relative term, meaning that how an individual used the framework at a previous company may be light years apart from how *you* envision using the system. They may have used different cadences or scoring mechanisms, for example, that aren't consistent with your plans.

REMEMBER

You want to ensure that your ambassadors are fully up to speed on how you'll be employing OKRs at your company because the last thing you need — and it's a documented organizational change killer — is inconsistency in approach to your rollout.

I've heard hundreds of examples of nifty corporate jargon over the years, but one of my all-time favorites is the word *voluntold*, as in, you've been told to volunteer for some activity or responsibility. If your entire group of ambassadors has been "voluntold" that they need to step up to the role, you're starting behind the eight ball.

Such a situation means that you're missing an opportunity to harness the energy and passion of people who truly care about OKRs and understand the value they can bring to your company. In selecting ambassadors, look for people who exhibit a true spirit of enthusiasm for the topic and are anxious to share that passion with others.

TIP

You may be tempted to recruit more junior-level employees to become ambassadors as a way of expanding their experience in the company, but don't forget that the ambassadors will serve as coaches and be charged with reviewing the OKRs of others, possibly including those of their boss. Will the people you're considering be comfortable critiquing the work of a superior?

Maximizing OKRs Success with Ambassadors

One of the best aspects of my job, and there are plenty, is watching people blossom right before my eyes. I've seen it dozens of times: an OKRs champion who may have reluctantly accepted the role but whose perseverance and insights not only keep the OKR train on the track but almost single-handedly deliver it to the promised land of focus and execution.

The same goes with ambassadors. An initial gathering of ambassadors may feature some awkward silence as everyone wonders what exactly what they should be talking about and how to help make this process a success. Then, over time (usually not much) the ambassadors grow, offering tidbits of what's working in their group or sharing a challenge that consistently holds them back. Others build on those thoughts, and soon a revelation emerges that can shift the direction of the entire implementation. Witnessing these transformations is a lot of fun.

I've just described yet another hidden benefit of OKRs: the development of your high-potential and hidden-gem employees. You score a true win-win as ambassadors gain confidence from being an integral part of your process, and that confidence translates into knowledge and insights that drive improved outcomes from the framework. Can you achieve OKRs success without ambassadors? Maybe, but why deprive yourself of a limitless source of energy — brainpower?

IN THIS CHAPTER

» **Discovering the most common choices for where to implement OKRs**

» **Considering other areas within your organization to create OKRs**

» **Determining how often to create OKRs**

Chapter **5**

Determining Where and When to Create OKRs

The song "Where or When," performed by "Ol' Blue Eyes" Frank Sinatra as well as many contemporary artists, came to mind as I wrote this chapter. "Where or When" was written for a 1937 Broadway production called *Babes in Arms,* and in honor of that, I'm going to write this entire chapter in the form of show tunes, so get those jazz hands limbered up. No, sorry to disappoint you — I don't offer any soaring lyrics or unforgettable rhymes in the chapter. I do, however, sing the praises of knowing where to create OKRs and how often to update them, which are critical decisions for a successful OKRs implementation.

In this chapter, I share the most common choices for where to create OKRs, including at the company level only, or for the company and business unit, or for the entire organization. However, just because these are common choices doesn't mean they're right for you. This chapter also considers other potential areas for OKRs use including pilot groups, projects, and support groups. Finally, you explore the best cadence for setting OKRs — annual, quarterly, or trimester.

Take your seat because the curtain is about to go up.

Determining When to Use OKRs

Regardless of the situation, people are awash in options and choices in the modern world. Not long ago, I decided it was time to get a new pair of jeans, so off to the store I went, thinking I could be in and out in less time than it would take to make a sandwich. Boy, was I wrong. Within minutes, I was overwhelmed by the options that awaited me: straight leg, straight taper, slim straight, slim taper, bootcut, wide-leg, yadda yadda yadda . . . the dizzying list went on and on. Later that same day, I visited my dental hygienist for a cleaning, which ended in an array of choices for polishing: mint, strawberry, orange . . . more choices! After that it was lunch with a friend, and don't even get me started on the phone book–sized menu we had to choose from at the restaurant.

Fortunately, when it comes to deciding where to begin creating OKRs, the number of choices is far less overwhelming, but unlike picking out a pair of dungarees (shout-out to my father, who always called them that), the stakes are considerably higher. You can't write out each department of your org chart on a piece of paper, throw them all in a hat, and have your admin assistant choose the lucky winner who will blaze the OKRs trail for the company.

On the contrary, you should give careful consideration to the best group or groups to lead the way on your implementation. That decision will hinge on the following:

>> The amount of sponsorship you have at the top

>> The availability of strategic background materials

>> Your desire to foster collaboration

>> Your philosophy on individual involvement in OKR setting

I cover your primary options, those used by most organizations, in the following sections.

Creating OKRs at the Company Level Only

First, let me define some terms. When I say "company-level," I mean OKRs that would exist at the very highest level of the company. So whether you're General Motors, Netflix, or Uncle Morty's Wax Emporium, company-level OKRs are those created and used to gauge execution at the very top of the house. Whenever possible (and sometimes it isn't, as I'll explain), drafting OKRs at the company level is the preferred way to kick off your efforts.

Some benefits to starting at the top level

Starting at the top has several benefits. Foremost is the fact that OKRs you create at this level make it crystal clear for your entire employee population what you consider to be the most important items for the organization to focus on in the days ahead.

Also, I can't overstate the communication value provided by these OKRs. Keeping in mind how few people can name their company's top goals, by creating a small number of OKRs at this level, you send a powerful signal of what employees should pay attention to. You also provide the context that all lower-level teams require to create their own, connected OKRs.

I was going to continue on to drift into my next point but I'm not sure you'd be with me. Your eyes may be seeing the words but your brain may be stuck on something I slipped into the last paragraph: "small number of OKRs" You're wondering, "What does he mean by 'small number'? Two? Eight? Fifteen?"

Allow me to turn the tables on you. What do you think is a small but appropriate number of OKRs at the company-level? If you're like most of the CEOs I've worked with, your estimate of the appropriate number of OKRs at the company will be very low, maybe two or three. If so, it's likely because you want to instill the discipline of focus in your organization, and you'd be correct in wanting this. However, when it comes to actually drafting the OKRs, if you attempt to tell your story of success with such a succinct number of OKRs, the tendency is to lump concepts together or devise such generic OKRs that they could fit any company in the world, Uncle Morty's Wax Emporium included.

The number is also impacted by your current situation. If you're in crisis mode and mere survival is your goal, perhaps one or two well-chosen OKRs is exactly what you need. If, however, you're in steady-state, moderate-growth mode, you may be able to balance four to seven OKRs.

REMEMBER

The old adage "less is more" applies to company-level OKRs. An abundance of OKRs at this level results in a lack of focus and prioritization, causing confusion and skepticism in your employees as to what truly matters.

More benefits of starting at the top

Having settled the number of OKRs quandary, you can consider a couple of additional advantages of starting at the top level. An obvious benefit is the accountability that it yokes to your executives. It is their responsibility to see these OKRs through, demonstrating success that lifts the entire company.

Also, wins at this level will go a long way in generating enthusiasm for OKRs throughout the company. After people see the impact of OKRs at the very top, they'll be anxious to create their own OKRs, making it clear for all to see how their unique piece of the puzzle fits into place.

Now for the disadvantages of top-level OKRs

Although beginning at the top with your OKRs offers some clear benefits, you should also consider some potential disadvantages before automatically making it your default choice:

>> **The potential of creating generic OKRs that could apply to any organization:** The lack of specificity will greatly reduce the power of those OKRs to inspire lower-level teams, and may in fact signal to everyone that the status quo is just fine and your company's biggest aspiration is to be like everyone else.

>> **The possibility that your OKRs will be irrelevant:** This possibility comes into play if yours is a very large organization with dozens (or more) of business units around the world, each the size of significant businesses on their own. Think conglomerates with assets spanning the globe. For these companies, job one of the corporate group is allocating resources effectively, and most if not all of the metrics are financial in nature, providing little in terms of guidance or inspiration for lower-level groups.

Prerequisites for company-level OKRs

If you determine that company-level OKRs are the way to go for you, be aware of a couple of "must haves" before convening your C-suite colleagues for a drafting session. The first requirement is access to, and the participation of, your CEO. (See Chapter 4 for details on the imperative of executive sponsorship). If you can't rouse the sincere support of your CEO, you should reconsider not only starting at the top, but starting OKRs at all.

A second prerequisite for company-level OKRs is the existence of some form of strategic plan for the organization from which you can derive the OKRs. OKRs shouldn't be created in a vacuum. If you're sitting around a boardroom table engaging in blue-sky brainstorming and pondering, "Hmmm, what should we do?" you have a problem.

OKRs will help answer the question, "To successfully execute our strategy, what has to happen?" but only if you have a strategy in the first place. The word *strategy* can be tricky, though. You don't require a 300-page leather bound, gilt-edged report from the head office of a global consulting firm. Some answers to basic questions like, "What do we sell?" will get you on track. See Chapter 6 for more on strategy and OKRs.

WARNING

OKRs are a strategy-execution system, not a strategy-formation system. If you're relying on the process to help you create a strategy, you're putting the cart before the horse.

Creating OKRs at Both the Company-and Team Levels

A second option for where to create OKRs is at both the company and business unit or team level, which provides the obvious advantage of involving lower-level groups, thereby upping the odds of execution because more people within the organization are creating aligned OKRs. Although this section's heading suggests that OKRs would be created simultaneously at both the company and team levels, there should be some lag time between those efforts. Company OKRs are written first, widely communicated to ensure understanding, and only then, after that context has been created, should team-level OKRs be considered. Most of my firm's clients choose this option (company and team OKRs) when embarking on an OKRs process.

Deciding which teams and units to include

Should you decide to go the route of OKRs at both the company and team levels, your next order of business will be defining the word *team*. I'm using that word in a very generic sense because as far as I know, no universal terms exist for creating a company's organizational chart. For example, engineering and IT may be business units at your company, or they may be called departments, squads, or teams.

Rather than focus on the titles appearing on your org chart, a simpler approach is to determine how far down the chart you want to go with your initial foray into OKRs. Maybe it's the first level, those reporting directly to the CEO; or perhaps you'll go two levels down on the chart. The obvious caveat is that the deeper you go, the more complex your rollout becomes, and you need to carefully consider how much complexity you can take on as you're getting your feet wet with OKRs.

A phased approach, going one level at a time, is the most conservative and likely the safest route; my experience shows that most organizations are excited to expose as many people as possible to the power of OKRs. Thus, going deeper faster has major appeal.

Deciding between following the org chart or linking dependent teams

If I had been writing this book back in, say, 2016, this section probably would have ended right here. Pick your teams and swish-boom, move on to the next section. But having worked on hundreds of engagements with organizations all over the world, I know it's not that easy.

You have another fundamental question to answer after you've chosen who will create OKRs at the team level: Do you write OKRs based simply on titles in the org chart? For example, Sales would create Sales OKRs, Marketing would create Marketing OKRs, and so on. Given its simplicity, this approach was the default answer for many organizations as OKRs rose to prominence, but a downside quickly emerged: Creating OKRs in this way had a tendency to reinforce silos and discourage cross-functional collaboration, which is anathema to the spirit of OKRs. (So glad I could slip the word *anathema* into the book!)

Simply following the org chart may not be your best alternative for drafting team-based OKRs. Another option is to find teams that are highly dependent on one another and create OKRs for the merged entities. For example, in most organizations, the Sales and Marketing teams must work closely together in order to drive demand and revenue. Marketing finds the leads and supplies media and collateral, which supports Sales's efforts to convert interested onlookers into paying customers. In this case, it could make sense to create OKRs for Sales and Marketing as one cross-functional unit, which of course enhances collaboration and diminishes the silo mentality.

A potential challenge with the dependent-teams approach is the fact that in modern organizations, the pairings aren't likely to be so clean because of the vast web of interconnectedness among most teams operating today. When I ask teams who they depend on for success, they rarely isolate their response to one other team. There's often a dominant partner, but other dependencies exist as well.

TIP

In deciding whether to use the dependent-teams method, determine whether the core relationship or partnership among two teams is strong enough to warrant working together on creating merged OKRs. In other words, if they can't be successful without one another, there is a legitimate case for merged OKRs.

Creating customer-based OKRs

And now, in the spirit of a 3 a.m. infomercial peddling that hydrospa hand massager you just can't live without: But wait, there's more! You may also want to create team-based OKRs in reference to specific customer segments, or points along the way of the customer's journey with your company. An online retailer, for instance, could create OKRs for teams aligned with the checkout process, or the subscription process, or something else. Doing so has the advantage of driving collaboration among teams devoted to a specific outcome, but on the flip side it's not immune to the difficulty of ensuring that the relationship between the groups is strong enough to warrant shared OKRs. (In case you're wondering, I didn't make up the hydrospa hand massager; QVC really did sell them at $40.)

Creating Individual OKRs for the Entire Organization

Encouraging OKRs at the organization-wide level includes, of course, the controversial practice of having individual OKRs. You may be thinking, "Google uses individual OKRs, right? So shouldn't everyone?" And besides, is the question of using individual OKRs even up for debate, and what makes it a "controversial practice"?

Yes, Google does it, but you may not want to

Google, the poster child for all things OKRs, does have a history of using the framework at the individual employee level, but you have to keep in mind that OKRs were literally baked into the culture of Google practically from day one through John Doerr's influence with the founders. The system grew along with the company and has become an ingrained part of their culture, which is something most organizations cannot say. But even within the Googleplex, there are whispers of discontent over the practice, and some question its value. Most organizations should consider individual level OKRs optional, if they consider it at all.

If you do believe that individual OKRs are right for your company, it's most likely because you can envision the system driving alignment throughout the entire enterprise. You also likely subscribe to the notion that giving employees the chance to write an OKR will boost their support of the system because they will no longer see OKRs as a "corporate thing" but something that they themselves engage with and can potentially benefit from. Both are valid points, but on the "pro" side of the ledger, that's all I've got. Switching to the "con" side, however, reveals a host of potential problems with individual level OKRs.

I'll use an example of an individual OKR to introduce some challenges with the practice. Following is one from a software engineer — and I'm not picking on engineers; I've seen similar (in tone, style, and direction) from finance professionals, marketers, HR staff, you name it:

Objective: Improve my programming skills to help the company release products faster.

Key results:

1. Read the five most popular books on programming on Amazon.com.
2. Take three courses on programming languages.
3. Attain Oracle MySQL certification.

When charged with creating OKRs, most individuals will automatically default to personal development goals like those above. Absolutely nothing is wrong with personal development, and of course everyone should be actively encouraged to set goals for improvement. However, if you're hewing to the true intent of OKRs, your aim is to demonstrate business impact. The key results in the preceding example are binary "outputs" that fail to demonstrate how this programmer is contributing to the company's goal of releasing products faster in a quantitative fashion.

TIP

Determining and communicating your OKRs philosophy, whether or not you'll allow personal development goals as part of OKRs, will help ensure consistency in the OKRs created across the organization.

More issues with individual OKRs

If you decide to opt for individual OKRs in your company, be prepared for an avalanche of OKRs similar to what I present in the preceding section. If you accept these as valid OKRs, you're sending a clear signal about the OKRs philosophy that you've decided to adopt, and you can expect most OKRs that follow to be consistent with that philosophy.

Another problem is one of redundancy. It's very likely that personal development goals are already being tracked in an HR system for performance-review purposes, so having the same goal in two places serves no purpose and will most likely lead to confusion and skepticism over the value of OKRs.

Here are some additional challenges you can expect to face if utilizing individual OKRs:

>> **Artificially low targets:** Regardless of whether you're linking OKRs to compensation or performance reviews, after you introduce accountability to individuals, you can expect human nature to kick into high gear and self-preservation to take hold. The vast majority of people will choose conservative targets that they're likely to achieve rather than put themselves, their reputation, and their future with the company on the line by shooting for the moon.

>> **The Michelangelo problem:** In Chapter 4, the story of how Michelangelo required numerous assistants to complete his work on the Sistine Chapel illustrates that fact that the corporate world has no "lone rangers." Getting results requires people to come together to solve complex problems in innovative ways. It's exceedingly difficult for one person's OKR to have a material impact on the business's prospects.

>> **Individual focus:** I've yet to work with a company that creates only individual OKRs, with no company or team-level OKRs in place. If your organization has all three levels, you open the distinct possibility that folks will emphasize their own OKRs, ignoring the team-level goals and destroying any chance at gaining the synergies of collaboration. Once again, that's human nature working against you.

Before you write me off as a complete downer when it comes to individual involvement with OKRs, let me redeem myself by noting there are ways to involve people in the process without having them actually create OKRs of their own. For example, when you have OKRs at a team level, different individuals within the team may own each key result, providing them with a direct line of sight to the objective and a chance to make an impactful contribution through the success of their key result. It's entirely possible that not every single employee will own a key result, but keep in mind that achieving most key results also entails accomplishing certain tasks or activities. You can enlist additional individuals to take part in completing those tasks.

Considering Other Options for Where to Create OKRs

Most organizations will choose one of the areas outlined in the preceding sections to begin their OKRs expedition but, for whatever reason, they may not be the correct choice for you. Fortunately you have additional options to choose from:

>> Pilot groups

>> Project OKRs

>> Support-group OKRs

In the sections that follow, I delve into these three additional candidates for the creation of OKRs.

Piloting at a business unit or team

When I talk about pilots, I'm not referring to the hero on the Hudson, Sully Sullenberger, or the first episode of Netflix's latest must-binge series. A pilot in the OKRs context refers to the practice of implementing OKRs in just one or two business units or teams as a test of the system to determine whether a wider rollout across the organization is justified. If things go well with the pilot, you'll likely enlist other groups to create OKRs and make it an organizational imperative, whereas if the pilot groups fail to produce the expected benefits, you may say sayonara to OKRs. In other words, pilots are a relatively low-risk, low-cost method of determining whether OKRs are right for your company.

Advantages of a pilot program

Taking the pilot approach offers a number of advantages, including the aforementioned low-risk, low-cost nature of the rollout. Typically, pilot implementations aren't launched with as much fanfare as a full-scale, company-wide implementation. Not that you're conducting some sort of back-alley transaction, but because the work is confined to one or two groups, you don't need to widely communicate the effort throughout the company. You thereby both lower the actual financial costs of planning and communicating, and reduce potential reputational risks and costs if things don't pan out. Here are a few more potential upsides of a pilot approach:

>> **You can show proof of the concept:** A small-scale pilot allows you to test in real time whether OKRs are a good fit for your organization given what is happening in your environment, your history of goal setting, and other considerations. You may embark on the pilot with high hopes of greater focus only to

discover that your already robust KPI system (for example) provides ample information for strategic analysis and decision making, and OKRs are mostly redundant. Conversely, the pilot groups may demonstrate very quickly that OKRs enhance focus through a determination of, and emphasis on, what is most critical, while also improving collaboration within teams.

>> **You can show quick wins:** A successful pilot will highlight the benefits of OKRs, and those early wins will go a long way in driving interest and enthusiasm from other groups wanting to experience the benefits themselves.

>> **You can generate enthusiasm:** Related to the previous bullet, if the pilot groups find early success with OKRs, you can be sure that success will quickly grab the attention of other groups within the company who want to pour a little of the secret sauce on their operations as well. Interestingly, however, this seeming advantage has an evil twin lurking in the shadows, something a client of mine once described as "bootleg OKRs." The "Beware of bootlegged OKRs" sidebar explains this problem.

BEWARE OF BOOTLEGGED OKRs

With apologies to anyone who doesn't follow it, here's an American football analogy: The National Football League (NFL) is notorious as a "copycat" league: The minute one team seizes on a new way of running an offense, or creates a devious defensive blitzing scheme, the newfangled practices pop up on every sideline in the league within a matter of weeks. Business units and departments within companies aren't that different — except, of course, for the lack of $20 million salaries and cheerleaders rooting them on from outside their cubicles. When one group finds that something works well, others want to jump on board as well.

When a client of mine began with an OKRs pilot, the selected team showed early promise with the framework, garnering attention from pretty much everyone in the company. Cue the copy-catters. Before long, unprovoked and not yet invited to the party, other groups began creating OKRs. That's a champagne problem (groups enthusiastically wanting to jump on board the OKR train), but a problem nonetheless because those outside the pilot were implementing OKRs inconsistently. Soon, scattered methods of writing OKRs, scoring them, and reviewing results popped up, which led to confusion and ultimately frustration, potentially dooming a wider rollout.

Although you never want to dampen enthusiasm for any type of change effort, you also don't want that unbridled excitement to damage subsequent efforts to implement OKRs. If you employ a pilot and find that it's drumming up interest across the company, take the opportunity to then provide lots of information on what's to come in a potential wider rollout but discourage the active use of OKRs until a formal set of guidelines is in place.

Pilots, especially those showing early success, will generate a lot of interest from other areas of the company. Be prepared to communicate the larger plan for OKRs to ensure that the eventual rollout is conducted in a consistent way.

Disadvantages of a pilot program

On the disadvantage side of the pilot ledger, your team or teams may write OKRs that are completely unachievable, fail miserably in their attempt to reach them, and hence extinguish any chance of a wider rollout because their flaming mess makes it abundantly clear that "OKRs don't work." You can mitigate this possibility with coaching, either from an internal expert or an external consultant, who can guide the pilot team(s) in creating stretch, but realistic, OKRs.

One final issue with a pilot is the chance that you simply choose the wrong teams to engage in the process. For example, I strongly recommend against piloting with your Legal team. I have nothing against lawyers or the legal field in general, but in the corporate context, much of their work tends to be fairly routine and predictable making it less amenable to the "test, innovate, and stretch" mantra of OKRs.

Ditto for the Finance department. Again, I'm not taking shots at these groups; although I retired my calculator many years ago, my background is in finance, and I love a good spreadsheet as much as anyone. When determining a pilot team or teams, ensure that they have a line of sight to your customers (meaning that their actions impact what you sell), engage in a variety of activities, and are open to experimentation.

If a pilot approach seems to fit the bill, you'll need to have the following three things in place:

>> **Executive sponsorship:** This requirement never seems to go away does it? Even if your pilot team is located on an ice floe in Antarctica, thousands of miles from corporate headquarters (in other words, out of sight and relatively out of mind), trust me, word will still get around that they're trying this new thing called OKRs. The rationale for the effort will need to be communicated by a senior executive who, as detailed in Chapter 4, explains why the pilot is taking place now as well as the ultimate possibilities for OKRs at your company.

>> **A champion:** This requirement doesn't go away, either! Someone will need to play the lead in this production, ensuring that quality OKRs are created, a check-in process is instituted, and retrospectives that focus on learning are conducted at the end of each period. Chapter 4 explains the role of champion in detail.

>> **Time:** Humans are an impatient species; it's as simple as that. I'm reminded of a joke about someone who reads recipe instructions directing them to put a dish in the oven and bake at 300 degrees for 10 minutes. Most people would think, "I don't want to wait ten minutes! Hmm . . . what if I bake it at 3,000 degrees for one minute? I'll just put it in the kiln over here." I'm sure the results would be delicious.

Your OKRs need time to "bake" as well, with a healthy dose of patience required to iron out the inevitable kinks in your approach as you learn the ins and outs of OKRs and how best to apply them in your company. Give the pilot team (or teams) room to experiment and learn from the OKR experience before you judge whether the system will or will not work for your entire organization.

Using OKRs for projects

"Project" is one of those open-to-interpretation terms, so let me define it in the context of OKRs: A *project* is a long-term discretionary undertaking (spanning at least six months and sometimes multiple years); it occurs outside the organization's day-to-day activities and is designed to improve performance in an area of strategic importance. (Say that ten times quickly.)

Replacing the chairs in your reception area because the leather on the arms is cracking doesn't qualify as a project worthy of OKRs. I'm referring to big-ticket items, like installing an Enterprise Resource Planning (ERP) system, which takes extensive time and entails substantial human and financial resources to complete.

Using OKRs for projects is like piloting: another way to ease yourself into OKRs. Instead of creating company-level OKRs or deploying the system at the business unit and team level, you begin by creating OKRs for your firm's high-profile projects. Typically, you start by challenging yourself to describe the ultimate business impact you're hoping to achieve from the significant investment you're making in the project. Your answer to that question will help you frame the objective.

Next, you create a set of key results to measure that business impact. However, many projects of significant scale will take more than one year, so you don't want to "set and forget" key results; instead, the aim is to create OKRs for each quarter or trimester of the project's life span to gauge progress along the way.

In my experience, this method of OKR use has primarily been reserved for very large organizations with complex operations that are reluctant or unwilling to create company-level OKRs. Virtually all companies that are mammoth enough to have a global presence will have a portfolio of strategic projects, with very senior people attached as sponsors, that could be used as a starting point for OKRs.

Unless yours is a global behemoth, I don't recommend starting your OKRs process by aligning them with your strategic projects. My chief concern is that projects at this level tend to be very arcane, focused on one specific element of the organization's success, and therefore provide little guidance for lower-level teams to craft contributing OKRs.

Using OKRs for support groups

For the final time in this chapter, I'll begin by clearing up any confusion over the term I'm discussing in this section, in this case "support groups." First of all, I'm not talking about the kind of groups that help people through some sort of trauma (although if this book is assigned reading and you're really not all that into it, you may want to launch a support group for fellow readers . . . but I hope that's not the case). In the corporate context, *support groups* are departments that deliver services which, although not directly customer facing, ensure the smooth and efficient functioning of the organization. Finance, Legal, and Human Resources (HR) are prime examples.

In the "Piloting at a business unit or team" section, earlier in this chapter, I recommend against beginning an OKRs implementation with Finance or Legal. Here I expand that advice to suggest that you don't kickstart your rollout with any support group. Given the nature of their work, support groups can find it difficult to demonstrate direct business impact through the administration of their services, and as you know, the goal of OKRs is to show business impact. If you're a support group employee, you may be thinking, "Hang on here, mister, what we do is critical for the company," and you'd be right. I don't mean that support groups can't show business impact through their OKRs, but only that doing so can be more difficult than it is for a customer-facing group like Sales.

WARNING

If support groups create OKRs that simply mirror their business-as-usual activities, they (the OKRs) could remain the same forever, which violates the spirit of the framework. You want to ensure that support groups use challenges and opportunities to create effective OKRs.

All this begs the question, should support groups have OKRs at all? I'll pull my answer from the consultant's standard bag of tricks: "Yes . . . but." I take each of these one at a time.

The "yes" part of OKRs with support groups

Yes, support groups should absolutely have the opportunity to showcase their work and demonstrate their contribution to the company's strategic pursuits. Take an HR group, for example. Although much of their work is repetitive — hiring people, administering benefits, running employee surveys — they're not immune to challenges, and challenges are fertile ground for creating OKRs.

Recently, a client company was growing rapidly and needed to bring on new people quickly to help meet the demand they were seeing in the marketplace. Unfortunately, their relatively antiquated hiring process was better suited to their former slow-growth days, which made bringing on new people a slow and frustrating process. This is a perfect scenario for an OKR because a clear challenge exists, one that impacts the overall success of the business. The HR team created this OKR:

Objective: Improve the hiring process in order to reduce the number of days to hire a new employee.

Key Results:

1. Establish an employee bonus program for candidate referrals by February 1.

2. Increase job advertisements on social from two to four platforms.

3. Reduce the number of required interviews from five to three.

4. Decrease days to hire from 50 to 25.

This OKR is effective because it strives to solve a strategic challenge faced by the company (needing more people to satisfy growth) that HR is uniquely positioned to overcome (by improving the hiring process).

The "but" part of using OKRs with support groups

Now on to my "but" portion of the "Yes . . . but" answer to the question of whether support groups should have OKRs. Your support groups aren't likely to face a unique strategic challenge of the magnitude described previously (the HR example) for every period, and when no such significant hurdle presents itself, support-group OKRs tend to devolve into descriptions of business-as-usual activities (BAU). Although measuring the effectiveness of your BAU tasks is important, that's not the purpose of an OKR, so you need to determine whether simply creating an OKR in the absence of a significant opportunity or challenge is worth the team's effort.

Setting the Right Cadence for OKRs

When I was growing up, my family owned a soda (or, in that part of the world, pop) factory. As you can imagine, this made me not only a pretty popular kid but also a hyperactive one, thanks to a steady infusion of caffeine and sugar. I liked my pop cold, so I'd stick a warm bottle (soda wasn't in plastic much yet) in the freezer, planning to return to it later. But I'd often completely forget about it, and the next day, the freezer would look like a caramel-colored crime scene of broken glass and shards of frozen cola.

The potentially messy consequences of a problem I call "set it and forget it" doesn't just apply to absent-minded, soda-fueled kids. It's just as damaging to organizations hoping to unlock the benefits of OKRs.

When you create OKRs, the timeline for achievement can't be "whenever you get around to it," or "whenever it happens." OKRs are an agile goal-setting system, designed to respond to changes in your operating environment, and therefore you must limit the amount of time you apportion for completing the OKRs you set. In this section, I examine the most common cadences for OKRs, which fall along these lines:

>> **For company-level OKRs:** Annual

>> **For all lower-level OKRs:** Quarters or trimesters

Feel free to grab a drink before you get started, and make sure to check the freezer.

Timing company-level OKRs (Hint: Annual works best)

To prepare the ground for understanding the best cadence for company-level OKRs, here's a brief recap of the benefits of starting your OKRs implementation at this level: Starting at the top level enables you to

>> **Clarify your priorities** and areas of focus, scrubbing away any confusion over where people should be directing their time and attention.

>> **Demonstrate your senior leaders' commitment** to the process through the accountability required to see the OKRs through to completion.

>> **Provide a boost of enthusiasm** and buy-in for OKRs that will accelerate your efforts to align OKRs across the enterprise.

Sizing up why annual OKRs work best for the top level

For a couple of significant reasons, the default cadence with company-level objectives (I address key results later in this section) is annual. The first reason relates to size. Company-level objectives translate the organization's strategy and are typically substantial in scope, requiring generous portions of time and effort to complete.

Take, for example, a recent client of mine that was undergoing a major change in its operations. For years, this company enjoyed high market share thanks to relatively low competition in their industry. Not surprisingly, without the threat of competitors breathing down the company's neck, they became complacent, failing to maintain investments in customer service and innovation. They had basically devolved over the years into order takers, happy to collect their customers' money with little effort in moving the company forward.

This company's take-it-for-granted attitude is not a recipe for success in our turbulent times, with disruption lurking around every corner. Sure enough, new entrants to the market emerged and the company's market share began to tumble faster than a snowball down Mount Everest. The company embraced the idea of OKRs to help turn things around, bringing new focus and determination to the entire workforce. Their company-level OKRs related to the following:

- ❯❯ Deepening customer relationships
- ❯❯ Evaluating core units of their business to determine ongoing relevance
- ❯❯ Investing in research and development

These are substantial undertakings that can't be achieved overnight, or in a single quarter. They require significant effort and time, hence the reason for an annual cadence.

Allotting sufficient time for major shifts

There is a second rationale for keeping company-level objectives annual, which I'll introduce with an analogy and an admission of one of my (many) guilty pleasures: watching home-renovation shows on HGTV, that addictive wallpaper of TV networks. Watching some contractors tear apart and reassemble a house doesn't exactly offer nail-biting suspense, so producers ratchet up the drama, often with game-changing, last-minute design decisions. Just before a commercial break, the homeowners summon the harried contractor and tell them, "We've decided we want an open kitchen," forcing a cascade of major design changes. The sudden tension makes for compelling television, but it also drives a lot of change, confusion, and extra work for everyone involved.

Consider the corporate equivalent of such a dramatic change in direction. For instance, what if the company described previously suddenly decided, two months after creating their company-level OKRs, that they no longer wanted to focus on deepening customer relationships but were instead going all-in on better technology to process orders faster? Now the focus is driving operational excellence. Employees would rightly moan, "Whaaattt? You want us to do what? Oh, never mind . . . what was that headhunter's number?"

Such a change would confuse everyone as to the firm's true priorities. Also, any lower-level OKRs that were created to demonstrate alignment with deepening customer relationships would have to be rewritten, further alienating everyone.

In fairness to organizations operating in volatile circumstances, wild shifts in strategic direction are sometimes necessary to withstand sudden competitive pressures, stave off bankruptcy, or, on a more positive note, take advantage of a sudden change (perhaps in the regulatory environment) that provides a dynamic new opportunity. However, unless you find yourself in one of those highly dramatic situations, I strongly advise against any in-year shifts of annual company-level objectives.

Setting the cadence for key results

Thus far I've addressed company-level objectives, and made the strong case for an annual cadence, but what about key results? At the company level, a best practice is to adopt a dual cadence to ensure that you capture long-term business impact and the steps along the way that lead to that outcome. For example, harkening back again to the company discussed previously, one of their annual objectives related to deepening customer relationships. The first order of business was determining how they would know they've been successful in doing that; in other words, what is the business impact key result? They ultimately decided that one of the most critical key results was to increase the percentage of customers who purchased multiple products, and they assigned a target of increasing it from 20 percent to 40 percent over the course of the year.

In addition to this annual key result (which they monitored quarterly), they wrote additional key results each quarter to drive that outcome. For example, a first-quarter milestone key result focused on studying current customers to discover the top three pain points. Each quarter, the company created key results that they believed would help drive the ultimate impact result of increasing the percentage of customers buying multiple products. This dual-cadence approach ensured that they were simultaneously thinking long and short term.

Determining whether quarters or trimesters are right for you

I'm proud to say that my father served in the Canadian Navy, and despite the fact that I consider myself a patriotic son of both Canada and my adopted country, the United States, I was never drawn to the military life. That's probably a good thing for the safety and freedom of any country whose flag I may have served under because I would not have made a good soldier. Marching? Forget it; I'd never keep the beat and would inevitably have sent the entire line tumbling to the ground in my clumsy attempts to keep up. As for taking apart and reassembling a firearm — not a chance; I couldn't assemble a kid's building blocks.

All of which is to say that I'm reluctant to use a military metaphor, but if you'll allow me, even I know that it's the generals and admirals who draft the grand strategies that ultimately cascade down to the soldiers and sailors on the front lines and in the ships who carry out those orders. Those closest to the action adhere, of course, to the overall plans drawn up by their superiors, but when situations are changing right in front of them, they often have to alter their approach in recognition of what is taking place at the time.

In the corporate world, the C-Suite, led by the CEO, drafts the company's highest-level OKRs. As noted previously, these OKRs use annual objectives and both annual and quarterly key results. Lower levels in the organization are akin to the sailors and soldiers fighting a battle; they must be agile in their approach; hewing to the overall direction provided but reacting in real time to changes in their environment. For that reason all lower-level OKRs in a company almost exclusively adopt a shorter cadence, either by quarter or by trimester.

To this day, many OKRs practices adopted by organizations around the world can be traced to the initial choices Google made when rolling out the system at their inception, with cadence being one of them. Google runs on a quarterly cadence, and as OKRs grew in popularity, most companies accepted the 90-day window as the default for introducing the framework. The quarterly timeline ensured that business units, departments, and teams were agile in their approach, embracing each period as an opportunity to conduct a mini strategic-planning exercise of scanning their environment and updating OKRs in line with what was occurring in their world, all while attempting to ensure alignment with overall strategic direction.

The quarterly cadence isn't set in stone

Of course, none of that means you are required to operate on a quarterly cycle. One of the many things I love about OKRs is that it's an "open source" framework, meaning that no set rules or regulations must be followed in implementing the framework. It's not like the Finance profession, which has to adhere to generally accepted accounting principles when compiling financial statements in order to ensure consistency and transparency — unless you're a failed crypto darling or a devotee of the Madoff school of accounting, but that's a different story. With OKRs, you get to decide on the cadence that's best for you, and for many companies, 90 days isn't the right answer.

The challenge most organizations face in using a quarterly cadence for OKRs is the simple fact that everyone can relate to: time flies. Ninety days seem to zip by in the blink of an eye, making it sometimes difficult to achieve the business impact you've described in your objectives. And pragmatically, the calendar often works against you in your desire to drive breakthrough results with OKRs. The fourth quarter is especially challenging in the United States, for example, because many people take most of the Thanksgiving week off from work, so companies lose several days in November. Likewise for the December holidays. The time to show results in the fourth quarter shrinks from 12 weeks to something closer to nine or ten. Similarly, summer holidays reduce execution windows in the mid-year period.

TIP

Although a quarterly OKRs cadence has always been the default, you should carefully consider the pace of change in your business and industry, and the impact of statutory holidays and vacations on your ability to execute in a timely fashion before determining your own organization's cadence.

The trimester as an alternative

Many organizations are now turning to four-month, or 120-day, periods called trimesters when creating OKRs below the company level. The additional weeks offer immense breathing space for setting, executing, checking in on, and reviewing OKRs. In practice, most teams work with a mix of milestone and metric key results. Frequently the milestones, which are critical drivers of the metric, business-impact key results, take significant time to achieve. The longer cadence of trimesters provides the opportunity to ensure that milestones are properly executed, thereby offering time for the metric key results to be realized. The extra time also allows you to make in-period interventions if key results aren't trending in the right direction.

A 16-week cadence may also reduce a phenomenon that is not often talked about but certainly present in many companies: goal fatigue. Setting audacious OKRs for 90 days with the weighty expectation of achieving them only to then be required to create yet another set of stretch OKRs 90 days later, and then 90 days after that, is a daunting and grueling task for most teams that can't be overcome by just toughing it out or holding all-night, caffeine-fueled brainstorming sessions. Simply coming up with new and innovative OKRs can prove challenging in such a compressed window of time.

REMEMBER

Stretching the process to four months instead of three may not seem like a large difference, but tactically, pragmatically, and psychologically, it offers enough additional space to let in the creativity required to craft and execute sound OKRs.

Setting the OKRs timeline

Perhaps you have regular rituals that you wouldn't dare skip in your daily routine. One of mine is quiet time in my favorite chair with my espresso after lunch. I can't imagine a day without this refreshing, energizing ritual.

To succeed with OKRs, you need to build rituals as well — standard practices that bring the system to life. Such rituals include the following:

>> How often to check in

>> How to score

>> How to create alignment

>> When to set your OKRs

In this section, I focus on team-level OKRs because your company OKRs will most likely be set based on the preexisting rhythms of your annual strategic-planning process. (I discuss alignment and other necessary rituals in the chapters ahead.)

Because individual organizations will kick off their OKRs efforts at different days and months of the year, there is no universal protocol for OKR setting. Therefore, with the following timeline, I assume a steady state of OKRs in your organization, meaning that your implementation is under way. With that caveat, here is a standard timeline you may want to follow each period:

>> **Two weeks before the end of the current period:** Begin deliberations on OKRs for the next period:

  • Scan your operating environment

  • Share relevant information on any changes taking place

  • Meet with the team to create draft OKRs

  • Outline any dependencies with other teams

>> **One week from the end of the current period:** Meet with any dependent teams to converge on shared OKRs. If you can't come to agreement, escalate any differences of opinion to your respective leaders.

>> **First week of the new period:** Resolve all dependencies and have your OKRs approved by leadership. With your OKRs finalized, it's time to start executing!

As noted previously, this timeline focuses exclusively on setting OKRs. You also need to consider the timing of OKRs check-ins and an end-of-period retrospective. Both will impact your selection of OKRs, and I discuss them in detail in Chapter 11.

Chapter **6**

The Raw Materials of OKRs: Mission, Vision, and Strategy

The terms *mission, vision, and strategy* are some of the most misunderstood, overused, and universally mocked terms in the business vocabulary. But understanding these three components of business is necessary to creating compelling OKRs. After all, mission, vision, and strategy should be the guideposts for everything your business does. Without these guideposts, you can't come up with meaningful OKRs that will drive your success.

In this chapter, I flip the script on these much-maligned terms by digging deeper into the power of each, showing how to create them and outlining exactly why they are critical to creating effective OKRs.

Agreeing on the Definitions of "Mission," "Vision," and "Strategy"

Organizations love to throw around the terms "mission," "vision" and "strategy," often in the absence of any deep thinking about their customers, markets, or competition. It's as if a lyrically composed mission, technical vision, or fluff-filled strategy statement can cover up for a lack of deep thinking and analytical rigor. News flash: They can't. Organizations that engage in that soft thinking are missing out on the tremendous benefits of

» A truly inspirational mission that makes your purpose clear

» A compelling vision of the future

» A well-thought-out strategy that will vault you to the top of your industry

The biggest hurdle to overcome with these terms is simply defining them clearly. If there are three terms with more potential definitions out there, I don't know what they could possibly be. Ask ten different people to define strategy, for example, and you're likely to get ten different answers. And the sad part is that those ten people could all be working in the same company! You have no way to derive value from a mission, vision, or strategy without universal agreement on what each represents and how best to use them in your organization. So I want to start at the very beginning — it's a very good place to start — and define these terms.

WARNING

In this chapter, I provide definitions of the terms "mission," "vision," and "strategy" based on my 25-plus years of experience as a practitioner, author, and consultant to more than 500 organizations. These are the definitions I've seen successfully utilized at countless organizations. However, if you choose to use a different definition for any of the terms, that's okay, with one enormous condition: You use the definitions consistently across the company and over time. Inconsistent definitions will undoubtedly lead to confusion and skepticism.

» The *mission* represents an organization's core purpose; that is, why it exists. It goes beyond the goal of making money if you're a for-profit company. Something deeper propels you, and that something is the mission.

» A *vision* is best thought of as a word picture of what the organization ultimately intends to become, maybe five or even ten years into the future. Whereas the mission can be somewhat abstract, the vision is concrete, using the sheer power of numbers to outline the desired future.

» *Strategy* represents the broad priorities adopted by an organization in recognition of its operating environment and in pursuit of its mission and vision.

Great, I've defined the terms, but these definitions really just scratch the surface of their potential. The rest of the chapter focuses on why you need each of these pieces, how to create them, and how they relate to the OKRs you're going to write.

Mission: Stating Why Your Business Exists

Here's a fun fact: If you were starting a company back in the 19th century, receiving a corporate charter wasn't a matter of filling out some forms, paying fees, and boom — you're in business. No, charters of that era were considered a privilege — and with that privilege came the obligation to serve the public interest. In other words, the company had to demonstrate a greater purpose. That purpose can be described as a mission: how your company's existence is making the world a better place in some way.

Even in today's Wall Street–driven, "make your quarterly numbers or else" world, there is still a place for the mission statement, which describes how an organization is indeed serving the public interest and why it matters. The mission should be written to stand the test of time — maybe a hundred years. Here's an example, from Marriott:

To make people away from home feel that they are among friends and are really wanted.

The hotel industry may change dramatically in the decades to come. Who knows — in 50 years we may be checking in at the Space Station for our suite on Mars. But Marriott's mission will stand the test of time; travelers will always want to feel they are among friends and really wanted, and that guidepost will motivate everyone at Marriott — from top to bottom — to provide the service necessary to meet that lofty standard.

Yes, you need to take the time to create a mission statement

Why people work is probably far too philosophical a question for this book, so without going too deep down the existential rabbit hole, I think we can all agree that purpose and fulfillment don't come exclusively from our salary or bonus checks. Most of us want to make a difference, whether that comes in the form of making our customer's lives a little better in some way or safeguarding the planet for future generations. The mission your organization creates will represent the collective embodiment of that desire; and that's a powerful force!

Enlightened leaders have always recognized and taken advantage of this tremendous motivational tool. David Packard, co-founder of Hewlett-Packard, is a prime example. Way back in 1960, he had this to say about the topic of purpose:

A group of people get together and exist as an institution that we call a company so they are able to accomplish something collectively that they could not accomplish separately — they make a contribution to society . . . do something which is of value.

A CLASSIC EXAMPLE OF FULFILLING A MISSION

An inspirational leader who recognized the power of a higher purpose was George Bailey. You're probably wondering, *"George Bailey . . . hmm . . . where have I heard that name before? Microsoft? Apple?"*

You haven't read about him in the *Wall Street Journal* or *Forbes*. George Bailey, portrayed to perfection by Jimmy Stewart, is the lead character of my all-time favorite Christmas movie, *It's a Wonderful Life*, from 1946. If you haven't seen the film, well . . . you probably haven't had your TV on during Christmas Eve for the past 50 years, but that's okay; read on for the pertinent details.

George runs a family-owned savings and loan company. He's desperate to escape the confines of his small town and what he views as a "two-bit" operation, but circumstances conspire to keep him chained to his desk in his hometown of Bedford Falls. At one point in the film Mr. Potter, the evil, money-grubbing villain who is eager to take over the Savings and Loan, gives George an offer that he seemingly would be crazy to refuse: a princely salary and perks that would instantly make him wealthy and successful beyond his wildest dreams. But the catch is that he has to close his bank.

So does George accept the offer and turn his back on the patrons of his lowly Savings and Loan operation? Not a chance; he realizes almost instantly that there is more to life than money and prestige. He rebukes Potter's offer, noting the admirable purpose of his company: giving decent, hard-working people the chance to own their own homes. That mission is greater than any one person, and it propels George to turn down an offer that would have put him on Easy Street. That's the power of a mission, and it extends beyond the imagination of Hollywood screenwriters.

A more recent example comes from Google's former senior vice president of People, Laszlo Bock, who described Google's mission, "To organize the world's information and make it universally accessible and useful," as being the cornerstone of the company's culture.

You may think that identifying your business's mission sounds a little too "soft." After all, business is a battleground, right? You slug it out in the trenches to win market share and create value for your shareholders; end of story.

Not quite. Today more than ever, employees have a choice of where they work and to whom they'll devote their human capital. Organizations are in a war for talent, and the balance of power has shifted dramatically from the buyers to the suppliers — your employees. It turns out that your team members really do care about what you stand for and why you exist. In one survey, for example, about 80 percent of people said that they expect CEOs to be personally visible in sharing the company's purpose, and around 75 percent want CEOs to discuss how their company benefits society. In another survey, employees considered purpose (mission) to be more than twice as important, on average, as traditional motivators such as compensation and career development. The bottom line: Mission matters.

OKRs are best used to drive visionary thinking and innovative ideas. The truly gifted among us may have the cognitive horsepower to generate flashes of brilliance on a whim, but most of us don't possess that capability. Instead, we need coaching, a little prodding, and some guidance on the path to inspiration. The mission can serve as your beacon, clearly outlining to everyone why the work they're undertaking matters, and inspiring them to demonstrate their contribution every day.

Knowing what makes an effective mission statement

Auto racing has a saying: "To finish first, first you have to finish," meaning that if you hope to stand on top of the podium celebrating a race win, the first order of business is simply avoiding a crash and finishing the race.

Applying that logic to mission statements, to have an effective mission statement, you must first *have* a mission statement. So if you don't currently have one, or if your existing mission was created and last reviewed sometime during the Clinton administration when your business was in entirely different circumstances, here are two methods for establishing your unique mission:

>> **Method 1 — The Mission Template:** Many mission statements consist of three distinct segments. Completing them with responses that fit your company is a great way to kickstart the discussion of your mission. Here goes:

- **We exist to** (primary purpose, need served, or problem solved)

- **For** (primary customers or stakeholders)

- **So that** (long-term outcomes determining success)

>> **Method 2 — The 5 Whys:** To use this approach to mission development, start with a descriptive statement such as "We make X products" or "We deliver Y services." Then ask, "Why is this important?" five times. A few "whys" into this exercise, your true mission begins to emerge. This process works for virtually any product or service organization. A waste-management company could easily move from "We pick up trash" to "We contribute to a stronger environment by creatively solving waste-management issues" after just a couple of rounds.

WARNING

Don't attempt to write your mission by committee. Take it from me, it's impossible to get a group to agree on the temperature in a meeting room, let alone come to agreement on your core purpose. Five or six people attempting to develop a concise and powerful statement is a sure recipe for compromise, confusion, and endless wordsmithing. It's okay to bring together a group to brainstorm initial concepts, but then have one or two people craft a statement that a larger group can then evaluate.

In case you need a little inspiration, here are the mission statements of some well-known organizations:

>> **Merck:** To preserve and improve human life.

>> **3M:** To solve unsolved problems innovatively.

>> **Microsoft:** Our mission is to empower every person and every organization on the planet to achieve more.

>> **Sony:** To experience the joy of advancing and applying technology for the benefit of the public.

>> **Amazon:** To be Earth's most customer-centric company.

>> **ING (Financial Services):** Empowering people to stay a step ahead in life and in business.

You're not writing the great American novel here, and volume is not the goal. Keep your mission statement relatively short; a good target is 20 words or fewer. Anything beyond that amount risks the dreaded MEGO effect ("my eyes glaze over") when people read the statement. The mission should be short enough to easily memorize.

Okay, so now you have a mission. Great job! But to ensure that it serves its purpose of acting as your long-term compass, keep the following characteristics in mind:

>> **It's focused:** The late business guru Peter Drucker, author of dozens of influential books over his long and distinguished career, once said that one of the biggest mistakes organizations commit is turning their missions into "hero sandwiches of good intentions." I love that, and I've definitely witnessed it over my long and less distinguished career. The tendency when writing mission statements is to cram them with every imaginable noble deed the writers can dream up. But that's not the point here. Your mission statement should be *your* mission statement — a focused declaration of your unique purpose, not an attempt to be all things to all people.

>> **It inspires change:** I noted earlier that your mission should be written to stand the test of time, but that doesn't mean it shouldn't inspire change along the way. Take Walmart Canada as an example. Their mission is "To save Canadians money to help them live better." The world of retail is constantly shifting, and Walmart has to adjust accordingly. However, you can bet that 20, 50, or 100 years from now, people will still want to save money to live better.

>> **It's easy to understand and communicate:** A mission statements can easily become a canvas for "Buzzword Bingo." If your statement is crammed with words like "synergistic," "sustainable," "engagement," "cross-pollination" (is that even a thing if you're not a bee?), and so on, then look out, because I'm about to holler "Bingo." For this exercise, set aside that thesaurus and rely on simple language that everyone can understand and most important, that reflects the culture of your organization.

Your mission statement should reflect your organization. You can't copy the statement of another company and hope that echoing their words will transform your company. After you've composed a draft, try this quick test to ensure that the mission is ready for prime time: Share your statement along with that of a competitor and see whether employees can tell the difference. If they're scratching their heads trying to figure out which is which, it's back to the whiteboard for you!

If you already have a mission statement

If you can't immediately bring your mission statement to mind, that doesn't necessarily mean it doesn't exist. I've lost count of how many times I've visited a client, asked to see the mission statement, and been greeted with, "We don't have one." But then, just moments later, someone bravely says, "Actually . . ." and the story of the long-lost mission statement surfaces. Usually in these cases, the task of writing the mission was delegated to a subteam, often from HR; the statement was created, put in a PowerPoint presentation, shared once, and never seen again. So you may have some digging to do before you declare that you don't have a mission statement.

If you do have a mission, whether it was created yesterday or 20 years ago and is now gathering cyber dust on a long-retired laptop, it's always a good practice to reevaluate it in light of your decision to embark on the creation of OKRs. The first step is to simply examine what you have with respect to its adherence to the characteristics I describe earlier in the previous section. In addition, does it clearly represent your company and culture?

Here are a few additional items to consider when putting your current mission under the microscope:

>> **Make sure that it's current.** I've noted that mission statements should stand the test of time, but if yours was written when you sold ice skates and you've since ditched the blades to market boots, it's a good idea to rewrite the mission so that it reflects what you actually do.

>> **Leverage the wisdom of the crowd.** Before writing a new mission, give your employees the chance to share how they would write the statement. Send out a simple survey asking everyone to describe the company's core purpose — that is, why it exists. The responses may surprise and enlighten you.

>> **Determine how the mission fits in.** Have you noticed that pretty much everything around us is growing? For example, if you head over to your local casual dining restaurant, you'll likely be greeted with a menu the size of an old Manhattan phone book. Of course, you'll probably pay for the meal with your credit card. You know, the one whose agreement you barely skimmed that has mushroomed from about 400 words in 1980 to more than 20,000 today. Unfortunately, it's happening in the corporate world as well. Many organizations will have mission, vision, values, strategy, imperatives, pillars of excellence, KPIs, OKRs, Balanced Scorecards. The list goes on and on, and often there are significant redundancies among the documents. Needless to say, this is overwhelming and confusing for employees who crave, above all else, clarity and transparency. Ensure that your mission is properly positioned and not competing with similar sentiments for employee mind share.

REMEMBER

Although mission can seem like "soft stuff," distracting you from the real work of business success, it does matter — to your employees, your customers, and your community. Jim Collins, the bestselling author of *Good to Great*, sums it up nicely:

The question of mission has become, if anything, even more important as our world becomes increasingly disruptive and turbulent. No matter how much the world changes, people still have a fundamental need to belong to something they can feel proud of. More than any time in the past, people will demand that the organizations of which they are a part stand for something."

That quote started out as good, but I'd say it went to great. Thanks, Jim!

Vision: Creating Your Picture of the Ideal Future

On May 25, 1961, NASA pilot Joseph A. Walker guided his hypersonic Air Force X-15 to an astonishing 107,000 feet above sea level. This was quite an achievement, but back in Washington, D.C., someone was setting their sights on going a bit further into space; a mere 1.26 billion feet further, to be exact. That man was President John F. Kennedy, and on the very day Walker was soaring above the earth, Kennedy addressed a joint session of Congress to lay out his audacious vision of sending a man to the moon. Specifically, he said: "I believe that this nation should commit itself to achieving the goal, before this decade is out, of landing a man on the moon and returning him safely to earth." He went on to acknowledge that it would be neither cheap nor easy, but in achieving the goal, the entire country would feel a sense of national pride because, indeed, everyone must work to put that man on the moon.

The nation took up Kennedy's challenge, with engineers solving seemingly unsolvable challenges, scientists and machinists fabricating parts for space ships that had previously existed only in the minds of science fiction authors, and a small group of brave people training diligently for the historic mission. And against all odds, it succeeded. On July 20, 1969, Neil Armstrong lowered his ladder from the Apollo 11 capsule and became the first human to walk on the surface of the moon.

I can't think of a better example of the power of vision than the moon expedition. The President's inspiring language, the specificity and boldness of the target, and the fact that it was bound to a clear time frame are all hallmarks of a rousing and effective vision statement. The very good news is that the advantages of a vision aren't the exclusive domain of those dreaming about the conquest of galaxies far, far away. Every organization can seize upon the power of vision to galvanize their people around a lofty goal. Ready to blast off? Onward!

Understanding the ins and outs of vision statements

You've written your mission statement, and everyone loves it; they're fired up, passionate about why they do what they do each and every day while living your core purpose. That mission is a necessary, but not sufficient, ingredient to take your organization to the next level of success. Now it's time to harness the energy from your mission and focus it in one laser-like beam of inspiration called your vision statement.

The mission statement, although engaging and inspiring, can often appear a bit abstract. Take, for example, Merck's mission: "To preserve and improve human life." That's a terrific representation of the company's core purpose — that is, why it exists, but on its own it won't guide employees to a specific destination.

That's where the vision statement comes in. Think of vision as a word picture of what the organization intends to become. Not by tomorrow, because you need some time to reach your destination. But maybe 5, 10, or even 15 years in the future. The vision may encompass financial targets, markets served, and innovative new products or services, just to name a few possible elements.

With a captivating shared vision, everyone in the organization, from the shop floor to the C-Suite, has a collective mental framework that will help them shape their desired future. Vision should always follow mission, your *raison d'être*, because a vision without a mission is just wishful thinking that isn't tied to, or in the service of, anything enduring or meaningful.

Knowing what makes an effective vision statement

Before I dig into the attributes of an effective vision statement, here's a look at two examples. The first is based on a high-performance bicycle company. They offer the kind of bikes that competitive cyclists, those in world-class events like the Tour de France, depend on for speed and reliability. But the company's main source of revenue comes from selling bikes to weekend-warrior MAMILs. I'll probably lose you if I don't spell out the MAMIL acronym, so here goes: It stands for Middle-Aged Men in Lycra. I'm sure you've got a visual. Some very athletic types but a good mix of dad-bods in there as well. Of course there are plenty of women cyclists, too, but I guess MAWIL just isn't as catchy an acronym. Back to the company's vision: "By 2025, we will achieve our triple-double: Double our revenue, number of riders, and races won."

Here's a second example. This one is based on a company in the industrial supply industry, and fortunately no acronyms are necessary to describe their customers. Their vision is as follows:

"Across four generations, our proprietors and devoted staff have constructed a business that fills us with pride. We offer best-in-class services in our selected domains, consequently fostering fulfilling professions and financial advantages for shareholders and employees alike. The owners have a vision for the future, aiming to expand upon this esteemed legacy of triumph by cultivating and implementing the utmost standards of: honesty, reliance, and reciprocal admiration; an enterprising mindset coupled with cautious administration; empowered personnel and an acceptance of setbacks when ambitious endeavors fall short; ongoing education and reinvention within the organization; cooperative alliances — achieving victory collectively with strategic suppliers, customers, and personnel; and excellence in our chosen fields both internally and externally."

I refer to both those examples in illustrating the key attributes of an effective vision statement, which I outline in the following section.

Quantified and time bound

A vision statement must go beyond platitudes and be concrete in describing the ideal future envisioned by the organization. That means using actual numbers, whether in the form of a time period, dollars, percentages, and so on. The bike company's vision statement, given in the previous section, fulfills these requirements by declaring 2025 as their target date and outlining what they expect to achieve in terms of revenue, riders, and races won. They don't provide actual numbers for the latter three items, but that decision reflects more of a style choice than a violation of the rules of vision writing.

That distinction points to a choice you'll need to make as well. That is, they could have outlined the actual revenue, number of riders, and number of race wins they hope to achieve, but they chose to focus on the word *double*, and even drew on the idea of a "triple double." A vision must be memorable, and rather than have people commit three different numbers to memory, the bike company opted to keep the statement simple and rely on the power of doubling.

There is no right or wrong approach to this choice. Its suitability will depend on your culture and, of course, your actual vision. If, for example, you include just one element in the vision —a revenue figure, say — then it makes sense to include the actual number. If you have multiple elements to your vision, as in the bike example, using a catchy phrase may be the best alternative.

A vision statement should be

>> **Concise:** If you read my example of the industrial supply company's vision statement in the previous section, how much do you remember? (Don't look back!) You may be able to recall a stray word here or there, but the gist of the thing? Forget it, unless you have a photographic memory. (Mostly, only kids have that, and I doubt you're a kid reading this, so I doubt you recalled much of the vision.) It's just too long. Way too long.

The best vision statements seize your attention and immediately invite you in. When Muhtar Kent assumed the CEO position at Coca-Cola in 2008, his reply to a question about his top priority moving forward was, "Establishing a vision . . . a shared picture of success. We call it 2020 vision, and it calls for us to double the business in ten years. It's not for the fainthearted, but it's clearly doable" (see Muhtar Kent, "Shaking Things Up at Coca-Cola," *Harvard Business Review*, October 2011). Kent's vision is both concise and powerful. Notice, also, that it's quantified and time bound.

>> **Verifiable:** If you include numbers in your vision, this point should be a slam dunk for you because numbers are, by their very nature, verifiable. You either hit them or you don't. If your statement is chock-full of phrases like "leading edge," "top quality," or "best in class," you're in trouble, because they are not objectively verifiable. "Leading edge" could mean a hundred different things depending on your industry, product and service mix, maturity of the marketplace, and more.

In the two example visions I present in the previous section, the bike company's has a number of verifiable elements, whereas the industrial supply company's vision is filled to overflowing with subjective phrases like "enterprising mindset," "empowered personnel," and "cooperative alliances." All such phrases are open to interpretation and therefore not verifiable.

REMEMBER

Strive to make your vision statement about 20 words or fewer.

>> **Inspiring yet feasible:** I put these two elements together because they represent a challenging tightrope that you have to walk if you hope to create an effective vision statement. Of course, your vision must arouse the collective passion of the entire organization, lifting them up to the possibilities of a grand future. However, if the statement is clearly not bounded by reality, you'll quickly invite skepticism and doubt, the very Kryptonite of vision accomplishment.

I've seen this process in action with clients over the years. One example is of an organization in the fintech (financial technology) space, newly formed with lots of A-list investor backing and a service that seemed destined to blow the competition out of the water. But nothing about its offering had actually been proven in the marketplace. The CEO brought his team together and within seconds proclaimed the vision to be reaching $1 billion in revenue in the next 18 months. If the moment had been captured in a movie, it would surely have featured a spit-take of someone spraying a drink all over the room in reaction to the CEO's crazy notion.

This was a company that at that point had about three paying customers and was embryonic in its overall development. Heck, it took Facebook five years to reach a billion dollars in revenue. Despite loud and reasoned protests from his team, the CEO put his foot down and the vision was set.

But it didn't prove to be inspirational. On the contrary, this company never really got off the ground, and eventually, investors lost an ocean of money. Of course, you can't pin its downfall solely on a poorly constructed vision statement, but the CEO's weak grasp on reality and his unrealistic goals surely didn't help the team as it struggled to find its way in the market. Your vision has to be grounded in reality, and for that to happen, you need to do your homework. Start by asking yourself these questions:

- What is the total addressable market in your space?
- What are your core capabilities and strengths?
- Is the overall market growing or declining?

These and other questions will help you create a vision that inspires your team with a great challenge but makes it clear that you can indeed achieve it.

Brainstorming your vision statement

One of my hobbies is screenwriting, specifically feature films, and like anyone who has ever opened a new document and started typing away on their magnum opus, I stop occasionally to practice my acceptance speech at the Academy Awards. And trust me, it's a good one! I thank my family, of course, and everyone who supported me along the way, but also show my gratitude to Steven Spielberg for recognizing my talent and giving me the opportunity to work with him. Yes, it gets that detailed, and more, much more. It may sound a little crazy, but every time I return to the laptop after this pleasant reverie, I have a renewed sense of purpose. That glimpse into a magnificent future of hobnobbing with Spielberg and polishing my Oscar never fails to pump me up and stimulate plenty of new ideas. Essentially, I'm creating a vision for the future.

The organizational equivalent of my process can be just as fun, entertaining, and productive. Think of a business magazine that you consider prestigious and influential. It may be *Forbes, Fast Company, Harvard Business Review* — any will do. Imagine it's five years from now and your company is featured on the cover. What's the headline? What have you done to see your logo and name emblazoned on the front of that magazine? Did you grow to previously unimagined heights? Did you create a breakthrough product or service the world can't live without? Did you create a new market where nothing existed in the past?

Brainstorming the text that appears on the cover is a great way to kickstart your visioning exercise. Chances are, it will lead you to consider revenue or profit aspirations, innovation, design, and a host of other possible elements of your success that you can encapsulate in your own vision statement.

TIP

Writing the vision shouldn't initially be confined to the C-Suite. Start by polling your employees and getting their input. Including your entire organization is a great opportunity to create excitement about the future and give everyone the chance to voice their opinion on your way forward. After you have lots of input, the senior team can write the final vision.

One of my favorite CEOs of the past 20 years is Alan Mulally, who led the Ford Motor Company from 2006 to 2014. His tenure included the historic financial crisis of 2008, which ultimately caused crosstown rivals General Motors and Chrysler to file for bankruptcy. With Mulally's steady hand at the helm, Ford was the only one of the big three auto makers not to ask for a government loan, and the company was eventually able to see its way through the crisis. Mulally was lauded with many awards for his leadership, including chief executive of the year in 2011. How did he do it? By starting with vision. Here's how he put it: "What I have learned is the power of a compelling vision . . . . The leader's job is to remind people of that vision, make sure they stick to the process, and keep them working together." It worked for Ford, and it can work for you — the power of vision!

Strategy: Getting Your Priorities Straight

A quick look at my bookcase reveals that probably a quarter or more of my book collection relates to the topic of strategy. And that's just my physical books. My Kindle app holds dozens more on the topic.

But if you were to do nothing but read 24/7, you could never keep up with the raging river of ink devoted to strategy. People write about what it is, how to create it, why it matters, and every other conceivable notion related to what is probably the most widely used yet least agreed upon word in the business lexicon. Because it's such an enormous subject, with literally hundreds of books, thousands of papers, and countless highly paid gurus devoted to its study, grappling with strategy can be confusing and overwhelming to even the most seasoned business leaders. Given the vastness of the landscape, I can't provide a comprehensive overview of the topic in these pages. But what I can do is demystify it for you.

First, a simple definition of *strategy:* the broad priorities in recognition of its operating environment and in pursuit of its mission and vision. Here's a breakdown of that definition:

>> **Broad priorities:** These represent your decisions regarding critical questions such as which customers to serve, what markets to enter, why your customers choose to buy from you, and more.

>> **In recognition of its operating environment:** Strategy isn't created in a vacuum. You must have a firm grasp of what is taking place around you in order to determine those aforementioned broad priorities. For example, consider these questions:

- Is your overall market growing or receding?

- What is the state of innovation in your industry?

- Are regulatory issues looming that could impact your position in the marketplace?

>> **In pursuit of its mission and vision:** Your strategy should be consistent with your mission and vision. Take the plant-based food company, Impossible Foods. Their stated mission is, "To make our global food system truly sustainable." They believe that using animals to "make meat" is a destructive technology that is extremely harmful to the environment. Therefore, their strategy is unlikely (one would hope) to relate to cutting corners in manufacturing, possibly increasing carbon emissions, in order to save a few bucks.

With a definition of strategy in hand, the following sections dig deeper to examine the intersection of strategy and OKRs while reviewing a number of questions you'll need to answer to create your own strategy.

Understanding why strategy is critical to OKRs

When I started my career, around the time the San Francisco 49ers were dominating the NFL (you'll have to Google the 49ers and then try to figure out which era of dominance I began my career in to see how old I am), companies often created strategic plans spanning a decade or more. The pace of just about everything was slower then, and defaulting to the comfort of the status quo when it came to the future was a perfectly acceptable and reasonable approach for many organizations.

But as they always do, the winds of change accelerated, primarily with the advent of the internet and the era of speed it ushered in on virtually every front. Strategic plans necessarily became shorter. And shorter, and shorter — to the point that pretty much every company now reviews their strategy at least annually to ensure that they're keeping pace in our VUCA-infused (volatile, uncertain, complex, ambiguous) world.

The question you may be wrestling with, based on the ever-increasing rate of change in the world and probably your industry, is this: Does strategy even matter anymore? When any competitive advantage you eek out today could be erased by a nimble competitor tomorrow, and predicting the next breakthrough product or service to take the world by storm is impossible, why expend the effort to try to carve out your view of the future?

However, the fact is (cliché coming) that thinking strategically may be more important now than ever. The pace of change occurring today doesn't lead exclusively to puzzling challenges; for those who are prepared, it provides ample opportunities as well. The problem is to separate the signal from the noise and isolate your focus on the opportunities you're best suited to take advantage of both now and going forward. What you can't do is chase every possible opportunity that is dangled in front of you (what many of my clients call the "shiny object syndrome").

Strategy provides boundaries, helping you determine not only what you should do but also, just as critically, what you won't do. The entire organization requires a shared view of where you're going and how you plan to get there. Only then is it possible for every team, and maybe even every individual, to determine their unique contribution to your success through aligned OKRs. Without the benefit of a strategy, your organization is like a rudderless boat, bobbing from wave to wave but getting nowhere.

WARNING

If you read the previous section and thought, "Well, I don't really know the strategy but I'm pretty sure Dev or Kate (fill in the name of your CEO) does," you're in trouble. The inimitable baseball pitcher Bill Lee once said this about money: "It's like manure, only good when it's spread around." The same can be said of strategy.

Getting started with strategy

Here's the good news: You really need to answer only a few core questions to create a strategic plan for your company. Ready?

1. What do you sell?

2. Who are your customers?

3. Why do customers buy from you? What is your "value proposition?"

Now, if you're a glass-half-empty kind of person, you've got some bad news coming up, but if you're a glass-half-full type, I have even more good news: Extra questions! Providing answers to a number of other questions will give you input for your responses to the preceding core queries. But before I get to those additional questions, I expand on the big three already listed.

What do you sell?

The question "What do you sell?" is really as basic as it sounds. Every company, regardless of the industry they compete in or where they're located in the world, has to determine the mix of products and services it will provide in the marketplace. The trick is deciding which products and services you'll place more emphasis on in the future, and which you'll place less on.

Who are your customers?

When answering the question, "Who are your customers," you need to look beyond your current roster of buyers and once again decide which customer groups (and geographies) to place more emphasis on in the future, and which deserve less of your attention.

Why do customers buy from you — what is your value proposition?

Why customers buy from you — your value proposition — is perhaps the most important of the core questions because it forms your basis of distinction in the marketplace. Fortunately, only a couple of choices are available when answering the question. You can either compete on the lowest cost of ownership for your customers, or attempt to offer a truly differentiated product or service. Companies that focus on lowest cost are relentless in their pursuit of capabilities and processes that allow them to standardize operations. Two great examples are Walmart and McDonald's. Both companies have taken operational excellence to the extreme in their constant drive to keep prices relatively low for their customers.

If you choose to compete on differentiation, you have two potential roads to follow. The first is known as "customer intimacy." At first the word "intimacy" may seem a bit strange (and creepy) in a business setting, but it simply means building long-lasting and deep relationships with your customers, primarily as a result of outstanding service. The department store Nordstrom is a great example; their customer service is legendary, as I can attest to; see the "Paul goes to Nordstrom" sidebar for details.

The second choice for differentiators is to compete on the superior functionality of your products and services. Cutting-edge design, bleeding-edge technology, and superior functionality are all hallmarks of these "product leading" companies. Does a certain fruit-inspired outfit spring to mind? Apple, of course, is the poster child for this type of value proposition. You pay more for their products, but with that price tag comes an expectation of exceptional design, ease of use, and outstanding functionality.

PAUL GOES TO NORDSTROM

One day, in an attempt no doubt to procrastinate on some important project, I decided to accompany my wife to the mall for a shopping expedition. Our first stop was Nordstrom, and having no list of items to shop for, my plan was to wait for my wife in one of the very comfortable customer lounges — cozy alcoves decked out with over-stuffed chairs, often close to someone playing standards on a baby grand piano.

It was a very relaxing atmosphere indeed, one I planned to immerse myself in, enjoying the relaxing tunes and engaging in that age-old pastime of people watching. The first 20 minutes or so went well, but then boredom crept in and I decided to stretch my legs and browse the store. I made my way to the Menswear department and soon received a casual but warm greeting from a sales associate. Small talk ensued, during which I mentioned that I had no intention of buying anything; I was simply killing time while waiting for my wife. At some point I either gave the associate my name or he subtly and skillfully extracted it from me. Leaving me for a few moments, he mentioned on his return that I hadn't purchased anything in a while (no doubt having looked me up in their system), and suggested we simply stroll the department while he pointed out some of the latest fashions. Again, no pressure.

You probably know where this is going. Fast-forward about 40 minutes: My wife is wait-ing impatiently for me, and here I come saddled with two enormous shopping bags overflowing with the 1,500 dollars' worth of clothes I just bought. Great service, building on an existing relationship with the brand . . . customer intimacy in action!

Playing 21 Questions

One of the first pieces of advice I received from the crack *For Dummies* editorial team was to ensure that I'm always providing answers, not questions. "Dummies readers expect answers" they told me. Yet here I go with a whole section of ques-tions, and to make it even worse, I'm suggesting we play 21 questions instead of 20 — who ever heard of that? But sometimes the answer to a challenge (in this case, setting a strategy) can be found only by tackling a series of challenging questions. I provided the big three earlier, and in this section, I supply "subques-tions" that you can use as input to cracking the code for each of those founda-tional strategy questions.

You may notice that I don't include any queries on competition. That's inten-tional. I'm in Jeff Bezos's camp on that one, who says, "If you're competitor-focused, you have to wait until there is a competitor doing something. Being customer-focused allows you to be more pioneering." If you take the time and effort to ponder, dig deep, and come up with answers to the questions that follow, you can forge your own, unique path, thereby making the competition irrelevant.

Subquestions for "What do you sell?"

In this section, I offer a number of questions specifically related to your product and services, challenges, and trends. Answering them will help you determine the best response to the overall question, "What do you sell?"

1. Has your business had any exceptionally successful products or services? If so, what are their characteristics? Your task with the question "What do we sell?" is to determine which products and services you'll place more and less emphasis on. Therefore, it's important to determine which products and services have been most successful, and why.

2. Have you had any exceptionally unsuccessful products or services? If so, what are their characteristics? This is the inverse of the preceding question.

3. Do any of your customers significantly modify your products and services for their own use? This question helps identify potential product and service modifications and new product innovations.

4. Which products and services produce the highest profit margins? Self-explanatory.

5. Which products and services produce the lowest profit margins? Self-explanatory.

6. What are the primary challenges you face regarding your product and/or service mix? Illustrative responses: stale product/service line, commoditized offering, increasing competition lower margins, and so on.

7. What are some key trends taking place inside and outside your market space that could impact your offerings? This question prompts you to look outward and determine how current trends may impact what you sell.

Subquestions for "Who are your customers?"

Getting to the heart of whom to serve is essential for any business. In this section, I provide several questions that will help you determine who represents the best market for your products and services.

1. Who buys from you now? This question, and the next, challenge you to examine current customers and the determinants of success.

2. Where (geographic markets) do you sell most successfully, and why?

3. Do you have any very unsuccessful customer segments? If so, why have you been unsuccessful in serving these customers? The inverse of the two preceding questions.

4. Are there any customers your industry prefers not to serve? If so, why? This question seeks to identify potential new customer groups.

5. Do any customers groups require significantly more or less support than others? Answering this question can shed a light on customer profitability.

6. Which customers' needs are changing most rapidly, and why? This question can be used to match changing customer behavior with your unique strengths.

7. Who will your customers be in the future? This could encompass demographic changes, new trends, and so on.

Subquestions for "Why do customers buy from you? What is your value proposition?"

Many strategy pundits consider the choice of value proposition to be at the very core of strategy development. The questions that follow will help you determine your value proposition for your organization.

1. How do your customers typically refer to you? This could be on social media, through your customer service interactions, and so on. Are they talking about your great service? Your fantastic products, or your unbeatable prices?

2. If you were to build your organization from scratch today, how would it be different, and what would you do differently? Changes could reflect a modification to your value proposition.

3. What things do you do better than anyone else? Whatever you're best at most likely represents your core value proposition.

4. What disruptive technologies may open up new opportunities for you? Changes in the world around you could impact how you sell.

5. What specific skills or competencies do you possess that it would be difficult for your competitors to copy? Each value proposition is represented by core competencies (such as, product-leading companies excel at innovation).

6. What must your organization be able to do in the future (perhaps two or three years from now) that is impossible to do today? If big changes are required, it may impact how you sell.

7. If you believe you are (or have to be) a little of all three value propositions — build long-lasting relationships, keep your prices low, and innovate constantly — I empathize, but sadly, it's not possible to excel in every domain. You simply can't be all things to all people. The resource requirements alone would be akin to stretching a piece of taffy from here to the moon. It's stretched so thin that at some point it's going to snap. Here's the question: What percentage of each do you think you are now? And, bonus question, what percentages would you like to see in the future?

3

Creating OKRs

It's time to embark on your exciting journey of writing OKRs that will drive focus, engagement, and alignment (to name just a few of the benefits) throughout your organization.

In this part, you find out why training and determining your OKRs philosophy are great places to start your efforts in creating OKRs. After laying that groundwork, I guide you step by step through the art and craft of developing effective objectives. Next I unlock the secrets of writing meaningful and measurable key results, including the types to use and the characteristics to adhere to. You also discover expert tips to supercharge your OKRs, and find answers to common OKRs-related questions that you're sure to get from your teams.

Chapter **7**

Preparing to Create OKRs

Have you ever made the decision to "wing it?" Maybe you showed up for a job interview without first studying the company (unfortunately, it turned out that seeing one of their commercials on TV didn't qualify as research), or you decided to head to the seventh game of the World Series in full team regalia, swinging the hometown pennant but absent a ticket. I'm a planner by nature but have been known to wing it from time to time, almost always with predictably bad results. (See the "Adventures in unpreparedness" sidebar for the painful details.)

Rigorous preparation is a prerequisite for success in the OKRs arena, where, despite the framework's inherent simplicity, rewards are never guaranteed. Without a doubt, the best ways to prepare your teams for OKRs glory are to provide training on the fundamentals of the model and to determine the OKRs "philosophy" that you'll use to guide your implementation. In this chapter, I examine both of these topics in detail so that when you're ready to introduce OKRs, you definitely won't be winging it.

Training Your Organization for OKRs Success

The iconoclastic business guru Tom Peters once opined, "Companies that don't encourage employee education of all kinds are dumb!" Need I say more? Maybe I'll add just a few words to build on Tom's blunt but sage advice.

There exists in OKRs land one enormous, hiding-in-plain-sight, success-devouring trap that any well-meaning organization can easily fall into, and that is, simplicity. It's true: OKRs are not a complex methodology requiring arcane language and indecipherable graphics to comprehend. In fact, the opposite is true. The model's easy-to-grasp terminology pretty much has you at hello. But don't let that seductive ease fool you; OKRs are teeming with devious devices that can throw you off course and derail your effort lickety-split. To get the most from your investment in the framework it's vital that everyone who will be using, or exposed to, OKRs understands the fundamentals of the system and knows how you'll be applying it in your organization.

In this section, I share with you why training is so critical, outline a comprehensive curriculum, and break down the merits and potential pitfalls of virtual training. Sound like fun? It is to me, because I love delivering training on OKRs and am very gratified when participants approach me after a workshop and say, "That was a great session, Paul; I really enjoyed it and learned a lot." And just as I'm about to blush with pride, they inevitably add, "Yeah, I was expecting it to be super boring." Follow the advice in this chapter and you, too, can defy the expectations of your learners and be the recipient of this classic back-handed compliment.

REMEMBER

Your training sessions can be both informative and fun. Be sure to build in plenty of opportunities for participant engagement throughout the session.

Grasping why training is critical

Here's a fun game to try at your next dinner party. Have one person be designated a "tapper," whose job it is to drum out with their fingers the rhythm of a well-known song, while a second person, the "listener," has to guess the song based on the tapper's rendition. Say the tapper decides to use "Happy Birthday" as the song. Do you think the listener would correctly identify it? "Happy Birthday" is a universally recognized song, one that is identifiable from just a few notes, so how hard could it be, right?

ADVENTURES IN UNPREPAREDNESS

Very early in my career, I was invited by a conference company to deliver a speech at a session in New Orleans. Sounded great! I accepted immediately. The challenge was my workload: I was swamped at the office and had very little time to prepare my presentation. No problem, I thought, I'll work on it on the plane. Fate had other plans for me, however. Two close friends decided they'd tag along with me on the trip, and one of them, who worked for the airline, secured us upgrades to business class. Air travel has changed a lot, but there was a time when traveling in business class was like holding a golden ticket that enabled you to whisk past the velvet rope into a hot nightclub where the fun and booze, never stopped. After three drinks, it was sayonara to the presentation. But in my "drinking thinking" frame of mind, I again determined that everything was perfectly fine; I'd create the presentation the next day, before the conference began. Did I mention it was the day before the Super Bowl and the city was basically one big party? I think you know where this tale of woe is headed. After making about a thousand new friends on Bourbon Street the next night, I slapped together a presentation at the last minute and, shock of shocks, the audience feedback on my effort was not stellar.

This experience provided a lesson I've never forgotten: Don't trust friends with connections. No, that's not it. The really valuable lesson is to always be prepared. Speaking of football, Super Bowl–winning quarterback Russell Wilson, when asked about his formula for success, advised that "the separation is in the preparation." In other words, to separate yourself from the pack, to elevate your performance, to grasp a Super Bowl ring the size of a steam gauge on the *Titanic*, you need to diligently prepare.

It turns out that researchers have tried this experiment in the field (how can I get that job?), dividing a group of people into tappers and listeners (see *Beyond Performance 2.0*, by Bill Schaninger and Scott Keller). The experimenters instructed the tappers to select a familiar tune like "Happy Birthday" and asked them to predict what percentage of listeners would correctly identify it. What would you guess? In the experiment, the tappers predicted that 50 percent of the listeners would guess the song. The actual percentage? About 2.5 percent! Apparently, as the experiment went on, the tappers became visibly upset with their listeners, frustrated that they couldn't guess such an easy song. Meanwhile, the listeners were equally frustrated, trying to decipher a tune from what seemed to them like a pitiful attempt at Morse code typing.

The gap between expectation and reality represented in this experiment is known as "the curse of knowledge." It sounds like a decent title for a Harrison Ford movie (*Indiana Jones and the Curse of Knowledge*) but it's a very real thing. After we know something, we find it extremely difficult to imagine not knowing it. As the tappers in the experiment were beating out "Happy Birthday," they were gleefully singing along in their heads, but the listeners heard nothing but random beats.

So what does all of this have to do with OKRs training? Plenty! The curse of knowledge has the potential to play out in dangerous fashion for any organization taking on OKRs and being led in the implementation by an executive or other senior leader who has previously implemented the system elsewhere. Just like the tapper drumming out "Happy Birthday," this leader assumes, likely based on some hasty communications and recommendations to read a book on the topic, that everyone in the organization will grasp the very simple concept of OKRs. In their mind, OKRs are the business equivalent of "Happy Birthday" — who wouldn't get it?

WARNING

Never assume that your employees will have the ability to write technically sound OKRs because the system isn't complex. Training in fundamentals is essential in ensuring quality OKRs across the organization.

Mastering the fundamentals

In reality — and everyone who has taken the time and effort to do OKRs the right way knows this — the system is not as simple as it appears; equal measures of art and science are necessary to effectively nail an implementation. An upfront commitment to training is critical to ensure that your organization understands the ins and outs of the framework, the subtleties of adapting it to fit your culture, and the technical aspects required to get the most from your investment.

In the later section, "Working with the Training Curriculum," I provide details on a curriculum you can follow, and it's heavy on OKRs fundamentals. When I say "fundamentals," I refer primarily to the ability to write a technically sound and effective OKR, one with an objective that clearly outlines what you want to do and why it's important. It also includes a set of key results that precisely demonstrates your story of success in achieving the objective.

Writing a solid OKR is foundational to achieving success with the model. If your organization rolls out the methodology but provides no training on how to actually construct a proper OKR, you can expect generic, business-as-usual objectives, along with vague key results that offer little guidance on execution and few opportunities to learn about your business.

Boosting confidence

Another benefit of training is that it builds the confidence of those who will ultimately be responsible to create OKRs in your organization, and that enhanced confidence will manifest itself in higher-quality OKRs. Most people have experienced the confidence-boosting power of training in their own lives. I know I have.

Several years ago I bought a fun little sports car and, enticed by the potential limits of what the machine had to offer, became interested in high-performance driving. I know, I know — classic midlife cliché, but hear me out; we're talking about OKRs, not my existential aging crisis. I decided to register for a weekend driving program that was held in the gigantic parking lot of a local stadium, filled with orange cones providing the lines we had to follow in various exercises. Going into the weekend, I had the right car and loads of enthusiasm, but not much in the way of actual skills. When I started out, it was a shocking case of "coneicide" as I flattened the orange pyramids left and right in my clumsy attempts to master the driving line. But as my instructor patiently guided me throughout the day, my skills increased, as did my confidence, and although I'll never grace the starting grid at the Indy 500, I came out of the weekend a much better and more confident driver.

By completing OKRs training, those drafting OKRs will experience a satisfying boost in confidence that not only will that lead to better OKRs but also bring the added benefit of motivating them to think more deeply about your implementation. After they master the fundamentals of the system, they'll begin to wonder how it can specifically be employed to drive alignment, enhance focus, and improve accountability within their part of the company. Often, your "trainees" will generate questions that the executive sponsor and OKRs champion didn't initially consider but that may have important consequences for the program's success.

TIP

Build ample time for questions into your OKRs training workshops. As participants begin to understand the nuances of the model, they will likely have questions about how to effectively implement it within the organization.

Speeding up learning

Finally, training will accelerate the learning curve for your OKRs champion and group of ambassadors. When I work with a client, we frequently have multiple training sessions in order to accommodate the most possible participants, and I strongly recommend that the champions and, whenever possible, ambassadors attend each and every session. I also encourage them to listen attentively each time, and not be distracted by email, Slack, or any of the hundred other attention-grabbing temptations that abound in modern offices.

Those who heed my advice are rewarded by picking up more and more nuances each time they go through the training, connecting the dots of OKRs and building their own personal knowledge base. I've lost count of how many times a champion or ambassador contacts me after the third or fourth session and says they've discovered something new every time that helped put more of the puzzle pieces together for them. And I know they're "getting it," because the champion or a chosen ambassador often addresses the group before turning things over to me, and it's clear from what they're delivering to the assembled group that their knowledge of OKRs has grown since their first exposure.

Preparing for training

Before I lay out what you should cover in various training sessions, there are some decisions you need to make prior to gathering your team, setting out the coffee, and firing up the projector. Outlined in the following pages are a number of items to consider before the actual training begins, along with my recommendations on the route I believe you should take.

Considering who should lead the training

Will you conduct the training yourself or have it led by an outside party? Putting a familiar face in front of the participants can increase their comfort level, and if the trainer is your CEO or another member of the C-Suite, you're very likely to have everyone's rapt attention from "Good Morning" all the way to "Thanks for coming today." A potential downside of using an insider is the "curse of knowledge" I describe in the "Grasping why training is critical" section, earlier in the chapter. If your executive used OKRs at another company and plans to train based exclusively on that experience, you have no guarantee that their roadmap for success will mesh with your organization's culture or overall goals for OKRs, and the training could produce confusion from day one.

Conversely, a skilled outsider who has extensive experience in the field brings something even an executive can't deliver: expert credibility. If I had a dollar or even a peso or ruble for every time I heard "We'd conduct the training ourselves but it will have more impact coming from an outsider," I'd be a wealthy man. And it's true that outsiders possess that shiny veneer of expertise no insider can match. They also bring actual experience from the trenches, and a credible outside consultant or trainer can use that battlefield knowledge to answer any and all questions that may surface during the training.

My recommendation? Go with an outside expert on OKRs. I can hear you from here, barely masking your contempt: "Of course you're saying that; you're a consultant!" That's true, but it doesn't outweigh the fact that you have one chance to make a first impression with your training, and you'd better get it right. You want someone who can deliver the theory, best practices, case studies, and idiosyncrasies of OKRs.

TIP

Unless you have executives or senior team members with extensive OKRs experience that is consistent with your goals for the implementation, use an outside expert to lead your training efforts.

Deciding who should receive the training

A very practical question to answer before you train is to determine exactly who will be receiving said training. The answer will, of course, depend on how you plan to roll out OKRs — whether it's just at the company level, at company and teams, for a pilot program, and so on.

The simple answer is that everyone who will be creating OKRs must be trained in the methodology. If you decide that you'll be creating company-level and director-level OKRs and that encompasses 150 people, then all of them should participate, but not in one big group. Split the sessions up with a maximum of 30 people in each. Anything larger than a group that size tends to become a lecture with scant participation from the audience.

Providing materials to be read before training

With your trainees identified and a trainer selected, another consideration is whether to issue pre-read materials to the attendees. I should note that "pre-read" is a very subjective term, considering that it could refer to a 350-word article or a 350-page book. There are pros and cons to both short and long materials.

A *BuzzFeed*-style article that's short, punchy, and can be digested in about five minutes has the obvious advantage of brevity, meaning it offers you a decent chance that people may actually read it. The downside is that it may have been written by someone who has zero knowledge of OKRs and was paid a hundred dollars to churn it out because the website it was found on deemed OKRs a hot topic. In that case, your people will get very little useful information to prepare them for an upcoming training event.

At the other end of the spectrum, and I've mentioned this previously, I have plenty of clients who require training participants to wade through an entire book, most frequently John Doerr's *Measure What Matters*. First, the bad news: More and more evidence points to the fact that people are reading fewer books all the time; in fact, in his book *Stolen Focus*, author Johann Hari notes that some 57 percent of Americans do not read a single book in a year. The average American (sorry to pick on the good ol' U.S. of A., but hey, I'm a citizen of that country, too), spends 17 minutes a day reading books, and a whopping 5.4 hours on their phone. Thus, unless your CEO conducts a rigorous examination process to determine whether participants have read the book from cover to cover, most people are unlikely to get through the entire thing. But on the positive side, if people do read a whole book, they'll arrive at your training session well-equipped to learn more and participate willingly. (And those of us writing books will certainly appreciate the effort.)

Fortunately, there is a third alternative to both short articles and long books. OKRs have become extremely popular, resulting in many credible voices offering a valuable perspective on the subject. Engaging in even a cursory amount of research leads you to OKRs primers written by people with legitimate experience in implementing the system, and these primers provide insights and observations to help prep your teams for a more in-depth training session. In fact, my website (www.okrstraining.com) offers a free download of an e-book called *The ABCs of OKRs*, which many clients use as a pre-read document before any training sessions are held.

Getting your training off to a good start

If you decide to use a consultant to lead your training session, here's how *not* to get off to a good start. Let me preface this story by telling you that I am a very punctual person. My parents didn't impart a lot of life lessons to me (I was the youngest of seven, so by the time I rolled around, it was pretty much like *Lord of the Flies* at my house), but my mother was a stickler for being on time. One year I made the Honor Roll in high school and was invited to a banquet along with the other high achievers to celebrate our scholarly achievements. (Picture a room full of awkward teens with braces, flood pants, and a tube of acne cream in their back pocket and you're there.) My mother was so concerned about getting to the venue early that we arrived before any of the other students or the teachers. Even the building's custodian was confused when he found us camped out at the front door hours before the appointed time.

I've carried that pathological sense of punctuality into my adulthood and, on the plus side, it typically does serve me well with clients. So you can imagine my shock and dismay one morning when, as I was sitting in my hotel room enjoying my second cup of coffee, I got a panicked call from my client contact telling me that the session was supposed to have started 30 minutes ago and everyone was wondering where I am. I had confirmed the time on numerous occasions, but apparently there was a last-minute change and everyone was informed — except me. Bit of a problem. I did my best to get there in half the time it should have taken, but I had lost the group's confidence in me and, despite my best efforts to regain it, the session never did get back on solid footing. Moral of the story: Please tell your consultant the actual starting time of any training sessions! Unrelated but also important moral of the story: Start on time. We're all busier than ever, so honor this precious asset by committing to beginning — and ending — your session at the scheduled hours.

Warming up with an icebreaker or introductions

Assuming that everyone, including your instructor, has arrived on time, your next decision is whether to start with an icebreaker as a warmup. I've experienced plenty of these over the years, ranging from simple introductions to game-like scenarios such as "Two truths and a Lie." I'm an innately curious person, so I enjoy that one, which involves trying to decipher which statement by someone is a lie after knowing the person for all of two minutes. It's always a reliable way to generate some laughs, which is a great way to increase everyone's comfort level with the session.

The challenge with including an icebreaker is, of course, time. Most training sessions, depending on the topics you choose to cover, will be scheduled for two hours, which may seem like ample time, but if you're fortunate enough to have an engaged group peppering you with questions, the clock winds down mighty fast. Therefore, although you want a warm-up to draw everyone into the session, you can't let it chew up too much of your schedule. My recommendation is to go with simple introductions instead of an icebreaker. Have each attendee give their name, position, how long they've been with the company, and whether they've had any prior experience with OKRs. With luck, a few people will have used OKRs at previous jobs and can attest to the system's effectiveness, which will provide a quick boost of confidence in the framework for other attendees who are hearing of OKRs for the first time.

WARNING

Even short introductions can be drawn out by talkative people, throwing your schedule for a loop. You'll find garrulous folks everywhere on the planet, including Mexico City where I once worked with a client organization filled with warm and friendly people. At the start of our training workshop, I asked them to provide brief introductions, but from the very first person on, they were inclined to provide a deep autobiography lasting several minutes. About three people in, the CEO stood up and hollered "*Rapido, rapido!*" The message was received and, thankfully, all subsequent introductions were much more to the point.

Including your executive sponsor

Putting aside timing, warm-up games, and introductions, the single most important thing you can do to ensure that your session gets off to a good start is to have the executive sponsor open the meeting. This simple act has the potential to create an enormous win by capturing everyone's attention from the start and priming them for a fun and engaging learning event that will kickstart the OKRs implementation. Sounds simple enough, and even logical, right? But you'd be surprised how often organizations miss this chance for a crucial early win in their OKRs campaign. What often occurs, instead, is what I call "Over to you, Paul" syndrome. It's so debilitating that it warrants a paragraph of its own.

"Over to you, Paul" describes a situation that any consultant reading this can surely relate to, and probably dislikes as much as I do. Here's the scenario: I'm scheduled to run an OKRs training workshop, usually my first interaction with a broader audience at the client's location, at, say 9:00 a.m. I get there nice and early, set up, and wait for the team to trickle in. By 9:05 everyone who is going to attend has arrived and, just as I'm expecting the CEO to provide a rousing change story and then introduce me to share the nitty-gritty of how OKRs can bring that narrative to life, the CEO looks at me and says, "Okay." As in, "You can start now." No introduction of the concept, no explanation of why everyone is sacrificing their valuable time, no introduction of this stranger at the front of the room. Nothing. What kind of a message is an executive sending, when they can't take five minutes to kick off what is supposedly a critical initiative for the organization?

Please, please avoid the "Over to you" syndrome at all costs and instead grab the reins and seize control of the session from the start by having your executive sponsor take the floor. Assuming that person is the CEO, they can welcome everyone to the event and, critically, take the opportunity to share why the organization is embracing OKRs, and how important this initial training effort is in launching a successful effort.

You cannot overcommunicate your "why OKRs" story. Be sure to start your training session by once again sharing why you've decided to use OKRs.

Working with the Training Curriculum

At least 50 percent of organizations reaching out to my consulting firm for assistance are failed "DIYers," meaning that they've tried to implement OKRs on their own but quickly discovered that it's not as easy as it seems, with problems mounting faster than the body count on an episode of the *Walking Dead*. When we ask what challenges they've encountered, an almost universal first response is, "The OKRs weren't as good as we'd hoped." OKRs are a seductively simple methodology, and I use the word *seductive* deliberately: If you look it up, you'll find that it means "enticing," "beguiling," and "captivating." Those words perfectly capture the allure of OKRs to many first-timers anxious to reap the rewards of focus and alignment but unaware (or unwilling to acknowledge) that some effort will be required to achieve those ends.

That effort begins with the ability to write an effective, technically sound OKR that features a compelling objective and set of key results that clearly demonstrate its achievement. As I note in the "Grasping why training is important" section, earlier in this chapter, if your organization rolls out the methodology but provides no training on how to actually construct a proper OKR, you can expect generic, business-as-usual objectives, as well as vague key results that offer little guidance on execution and few opportunities to learn about your business. So make sure all that doesn't happen by creating a training curriculum focused on mastering the fundamental skill of writing a good OKR.

Whether you conduct the training in person or virtually, I recommend a two-hour duration for the fundamentals course, which should provide ample time to cover your agenda. Speaking of the agenda, you have many options for how to order the items you'll present, including, for the extremely lazy among us, alphabetical. My approach, as you'll soon discover, is to bring everyone on board with a captivating opening, and then outline the fundamentals, provide examples, and let people play with the concept using a case-study format. The following sections offer information on each item of the recommended agenda — but definitely not in alphabetical order.

Starting with a story

Some people may see this section's title and think, "Oh, I have to start with a joke." As with most things in life, there are different schools of thought on whether opening any session with a joke is a good idea. Some experts say doing so is corny and outdated, whereas others suggest that a joke related to the content can be a fun way to win the crowd over to your side from the very beginning.

From the "corny and outdated" file: I once attended a seminar whose first speaker was clearly uncomfortable addressing a large crowd. (He was very well-regarded in his field, and everyone was anxious to hear from him.) After being introduced, the speaker walked slowly to the lectern and, head down, mumbled, "I heard you have to start these things off with a joke." He then stammered his way through an old joke, the one about two guys being attacked by a bear in the woods. One guy starts to run and the other says, "You'll never outrun that bear!" To which the second fellow replies, "I don't have to outrun the bear; I just have to outrun you!" Delivered with some comedic flair, it's good for at least some polite laughter, but this poor speaker's delivery was so awkward and stunted, it generated nothing but a few subdued chuckles and a cringe-worthy moment we couldn't wait to end. Sadly, I have to say that I think his poor beginning put a dent in his otherwise sterling credibility.

Unless you're certain you're a naturally funny person who can easily channel your inner Jerry Seinfeld, a better strategy is to frame your opening in the form of a story that encapsulates your key points. The best story is one you can return to throughout the presentation to emphasize important pieces of information. I've heard people invoke past presidents, great athletes, or even their own company's history to set up the session for success from the get-go. If no such stories spring to mind for you, conduct research on goal setting or great achievements of the past and you'll be sure to find a story that resonates with you and will win the hearts of your audience.

Giving your participants a history lesson

In a Chapter 1 sidebar, I provide a brief history of OKRs in five names. One of them rhymes with *trucker*. If you thought, "Mark Zuckerberg," please check out the opening chapter, where your history lesson awaits. (Go ahead; I'll wait.) Okay, I acknowledge that not everyone finds the history of OKRs as spellbinding as I do, but serving up an overview of the system's provenance to your audience delivers a very important lesson that you want to impart as soon as possible in your implementation: OKRs are not a fad.

The astronomical number of business books published every year is evidence that companies are hungry — nay, starving — for new approaches, and countless gurus out there are only too happy to concoct some convoluted magic bullet to solve every organizational ailment you suffer from. Some of these systems may catch on for a short period of time, but most will fall by the wayside before the author has even had a chance to cash their first royalty check.

As described in Chapter 1, the OKRs methodology is constructed on a mighty foundation of common-sense and time-tested principles. You'll want your people to know immediately that OKRs aren't some fly-by-night business equivalent of a get-rich-quick scheme, but instead has deep ancestral roots in proven business practices. You don't need your audience to read entire books by Drucker (rhymes with *trucker* — did you get that?), Grove, or Doerr to get the message across. A simple timeline from the 1950s to today with nods to each of those five names from Chapter 1 will sufficiently tell the story of the system's impressive past and very relevant future.

WARNING

Many people in your organization will view any new system being introduced as a fad and immediately dismiss it. Take the time and effort to acquaint yourself with the deep history underpinning OKRs, and share that with your employees.

Defining your terms

I hope you start your training session by bursting out of the gate with a strong start thanks to the inspirational (and relevant) story you kicked the session off with and then talking down the naysayers by proving that OKRs aren't a fad. When everyone is with you, it's time to pivot to some real fundamentals, and it doesn't get more fundamental than defining your terms.

You want to start with the objective, which, as noted in Chapter 1, is, "A statement of a broad qualitative goal designed to propel the organization forward in a desired direction." In my training sessions, I usually display that definition in a sizable font on my PowerPoint slide to underscore its importance.

Next you can break the definition down, emphasizing the critical nature of the word *qualitative* and noting that objectives are aspirational statements that don't include numbers. You can then unpack the word *organization*, noting that OKRs can be created at many levels of an organization. If, at this point, you know where you'll be creating OKRs, be sure to share that information with the group. Finally, be sure to stick the landing by spending some quality time with the last part of the definition: ". . . propel the organization forward in a desired direction." Make it clear that objectives are meant to drive the business forward in a way that ensures the execution of your strategy; objectives are not intended to catalog your day-to-day, business-as-usual activities.

Next, turn to the key results. As you may recall, a *key result* is a quantitative statement that measures the achievement of a given objective. The key results answer the question, "How will we know we've achieved the objective?" When you drill down on this definition, you want to focus on the word *quantitative*, making it clear that key results should be comprised of numbers, percentages, dollar amounts, or dates.

Illustrating an effective OKR with an example

This step in the training curriculum involves sharing an actual example and using it to illustrate the characteristics of an effective OKR. You can create an OKR that may be applicable to your own company, but my advice is to choose a more generic version because at this point, you want your audience concentrating on the fundamental aspects of writing an OKR, not getting sidetracked on the specifics of an example that may or may not accurately reflect your own operations.

I typically use OKRs from industries that are outside the client's domain but recognizable to most people, such as airlines, sports teams, or hotels. It's a safe bet that everyone in the audience has been on an airplane, are familiar with the overall workings of that industry, and can therefore recognize, and learn from, an illustrative OKR. It's important to involve the group as you work through the example, asking them why a certain key result is effective or ineffective, soliciting their opinion on what might be a better fit to measure the objective, and so on. The best way for them to learn is to interact with your content.

Distinguishing between the types of key results

Chances are, the example OKR you shared in the previous section featured both metric and milestone key results. In this portion of the training, you go deeper on each of those types of key results, providing definitions and helping your team understand when it's appropriate to use each type. Metric key results are those that contain numbers, dollar amounts, or percentages, and you'll always have at least one metric key result per OKR that measures the business impact portion of the objective. Milestones are perfectly acceptable key results on two conditions: 1) They include a date of completion; and 2) they are accompanied by at least one metric key result. Milestones should always drive, or lead to, metrics. For example, a Human Resources team could have a milestone key result of "Launch the new hiring process by January 31st," which they believe will drive the metric key result of "Decrease the time to hire from 60 to 45 days."

Sharing the characteristics of OKRs

There are many required attributes to ensure that your OKR is unleashing the potential it's capable of. I give you a thorough grounding in the characteristics in Chapters 8 and 9, but here are the main points. An objective (see Chapter 8) must be

>> Meaningful to the team or individual writing it

>> A stretch, but attainable

>> Doable in the time period allotted

>> Mostly controlled by the team

>> One that provides business value

The characteristics of an effective key result (see Chapter 9) include:

>> Quantitative

>> Aspirational but attainable

>> Specific

>> Descriptive of the story of success

>> Indicative of the business impact

Learning by doing

Earlier in the chapter, I relate how I once bought a fun little sports car and decided to jump into the world of performance driving. What I didn't tell you is that not only did I intend to channel my inner Mario Andretti, but I was also determined to do my own repairs on the car. For me, this was the very essence of a "BHAG" (big, hairy, audacious goal) because (and the biggest understatement you'll find in the entire book is coming up right now) I am not mechanically inclined. There is a famous story in our family of the time my brother (no grease monkey himself) and I attempted to fix a broken tail light on his Oldsmobile Cutlass. Two hours after hitting the garage for what we anticipated would be a ten-minute fix, we were drenched with sweat, blood-soaked, and surrounded by shards of glass. The project was soon abandoned, and we decamped to the backyard to lick our wounds with a cold beverage.

But this time, with my new little sports car, I vowed that things would be different. What did I do? I read books, scoured YouTube, and watched a buddy of mine do work on his car. Notice a trend there? While I was preparing myself, I wasn't actually *doing* any real repair work, and thus my skills didn't improve.

People enhance their skills only by rolling up their sleeves and *doing* something, whether it's attempting to install a performance exhaust system on their car (which I'm proud to say I eventually did) or mastering OKRs. In this phase of the training, it's time to challenge everyone to apply what they've learned thus far by creating an actual OKR.

I suggest the case study approach, once again using a different industry than your own. You want your folks concentrating on the mechanics of writing a quality OKR, not going ten layers deep on potential issues in their own department. As with the example portion of the training covered earlier, I recommend drawing on an industry that will be familiar to most of your participants. Airlines, hotels, and sports teams are reliable alternatives.

Say you decide to use a hotel company. To set up the exercise, create a document that contains a transcript of an interview between a consultant and the CEO of the company. The consultant can then ask the CEO questions about the company's strategy, and your trainees can use the CEO's responses to create at least one OKR. The document should contain at least five questions.

I absolutely despise books that do what I just did at the end of the last paragraph: Give you a piece of advice (create a case study) with no tactical guidance on how to implement it. But this is a *For Dummies* book, and in the Dummies universe, we stand with you, united in purpose and commitment. I will not leave you hanging. (If this were a cartoon, now would be the time for the cape-draped *For Dummies* mascot to stream into view.)

Coming up is a hotel-themed case study that you can use in your own training. The case is written in the form of an interview between a consultant and the fictitious CEO of the also fictitious hotel chain. In the case study, the CEO provides plenty of ideas for potential objectives and key results. But it's important to stress that participants are free to make up key results that may not appear in the document but that will be necessary to achieve the objective they created.

I recommend giving your group about 20 minutes to read the case and create at least one OKR. After the time has elapsed, you ask for volunteers to share the OKR they created with the group. It's important to emphasize the fact that there are no absolute right or wrong answers with the case; it's simply a way to play with the content, applying what people have learned in the training. In the report outs, you want to assess how well people construct the objective (does it have a business impact statement, for example?) and whether the key results actually measure achievement of the objective. A side benefit of the case study exercise is that it will inevitably bring out questions that wouldn't otherwise come up during the training.

Kick Off Your Shoes Hotels OKRs case study

» **Company Mission:** To earn our guests' loyalty by delivering unsurpassed boutique hotel experiences

» **Vision:** Within five years we will have 20 locations and $1 billion in revenue

» **Strategy:** Offer world-class amenities and premium experiences based on the location of each hotel

Interview with Melissa Jacobs, Chief Executive Officer

Consultant: We know that Kick Off Your Shoes Hotels has recently developed a mission, vision, and strategy and has chosen OKRs to help you successfully execute that strategy and ultimately realize your vision. In this interview, I'd like to get your input on what you consider the drivers of success. So, let me begin by simply asking you, what do you feel you must do well in order to execute your strategy?

Jacobs: There are a plenty of things we have to excel at if we're going to successfully execute our strategy, including the very basic necessity of having rooms available for our guests. Our chain is a mix of newly constructed hotels and refurbished properties, and both of those conditions bring challenges.

Consultant: Can you elaborate on the challenges?

Jacobs: With new construction there are always issues — it could be anything from poorly insulated windows to leaky faucets to cracked floor tiles. We need to ensure that once an issue is identified with a room, it is fixed as quickly as possible so that we can use it to accommodate guests.

Consultant: What about refurbished properties? What unique challenges do they bring?

Jacobs: Have you ever heard of the planning fallacy? It represents our tendency to underestimate the costs and timing to complete tasks. As good as we are at planning, it's not uncommon for a refurbished property to miss a proposed opening date because the construction hasn't been completed. We don't always anticipate and plan for unexpected snafus found in older properties. Going forward, we need to generate accurate forecasts, and we must also complete renovations on time and on budget.

Consultant: Your mission and strategy refer to world-class amenities and unsurpassed experiences. How do you make those things a reality for your guests?

Jacobs: Our strategy notes premium experiences based on the location of each hotel. That's an important point. Amenities and experiences we offer at our Palm Springs property are going to be very different from what a guest can discover in Park City, Utah, for example. In Palm Springs, we may offer golf or tennis, whereas in Park City the focus will be on skiing. We don't plan to build our own golf courses or ski hills, so we need to develop partnerships with high-end purveyors in each of our markets. We expect these partnerships to provide our guests with unsurpassed experiences, and that will in turn drive loyalty, market share, and revenue.

Consultant: Speaking of your guests, how do you attract them to your hotels?

Jacobs: The Yellow Pages.

Consultant: (Awkward pause). Okay, great idea.

Jacobs: I'm kidding. We've invested heavily in SEO (search engine optimization) to drive traffic to our site, and what's most important now is improving our website conversion rate, the percentage of site visitors that convert to bookings. The industry average is pretty sad, about two to three percent. We'd like to see our percentage closer to ten percent.

Consultant: That's pretty ambitious. How will you get there?

Jacobs: We have several routes to hitting that number. First, we're going to focus on growing our analytics capabilities so that we can fully understand how people currently navigate our site. We also plan to improve the checkout process so that, at a glance, guests will have a complete, easy-to-read-and-understand summary of their upcoming stay, with no fine print to worry about. Finally, we need to improve page-load time. Today's consumer is impatient; if they don't see the information they request almost instantaneously, they're off to another site. The research says four seconds is good, but we're aiming for a three-second page-load time.

Consultant: It's very clear you care deeply about the guest experience, but what does all this mean financially? Do you have revenue or profit aspirations?

Jacobs: Of course! Our goal is to increase total revenue per available room by maximizing occupancy, food and beverage sales, and partnership commissions.

Consultant: How do your people fit into this equation?

Jacobs: It's a cliché, I know, but a truism, that people are the most important part of any business, and that is especially so in hospitality, where there are so many one-on-one interactions that can make or break the guest experience. Because of that, the culture we're creating, and living, is extremely important to us. We want to foster a culture of inclusion, accountability, and engagement that allows everyone to bring their best selves to work every day.

Consultant: Sounds like a great place to work. How do you bring that culture to life?

Jacobs: Well, as you might remember from my appearance on *Undercover Boss* . . .

Consultant: Wait, you were on *Undercover Boss*? I love that show.

Jacobs: No, I wasn't on *Undercover Boss*. Again, kidding. How did you get this job, anyway? Doesn't matter. We grow our culture by ensuring that we're always listening to what our team members have to say. We do frequent engagement surveys and have several employee councils that offer recommendations to senior leadership. Whether they stay with us for their entire careers or go on to new adventures, we want to equip our employees with skills that will set them up for success.

Consultant: Thanks very much for your time today Ms. Jacobs, I really appreciate your insights. Ready to develop OKRs for Kick Off Your Shoes Hotels?

Jacobs: Let's do it!

As I note before the transcript, give your attendees 20 minutes to read the case and create at least one OKR. You'll be amazed at how creative people can be in embracing the case. I've had people actually — no kidding — write theme songs for the company!

Finishing strong

After you've finished the case study exercise, the best way to end your training session is to outline how to use OKRs to overcome a specific pain point faced by your organization. For example, if you're turning to OKRs in order to foster alignment, conclude with a discussion of how you'll employ OKRs to ensure that teams work together more collaboratively. If focus is your aim, sign off the session by outlining how the use of OKRs will ensure that you prioritize the most important things to move the company forward. Table 7-1 summarizes the training curriculum with recommended durations for each section.

TABLE 7-1   **The OKRs Training Curriculum**

Agenda Item	Summary	Recommended Duration*
Start with a story	Share a story or anecdote that encapsulates your key points	10 minutes
Give trainees a history lesson	Outline the history of OKRs, demonstrating that the system is not a fad	10 minutes
Define your terms	Provide definitions of an objective and key results	10 minutes
Illustrate with an example	Show an actual OKR from a generic company to illustrate key concepts	10 minutes
Distinguish between the types of key results	Define both metric and milestone key results, noting when each is appropriate	10 minutes
Share the characteristics	Provide the attributes of an effective OKR	10 minutes
Learn by doing (case study)	Give participants the opportunity to create an OKR for a fictitious organization	40 minutes
Finish strong	Share how OKRs will help you overcome a critical challenge	20 minutes

* Note that the recommended duration includes time for questions from the group.

Knowing whether virtual training is effective

About 20 years ago, I was invited to lunch with a consultant who also lived in the San Diego area. I almost performed a classic spit-take on the table when he revealed — no, gloated — that his business was 100 percent virtual and he had never met any of his clients face to face. My steadfast assumption had always been that consulting was a high-touch industry, meaning that you had to be in the room with the client in order to generate the desired results. I had never even dared to question this "brought down on stone tablets" theory of consulting, and despite his promises of greater efficiency with no loss of effectiveness, I went right on traveling two days of every week to meet clients all across the country and around the world.

That conversation always stayed with me, but at the end of the day, I believed then, and still believe today, that in-person training is preferable to any form of virtual interactions. When you're in the same room with your audience, you can read subtle cues that are impossible to detect on Zoom. You see when someone has their arms crossed stiffly across their chest, which often indicates that they're not on board with what you're presenting; or you see the person who is shifting nervously, anxious to make a point when the time is right. Or there's the telltale sign that a break is needed when you're getting more yawns than head nods as you share your points.

It took a global pandemic to change the way I, and virtually all consultants, engage with their clients. When Covid-19 became a reality, an accompanying truth was that meeting face-to-face with client organizations would be impossible for the foreseeable future. Overnight, our business model had to change, and we were forced to offer virtual training and facilitation to our clients.

Fast-forward to (blissfully) emerging from the pandemic, and thousands of organizations have embraced a hybrid model of work, with employees coming to the office only one or two days a week and toiling the rest of the time from home offices, vacation homes, yurts, and who knows where else. This new reality means that regardless of whether you're a consultant, freelancer, or corporate executive, virtual facilitation and training is most likely here to stay. So the question is, can it be effective? Despite my own past doubts and disbelief, my answer is a fist-pumping, enthusiastic yes. That said, the coming pages outline a number of factors to keep in mind to ensure that your virtual session is as productive, effective, and fun as possible.

Being prepared

I've delivered presentations in more than 25 countries and have witnessed a wide variety of cultural norms, from audiences who will rarely interact with the "authority" at the front of the room to crowds who barely let me squeeze a word in edgewise. One universal truth I've discovered, however, is that most audiences will give you at least the first five or ten minutes to win them over and get their attention. If you can start with a strong story, you stand a reasonable chance of having the group stay with you — perhaps not eating out of your hand, but at least attentively following your breadcrumbs. To get off to a robust beginning, you need to be prepared in four ways:

>> Thoroughly know your material
>> Offer interactive activities

>> Set expectations for everyone

>> Keep the training session relatively short (two hours)

I flesh out each of these prescriptions in the following pages.

Knowing your material

The most important way to prepare for training is to know your material inside and out. If it's clear two minutes in that you're basically just one chapter ahead of the group in an assigned OKRs book, your credibility will be shredded, and they'll be checking their email or making a PB & J sandwich before you get to the introductions.

A second form of preparation is technical. Regardless of the platform you're using — Zoom, Microsoft Teams, Webex, Google Meet — you must possess the ability to operate it competently. Knowing how to admit people, mute the group, allow screen sharing, and a host of other duties must be mastered before you start the session. One of the most embarrassing moments I've ever witnessed was at an in-person conference in Singapore when a senior executive of a tech company was on stage in front of hundreds of people to showcase his firm's latest breakthrough offering. But he didn't know how to run the presentation! Minutes passed, which must have felt like years to him. It was awful and cringeworthy, but you know how you just have to take a little sniff of that expired milk in the fridge before you throw it out? Same thing here: The entire audience couldn't take their eyes off this poor gentleman as he struggled to contain the very bits and bytes he had shepherded to life. It probably won't surprise you to know that I didn't rush to my broker to buy shares in that company.

TIP

Always conduct a dry run or rehearsal of the training session to ensure that the technology you're using is working as planned. You don't need to go through the entire presentation; just make sure you have covered the basics that will surface in the workshop.

Offering interactive activities

Hint: Making the training interactive doesn't mean asking "Any questions?" at the end of a two-hour lecture. As mentioned previously, one of the downsides of virtual exchanges is the fact that it's difficult to read body language; you never know for sure when someone (or, heaven forbid, the entire group) has mentally checked out. Therefore, including interactive activities throughout the session is vital. I involve the participants by reviewing an OKRs example and by conducting the case study portion of the training (see the earlier section "Kick Off Your Shoes Hotels OKRs case study").

Setting expectations for everyone

If you're leading the session, it's your job to make decisions on a number of things, including whether you require the participants to have their cameras on and their microphones muted during the presentation, and whether to allow screen sharing. A laissez-faire attitude of "do what you want" will be sure to wind up in some sort of time-consuming, potentially embarrassing, and utterly avoidable disaster.

Case in point: I was conducting a training session with a client, and they, not I, controlled the technology. I had suggested that people open their mics to ask or answer questions but otherwise keep them muted. The host didn't feel that this was a necessary precaution, and sure enough, about five minutes into my session, we had an "intrusion." The first word to shatter our nerves was "What?!" followed by "You're the most spoiled brat I've ever seen!" What followed was a parent-teenager screaming match of epic proportions, with some profanity tossed in to turbocharge the situation from distracting and annoying to extremely awkward. I stopped talking, hoping the silence may trigger the open mic'er to see there was something happening and realize they weren't on mute, but of course if you're engaged in a full-scale domestic battle with your kid, the status of your mic in an OKRs training session probably isn't top of mind. This embarrassing outburst could have been avoided by simply muting everyone before the session started.

Keeping the session relatively short

I use the word *relatively* in "relatively short" because every organization has different norms and customs when it comes to the duration of meetings. Specifically, I recommend two hours with no break for the training session outlined in this chapter. If you've carefully planned the flow of the presentation, included opportunities for engagement with the group, and you have the technology on your side, then the two hours should fly by.

Determining Your OKRs Philosophy

Back in college, I took an introductory philosophy course and will never forget the professor's first entrance and opening salvo to the class. He strode confidently to the front of the room, jaunty scarf flowing elegantly behind him, and after an obviously well-rehearsed dramatic pause, said, "Philosophy. Phila Sophia, love of knowledge." I felt as though a great bomb of knowledge were about to be dropped on me by this learned gentleman, but, alas, that's pretty much all I remember from the entire semester. It was important, however, because in that opening remark he reminded the class that philosophy means learning and questioning. It means not accepting something just because it's told to you, but using reason and logic to develop your own conclusion.

And so it is with OKRs. Certain "rules" appear to be unquestionable, but that's simply not the case. A wall of dogma has been built up around the methodology primarily through the influence of bestselling books and Google's pioneering use of the system. You possess the power and will to evaluate your own culture, apply logic and reason, and determine the guiding philosophy that you feel is most appropriate in implementing OKRs within your organization.

In previous chapters, I allude to some of the philosophical decisions you'll be required to make as you embark upon the path of OKRs. One of those, for example, is determining the cadence you'll use for your OKRs, whether quarterly, in trimesters, or some other period. In this section, I focus on what often turns out to be the elephant in the room of every OKRs implementation: whether to allow business-as-usual activities to serve as OKRs.

Weighing whether to use business-as-usual activities for OKRs

I'll start by defining what I mean by a "business as usual" (BAU) activity. A BAU activity refers to anything that represents a person's core job function, role, and responsibilities. For example, central to the role of a human resources executive are functions such as hiring new employees, administering benefits, and measuring employee engagement. A sales executive's BAU activities include calling on prospects, writing proposals or quotes, and following up with customers to maintain or grow existing relationships. So, should OKRs be derived from BAU activities? What do you think? Do you have a gut response to the question?

Drawbacks of BAU as OKRs

OKRs are, by definition, designed to propel an organization forward by measuring its true priorities — the actions that will drive learning and change. Pick your cliché here: focusing on the vital few in place of the trivial many; separating the signal from the noise; and so on. The point of OKRs is to move beyond the daily routine and isolate the new, bigger, different courses of action that you feel will drive the execution of your strategy.

Here are several problems with listing BAU activities as your OKRs:

>> **They never change.** One of the primary benefits of the OKRs methodology is the short cadence. Updating every quarter or trimester allows for agility and

swift reaction to changes in your environment, which is critical in an era of rapid disruption. Job roles and expectations, however, are for the most part fixed. Despite some variations from time to time, the metrics used to gauge success in standard activities are unlikely to alter over time. Therefore, by selecting BAU activities to serve as OKRs, you rob yourself of two of the system's greatest attributes: flexibility and prioritization.

>> **They don't promote innovation.** Building on the preceding point, if you choose to measure BAU chores as OKRs, you have little hope of introducing profound or meaningful innovation in your work because you continue to monitor the same activities. The targets *may* change, but without the experimentation inherent in stretch OKRs, you're likely to remain in a static and fixed relationship with your work.

>> **They rob you of autonomy and intrinsic motivation.** One of the most important characteristics of an effective OKR is that it must be meaningful to you. Research consistently demonstrates that people are much more likely to achieve goals that are self-selected, enjoyable, and imbued with personal meaning. I'm not suggesting that BAU activities aren't meaningful to those engaging with them, just that the metrics associated with such activities are rarely chosen by the individual performing the duties. OKRs, conversely, should result from a robust dialog between an individual (or team) and their superior. The team, those performing the work, know better than anyone what is necessary for improvement and are therefore best able to provide meaningful OKRs.

When BAU as OKRs may be appropriate

The case against using BAU as OKRs certainly appears to be open and shut, but . . . before you go issuing edicts and banning BAU as OKRs throughout your vast organizational empire, let me introduce a potential counterargument. Although goal setting is a ubiquitous practice for most, some organizations have never engaged in any type of formal goal setting practice. I know this because these outliers frequently contact my company with the desire to introduce OKRs. If yours is a company that has never instituted a process for setting goals, transitioning from that metric-deprived state to full-stretch, moonshot-type OKRs is like expecting to play first cello in a symphony orchestra after taking one lesson from your aunt who played in high school 40 years ago. It's too much too soon — a bridge too far.

In cases like this, it may be advisable, even preferable, to allow BAU OKRs in year one of your implementation as you're dipping your toes in the goal-setting pool and becoming acquainted with what it takes to create, and manage with, OKRs. The benefit is that every team and individual will be aware of what they're responsible for delivering, and they should be able to translate that awareness into a technically well-written OKR.

Think of OKRs maturity as a ladder, and this is the first rung you can comfortably put your foot on as you climb upward over time. In year one, everyone can become accustomed to the rhythm and process of measurement; then, in year two of your implementation, you can transition from BAU to more robust OKRs emphasizing innovation, experimentation, and stretch.

REMEMBER

The decision to allow BAU activities to create OKRs is not as simple as most pundits would have you believe. You must determine your current level of measurement maturity before deciding whether to allow BAU OKRs.

Creating a dashboard of "health of the business" metrics

Unless you're in the tiny minority of organizations that has never used any formal goal-setting process, I do recommend avoiding using BAU activities as OKRs for the reasons listed in the previous section. Unfortunately, my guidance alone doesn't mean you'll be able to stop people from attempting to populate OKRs with their day-to-day actions. For many, even after extensive instruction on the power of stretch OKRs, the reflexive response is to measure their current job responsibilities.

Let me propose an easy and practical approach for balancing day-to-day, BAU work with OKRs. It is simply this: Before you draft OKRs for the first time, create a dashboard of metrics that you can use to assess performance on your BAU activities. This dashboard serves two purposes:

>> **It provides a mechanism for tracking your success in the "blocking and tackling activities" of your day job.** And having such a mechanism is certainly important; both you and your boss need to know that "the trains are running on time" and you're on top of the responsibilities that have been assigned to you.

>> **You can use the BAU activities as a starting point for creating OKRs.** Examine what you do and ask, "How could I make a 10x improvement in that process?" or "What roadblock is holding me back from world class performance?" Your OKRs don't necessarily have to derive from BAU activities, but starting there can provide ample food for thought.

Here's a personal example. As the owner of OKRsTraining.com, I have a number of BAU activities that are vital to running the company: writing blogs; promoting our work on social media; creating client presentations; researching new trends in performance management; developing new business to grow revenue; and more. I have a dashboard of metrics that dutifully tracks these and which I monitor regularly. That dashboard includes measures such as revenue, website hits, social media impressions, number of new clients, blogs written, and several more. But are any of those my OKRs? No.

Instead, each quarter I challenge myself to isolate the one or two most important things I can do to drive success for the business. Those things don't necessarily derive from my BAU activities, but often they do. For example, in an effort to develop new business (a classic BAU item), we're hoping to expand our operations internationally, serving clients around the globe. I developed a specific OKR to help with that. The objective is

Find potential international affiliates to grow our business globally.

Of course, a number of key results accompany this objective as well. This OKR is new, different, quarterly in nature, and important enough to drive strategic change in the company — precisely what an OKR should do.

Chapter 8

Rolling Up Your Sleeves, Part 1: Creating Objectives

Chapters 1 through 7 cover, among other things, what OKRs are, how they differ from other systems, and how your organization benefits from the system. You also discover in those chapters how critical it is to outline your "why" of OKRs, and what roles you need people in your organization to play to make OKRs a reality.

In this chapter, you turn to the actual development and use of OKRs, and you begin by exploring how to create powerful objectives. I delve deeply into the different types of objectives, guide you step-by-step through the process of writing them, provide tips, and outline the characteristics you need to keep in mind to ensure that your objectives will drive the execution you expect. As the chapter title says, roll up your sleeves, because it's time to get to work!

Working with the Various Types of Objectives

Raise your hand if you love IKEA. Who isn't gaga (maybe even Lady Gaga is) over the Swedish home furnishing giant where, while strolling the yellow brick road of retail they've conveniently laid out on the floor, you can buy everything from meatballs to mattresses to *macetas* (that's Spanish for flowerpot, in case you're wondering). Not long ago, I made the trek to our local IKEA because I'd determined that my home office didn't have enough light (likely a pitiful procrastination strategy) and figured, where better to pick up a stylish yet low-priced lamp?

An added bonus of shopping at IKEA is the workout you get if, like me, you miss the department you're looking for the first time and have to loop around the entire airport-terminal-sized maze all over again. The second time was the charm for me, and after deliberating in front of the glowing choices for a seeming eternity of maybe 30 seconds, I found the lamp that was sure to infuse my office with both light and inspiration. I got home, eagerly tore the contents from the box, and fully expected to have the room lighted within ten minutes. Unfortunately, IKEA had (so I thought at the time) neglected to include a certain-sized Allen wrench that was instrumental in the process. Try as I might (and boy did I try), there was no way that lamp was going to be assembled without the right tool for the job.

Regardless of the endeavor, whether it's putting together a piece of furniture or creating OKRs, you need the right tool for the job. The very ambitious and essential job you're attempting to get done is executing your company's strategy, and to do that, you rely on different types of objectives. The actual definition of the objective won't change; it will always be a statement of a broad qualitative goal designed to propel the organization forward in a desired direction.

However, as you'll discover in the following pages, to execute objectives effectively, you need them to span diverse time spans. In this section, I outline how to best employ annual, quarterly or trimester-based objectives, and objectives that emerge due to unforeseen circumstances. And by the way, in case you work for (or are a raving fan of) IKEA and are thinking, "There is no way the right Allen wrench wouldn't be included," you're correct; I eventually found it amid shreds of cardboard on the floor and, hallelujah — there was light!

Looking ahead: Annual objectives

Annual objectives are those created at the highest level, representing the most important things that must be achieved for the organization to execute its strategy. As noted in Chapter 5, these company-level OKRs make the most essential items to focus on in the months ahead crystal clear to all the organization's employees.

The preferred cadence for company-level objectives is annual because you require stability at this level of the organization. These objectives provide the context for all lower-level objectives throughout the company; therefore, they set in motion all OKRs, from top to bottom, with every team determining how they can best contribute to the overall goals of the organization.

REMEMBER

Your people expect leadership to set a destination and stick to it with the required commitment and patience. If you were to change your company-level objectives every quarter, for example, doing so would require sweeping changes to all OKRs beneath them and surely cause confusion and skepticism from the entire employee population.

I'm not speaking theoretically here. I've witnessed the paralyzing effects of capriciously changing company-level OKRs mid-stream, and the damage it does to leadership's credibility. One company's leadership team decided to pivot to a strategy focused on innovation, hoping to jumpstart a moribund research and development process in order to churn out new products faster. A few months later, for no apparent reason, they shifted again to focus on lean operations, requiring a major shift in the accompanying OKRs. Employees were left scratching their heads and wondering, "What's next?"

Of course, there are times that may require you to alter your plans, but the circumstances that dictate such a change should be dramatic — the defection of a core customer upon whom you rely for a significant share of your revenue, for example. Or a natural disaster that significantly impacts your operations. Otherwise, whenever possible, stick with and relentlessly execute your chosen company-level objectives.

WARNING

Changing company-level objectives frequently leads to skeptical and confused employees who are uncertain of where to place their focus.

Although every organization will pursue different company-level objectives based on their unique strategy, most will include objectives in each of four perspectives of performance:

>> Financial
>> Customer
>> Internal processes
>> Employee learning and growth

In the end, you may decide not to include an objective (or objectives) in each of these four perspectives. However, it's important to at least consider each of them as you deliberate over your final set of objectives. What you want to avoid is a set of annual company-level objectives that focus on a single parameter of success; for example, all financial objectives. The problem with that approach is that it's unclear how you'll reach those financial goals. Your aim at the top of the house should be to tell a comprehensive story of your success, weaving together (whenever possible) objectives in each of the four perspectives.

Table 8-1 lists thematic examples of the type of objectives typically found in each of the four perspectives. Before you pull a "gotcha" by noting that none of them includes a verb or an "in order to" statement (and by the way, good on you for picking that up), I left those components out because they depend on each organization's specific strategy.

TABLE 8-1

Common Themes for Company-Level Objectives

Perspective	Common Themes for Objectives
Financial	Revenue
	Profitability
	Asset utilization
Customer	Customer acquisition
	Customer satisfaction
	Net Promoter Score
	Customer retention
	Market share
Internal processes	Operations
	Supply chain
	Research and development
	Marketing
	Branding
	Manufacturing
Employee learning and growth	Employee training and development
	Employee engagement
	Culture
	Access to required technology
	Implementation of OKRs

Facing the here and now: quarterly or trimester OKRs

Below the company-level, all teams and individuals charged with utilizing OKRs will typically use either a quarterly (90 days) or trimester-based (120 days) cadence for creating and executing the framework. The organization's highest-level OKRs should, barring very untoward events, remain stable throughout the year, providing the context that all teams and individuals require to create their contributing OKRs. At lower levels, however, it's preferable to employ a more agile approach to OKRs, using the truncated cadence for two reasons:

» To take advantage of emerging opportunities
» To overcome budding challenges

Here's a fun example of taking advantage of an emerging opportunity. A friend of mine is a proud descendant of Scotland who dons his kilt once a year to attend "Robbie Burns Night," a celebration of the 18th-century Scottish poet and lyricist, but mostly an opportunity for anyone with one one-thousandth of a strand of Scottish DNA to indulge in their favorite Scotch whisky and sing incoherently late into the night. My friend sent me a picture of him and a friend smiling proudly in their worsted-wool finery.

Imagine that you lead the Buying group of a fast-fashion clothing company and use OKRs to drive focus and alignment. Further imagine that my friend's kilt-bearing photo goes viral and ignites a frenzy of interest in kilts that quickly circles the globe. Suddenly kilts are everywhere. This is the very definition of an emerging opportunity, so regardless of last quarter's or trimester's focus, you should absolutely dedicate your next OKR to this critical shift in consumer preferences. Here's what that OKR might look like:

Objective: Secure reliable supply of kilts in order to meet store demand.

Key Results:

1. Research kilt manufacturers and meet with three potential vendors by April 15.
2. Select a vendor based on price and availability of supply by April 30.
3. Increase corporate inventory of kilts from zero to 100,000.
4. Increase the number of stores with kilts available for sale from zero to 100.

That's the power of agile OKRs created either quarterly or by trimester; they allow you to scan your environment and seize on opportunities, or, conversely, quickly deal with problems or issues that could soon mushroom into critical challenges.

A final word on whether to use quarterly or trimester-based OKRs. In Chapter 5, I list some of the challenges with 90-day OKRs and note that many organizations are now switching to the slightly longer 120-day trimester period. As far as I know, no research dictates which will lead to better results, so at the end of the day, the choice of which cadence to employ comes down to your current culture, the timeline you've used in the past for goal setting, and the overall rhythm of your company and industry.

Dealing with necessary on-the-fly objectives

In the previous section, I introduce a fast-fashion store Buying Director. (Here, I'll call him Bob). Before kilts knocked the fashion world off its very axis, Bob had been monitoring an OKR to drive better outcomes for his portion of the company. But because fashion trends don't always arrive conveniently at the end of a quarter, the kilt revolution took place in the middle of Bob's current 90-day period. Should Bob stand by, focusing on his current OKR, which of course has absolutely nothing to do with kilts, or should he abandon that OKR quicker than you can say *"Ma heid's mince"* (Scottish slang for "I'm a bit confused") and create an OKR like the previous section's example?

Without a doubt, in this situation Bob should put his current OKRs on the back burner and immediately devote his attention to the trend that is sweeping the globe. Organizations rely on OKRs to help them deal with change, and this is a change of the highest order, one with the potential to significantly impact Bob's business. He must not only pay attention to it but also act to capitalize on it with the help of a well-constructed OKR.

REMEMBER

You should use the OKRs framework as an agile goal-setting system, making you responsive to changes in your environment to ensure that you're focusing on what truly matters.

The kilt example represents the magnitude of a disruption that would necessitate a mid-period change in an OKR. Although OKRs are not a binding contract, and are subject to change in certain situations, for the most part they should be developed based on deep analysis and insights relating to your operating environment, and you should commit to pursuing them with rigor throughout the period, whether it's a quarter or trimester. Changing an OKR midstream because it appears too difficult is not an acceptable rationale, whereas having a hurricane wipe out your local distribution center, or acquiring a new customer who will represent 50 percent of your revenue going forward, are acceptable rationales. Again, that's the level of disturbance that should trigger a change in an OKR.

Walking through the Process for Creating Objectives

Full disclosure: I didn't personally come up with all of the section headers you see in this book, including the preceding one. A big shout-out goes to the *For Dummies* editorial team for assisting authors like me in turning what can be dry academic titles into something fun and inviting. I particularly like this title because of the notion of walking through the process. I love walking, whether briskly to get my heart pumping, dutifully getting in my 10,000 steps, or leisurely on the beach while enjoying my wife's company. Walks can be therapeutic and beneficial in so many ways.

The walk through the process of creating objectives is a mix of all three of these dimensions. I offer lots of specific actionable advice that you won't want to ignore if you hope to create powerful objectives (which should get your heart pumping a bit), but I also take my time to carefully lay out the steps in a way you can immediately understand and apply (that's the leisurely piece). Finally, I present a coherent process that, when followed carefully, will result in strong objectives every time (that's dutiful).

A *process* is a series of actions or steps taken in order to achieve a particular end, and the particular end you're striving for here is a set of actionable objectives that will drive the development of execution-aiding key results. The series of actions you take to achieve that end are the steps I walk (there's that word again!) you through on the pages that follow. You may be tempted, when creating objectives, to skip a step in the process — such as by going straight from asking the fundamental objective-setting question to using the formula to frame your response as an objective — but I urge you to be true to that definition and follow each of the steps to ensure the best possible outcomes for your company, unit, or team.

For the best possible outcomes, always stick to the sequential process for creating objectives outlined in the upcoming sections. With repeated attempts over successive periods, the steps will become second nature, ensuring the highest-quality OKRs each time.

Asking the fundamental objective setting question (based on the cadence)

ChatGPT, the chatbot introduced by OpenAI in November of 2022, has been getting a lot of headlines, in everything from local media outlets to the *New York Times*. In case you're not familiar with it, it's an artificial intelligence tool that you can query on any subject imaginable, and it provides an answer based on the incalculable number of terabytes of information at its disposal. I gave it a whirl asking nerdish questions like, "What is the best business book of all time?" Alas, none of mine were on the list. (Clearly this machine has some learning to do.) Then, apropos to this section, I typed, "What is the fundamental objective-setting question?" I fully expected to see a crude sentence packed with randomly generated nonsense that slapped together a bunch of business-speak but didn't amount to anything remotely relevant or usable.

Well, I guess the singularity is closer at hand than I thought, because ChatGPT's response was actually quite accurate. The bot replied to my question with the following: "The fundamental objective-setting question is 'What do you want to achieve?' This question helps in defining the desired outcome and serves as a basis for making decisions and taking actions toward achieving that goal." Maybe I should have asked the bot, "Would you please write an *OKRs For Dummies* book for me?" and saved myself a lot of trouble. (The publisher wouldn't have allowed it, though, and they certainly would have figured it out.) And fortunately, human ingenuity and know-how aren't done yet; I'm still needed to expand on ChatGPT's response with some insights that you'll require when creating your own objectives.

"What do you want to do?" or "What do you want to achieve?" are essential questions to ask, but you must also add an imperative qualifier, and that is the word *important.* I'm certain you could lay this book down right now and quickly brainstorm 20 things you'd like to do, whether you're thinking about your company or your personal life. When you add the word *important,* however, as in "What is the most important thing you can do?" the selection challenge is heightened significantly. Objectives, in the OKRs sense of the word, aren't simply a wish list of tasks you'd love to get to, but must also represent critical challenges you need to overcome, or enticing opportunities you have before you. In other words, objectives are the important things.

Whenever possible in this book, I supply examples to illustrate the key points made, but in this case it's difficult to do so because only you know your specific business situation, environment, challenges, and opportunities well enough to draft execution-aiding objectives. But from years of experience helping organizations draft objectives, I know how difficult starting from a blank slate can be. Having something to react to always seems to get the creative juices flowing and help people build on current ideas and generate even more appropriate objectives and key results.

In that spirit, when creating your annual, company-level objectives, a good place to start your analysis is the list of possible areas I outline in Table 8-1, earlier in this chapter. You may have challenges or opportunities that could be faithfully represented in objective form by some of the items I've included in the list of four perspectives (financial, customer, internal processes, and employee learning and growth).

Creating quarterly or trimester-based objectives at the business unit, department, team, or individual level can prove even more challenging because of the seemingly limitless choices of where to exert your effort. Once again, it's helpful to revert to those two golden words, *challenge* and *opportunity*. What specific challenges are holding you back right now? Difficulties that, if surmounted, would significantly improve your performance and appreciably amp up your contribution to overall success? Or, what opportunities have appeared on your horizon that, if fully exploited, would enhance your results? The fundamental objective-setting question truly does require a commitment to the basics of objective-setting choice: challenges and opportunities.

Making a list of possible objectives

Henry Kissinger, who served as Secretary of State under President Richard Nixon, had a speechwriter named Winston Lord. As Lord tells the story (https://www.youtube.com/watch?v=VekBG4KmUcE), when he would deliver a draft of a speech, Kissinger wouldn't even glance at the document, simply saying, 'Is this the best you can do?' Lord replied that he thought it was but he'd try again. The next day, he would return to his boss's office with a fresh draft and Kissinger would ask, "Are you sure this is the best you can do?" Once again, Lord would assure him he that he really thought it was but he would try one more time. This cycle repeated itself six times until Lord finally replied, "Henry, I've looked at every sentence; I've tweaked every colon and semicolon; I can't improve this speech anymore — it's the best I can do." Kissinger then looked at him and smiled, saying, "In that case, now I'll read it."

Kissinger must have been a fun boss, huh? Imagine trying to have lunch with a boss like him:

> Me: I think I'll have the burger and fries.
>
> Boss: Are you sure that's the best for you?
>
> Me: Maybe the burger with a green salad on the side.
>
> Boss: Are you sure that's the best for you?
>
> Boss: Right . . . tuna salad sandwich on whole wheat.
>
> Boss: Are you sure that's the best for you?
>
> On and on until . . .
>
> Me: I'll have a piece of kale, six chickpeas, and a glass of water.
>
> Boss: Wonderful. Now we can eat.

Joking aside, although Kissinger's constant demands of improvement may have been irritating to Winston Lord and others who reported to him, it represents a core principle to keep in mind when creating your objectives: Don't settle for the first thing that comes to mind during a brainstorming session. When drafting your first set of OKRs, there's likely to be at least one issue, challenge, or opportunity that has been rattling around in your subconscious for months, just waiting for the right moment to be unleashed. So naturally, when you put pen to paper or finger to keyboard, that is the first thing that will spring to mind, and you may be tempted to declare, "Done. Time to move. That was easy!"

Sure, maybe the first thing you write down as a potential objective is in fact the most important, but one of the most critical questions you can ask during this process is, "What else?" Take some time to widen the aperture on your thinking to ensure that you're seeing the entire field of possibilities and making an informed choice as to the truly important objective (or objectives).

So how do you make an informed choice? Use categories to help you come up with potential areas for objectives. For company-level objectives, once again consider the perspectives noted earlier in Table 8-1. Do you have customer issues or opportunities that must be addressed? What process challenges are holding you back? Do you have the right people armed with the right information?

For quarterly or trimester-based objectives, you can first draw on your newly created company-level objectives and ask, "How can I influence one or more of these?" That fundamental query may lead to numerous potential objectives. Creating a simple list of challenges and opportunities for your group will also yield multiple possible objectives. Adopting a broader frame of reference ensures that you are in fact choosing the most critical objectives necessary to drive the execution of your strategy. Then, and only then, will you know you're doing your very best and making Henry proud.

REMEMBER

Challenge yourself or team to generate several possible objectives to ensure that you're considering multiple angles, and then choose those that deliver the greatest value.

Sequencing your list

A few years ago, I was engaged by the Ophthalmology group of a very large global pharmaceutical company to assist them in creating OKRs. This group had never done any form of formal goal setting, instead relying primarily on a standard set of outdated KPIs handed down by headquarters. The group was very excited to harness the powers of focus, alignment, and engagement offered by OKRs. We began our day together with a training session similar to the fundamentals workshop outlined in Chapter 7, and they were only too happy to soak up as much knowledge as they could on the framework. By lunch, they were chomping at the bit to roll up their sleeves and create their very first set of OKRs.

Because it was a fairly large group, I split them into smaller teams and assigned each team the challenge of brainstorming one potential quarterly objective for the overall group. I gave them 20 minutes to create a draft objective, write it on flip-chart paper, and then return to the main room to tape their chart to the wall, at which point, each team was to report what they came up with.

When all the flip charts were posted on the wall and I had the opportunity to review them, at the first one I started to giggle. The giggles turned to full-on laughter as I reviewed the successive charts. What could possibly be so funny about draft objectives for the Ophthalmology group of a vast pharmaceutical enterprise, you ask? I kid you not: Every objective they submitted essentially amounted to "cure blindness." In 90 days, I might add!

Make the objective attainable

What the ophthalmologists had generated was lofty, visionary, and, if achieved, something that would literally change the course of human history, but it wasn't a realistic objective within the given time frame. Yes, OKRs are meant to encourage stretch thinking, but the caveat of attainability can never go too far afield. Determining the "size" of the objective is one form of sequencing the objectives you listed in the previous step. You should immediately remove any that are simply too big, broad, or outside the realm of possibility in the time frame. I'm not discouraging such bold proclamations, and in fact encourage you to think about the end goal for your team, unit, or organization. The issue is to recognize where they belong, such as with mission or vision statements, but not quarterly OKRs.

Consider the timing of various objectives

A second form of sequencing that can help when narrowing your list of potential objectives is simply timing. Some objectives must be achieved before it's possible for others to even begin, so it's best to set aside for future periods any objectives that you can't start before you accomplish others. This is true for both annual company-level objectives and quarterly or trimester-based objectives for departments, teams, or individuals.

For example, imagine an Accounts Payable group in a company that, because of obsolete technology, is forced to manually process some vendor invoices, which consistently results in costly errors. Management has therefore given the green light for purchasing a leading-edge software tool that promises to eliminate any vendor invoice processing errors. When brainstorming their quarterly objective(s), it wouldn't come as a big surprise to see this team consider the following themes:

1. Eliminate vendor invoice errors.

2. Reduce late payment fees from vendor invoices.

3. Install the new Accounts Payable software system.

4. Train Accounts Payable staff on the new software system.

So, which of those do they choose for the coming quarter? If you've ever gone through the nightmare of any large-scale software upgrade at your company, you probably recognize that installing the system and having it up, running, *and* producing results in the span of 90 days is about as likely as me — who couldn't build a birdhouse — being the next host of a home renovation show on HGTV. Therefore, numbers one and two in the preceding objectives should most likely be eliminated for consideration in the current quarter.

That leaves numbers three and four, and the decision hinges on whether the company feels they can both install and train their team in the course of 90 days. That's most likely a big ask, given the inevitable hiccups associated with new software. Therefore, the most logical objective would be one focused exclusively on having the system installed and ready for use in the quarter. Going through this simple, time-based sequencing exercise will ensure that you select objectives that are both stretch and attainable.

Choosing the most important objectives

Selecting your objectives — those of the greatest significance that are likely to have a profound impact on your success — is a considerable undertaking, one not to be taken lightly. Assuming that you've reduced your burden somewhat by eliminating at least a few possible objectives through the sequencing process, here are some things to think about when determining what will make the final cut:

>> **Consider your challenges.** You should focus your strategy as well as strategy execution on overcoming critical challenges that stand in the way of competing successfully in your chosen industry. Therefore, a good place to start when considering what objective, or objectives, you'll choose is to determine which are best positioned to assist you in slaying whatever dragons have been

holding you back in the past, or helping you erase any deficits in areas that require substantial improvement. Any objectives deemed to be high impact in terms of beating back critical challenges warrant serious consideration.

» **Look at your opportunities.** This point may be the "glass half full" equivalent of the previous bullet. At any given moment, every business or organization has opportunities for improvement, expansion, and innovation that, if seized upon, could vault them to the next level of growth and profitability. If you have a limited time to take advantage of those tantalizing opportunities on your doorstep those opportunities may serve as great raw materials for the creation of an objective.

» **Consider what you talk about in your organization.** If you were to catalog the most prominent keywords, phrases, and topics that surface again and again in management meetings, town halls, and Slack channels, what would they be? What are the hot-button issues that come up time after time but for whatever reason are swept under the rug while you fight the current operational fires or decide to wait until the time is right to attack them? Your answers to those questions may well represent contenders for objectives.

» **Ask what you are most likely to achieve.** A sweet spot for objective creation is often the Venn diagram of what you determine is critical to achieve and what, given your unique skills and resources, you are in the best position to achieve. When brainstorming possible objectives, you must take a long look in the mirror to ensure that you have the ability to turn the objective into reality. Objective setting is not wish fulfillment, but must be grounded in the reality of your current situation.

» **Think about what you're most passionate about.** In the past, I've set personal goals around getting up earlier in the morning as well as improving my cardio fitness routine. Here are two clues to help you choose which one you think I stuck to and achieved: 1) For most of my life, I've been a night owl; there was a time in my college years when I could tell you exactly what was on every channel at 2 a.m.; 2) I love hiking. So, with that limited information, what goal do you think I crushed?

If this were a game show, you'd win a small appliance if you selected the goal of improving my cardio fitness. I have no problem motivating myself to tackle the switchbacks while I'm ascending the foothills of San Diego, but there is no chance of me doing it in the pre-dawn hours because I'm not an early bird. It's human nature: People are more likely to achieve a goal they're passionate about. I don't, however, suggest making this the primary attribute when selecting an objective, because at times you must conquer the hard things in order to show progress. But if you're looking for a tiebreaker vote on potential objectives that fulfill other criteria in this list, passion can be your friend.

In the end, no secret formula exists for selecting the most important objectives. The process is necessarily messy and often subjective, which is okay so long as you apply the necessary care and discipline to the proceedings, taking your time to carefully consider the options and making an informed decision that you can confidently defend to your boss and other colleagues.

Using your formula

After you've whittled what may have seemed like an Everest-sized list of objectives down to a manageable number that you feel you can achieve in the next period, whether that's annual, quarterly, or a trimester, the job of objective setting isn't quite done yet. Based on experience, I'd wager that the objectives you've created are more akin to concepts or notions than true objectives. For example, you may have objectives that sound like "Launch V2 of the software," or "Be more customer focused," or "Innovate constantly."

WARNING

Objectives that don't follow the standard formula (verb + what you're going to do + in order to / so that) are highly likely to fall short of describing business impact and thus generate poorer-than-anticipated outcomes. Chapter 1 describes working with this formula in detail.

Every OKR created in your organization is like a fingerprint in that it will be unique to the team or individual that created it, signaling what they feel is most important for them to focus on in the days ahead. And that's exactly what you want: People determining their exclusive contribution to the company's success. What you don't want, on the other hand, is for every OKR in the organization to be written using a variety of formats — some with numbers; some with statements of business impact and others without such statements; some beginning with verbs and some not; and so on. To foster transparency across the organization, allowing for apples-to-apples comparisons among OKRs, they must be constructed using the same building blocks, and those are the three components in the standard formula.

Table 8-2 summarizes the process for selecting objectives.

TABLE 8-2 **The Process for Selecting Objectives**

Item	Keep in Mind
Ask the fundamental objective-setting question (based on the cadence: "What is the most important thing you can do in the upcoming period?"	Balance what you want to do with what you need to do.
Make a list.	Don't automatically select the first objective you consider. Ask "what else?" to ensure that you're examining all possibilities.
Sequence your list.	Look for any natural order of objectives, determining what must be done before another can be started. Also, be on the lookout for any objectives that are too big or broad for the time frame.
Choose the most important.	Analyze your list in relation to challenges, opportunities, topics of frequent discussion, current reality, and what you're most passionate about.
Use your formula: verb + what you're going to do + in order to / so that	Use of the formula across the organization will ensure consistency in approach and enhance transparency.

Exploring Other Ways to Help You Set Objectives

If I were asked, "Hey, Paul, what's the friendliest place you know?" my answer would not be a bar where everyone may or may not know my name; or the local coffee shop where I can order my half-caf, triple shot, extra-hot latte with almond milk, a shot of hazelnut, and foam art in the shape of a heart; or the weekend Farmer's Market, where I buy wild Enoki mushrooms. No, for my money, one of the friendliest places I'll ever find is a gym.

Since I began traveling full-time for work over two decades ago, I've visited a lot of gyms in cities all over the world, and I've yet to find one whose members are not willing to enthusiastically lend a hand when assistance is needed. If you're in a gym and see someone performing an exercise you think is interesting and you'd like to learn how to do it, I guarantee the person you approach will be happy to show you the ropes. Of course, the high watermark of this friendly attitude is the concept of the "spot." As you're struggling mightily to get that last rep of a bench press in, a friendly voice is hovering over you, exhorting you for "one more" and, if necessary, placing a guiding hand on the bar as you push through that last satisfying rep.

Sometimes people need a little extra help, a final nudge to get over the finish line, and that may be the case as you work through the process of creating your objectives. I'm confident the steps outlined in the previous section can get you to the promised land, but given the difficulty of the task, you may require an additional boost to spike your creativity. In the sections that follow, I offer a few additional ideas to draw on as you fashion your final set of objectives.

Using rituals

Have you ever noticed that before basketball players attempt free-throw shots, they almost always dribble the ball a specific number of times? Or they gently run their hand across their forehead, or even kiss the ball! Although these routines may seem like silly superstitions with little real-world value, I prefer to view them more positively as rituals. Do they work? They sure do! One study of free throws found that players engaging in consistent rituals were 12.4 percent more accurate than when they deviated from their standard sequence of actions (see *The Expectation Effect: How Your Mindset Can Change Your World*, by David Robson).

If you look closely, you'll find rituals everywhere, not just in sports. Beyoncé reportedly prays and performs a fixed set of stretching exercises before she performs. The famed and prolific children's writer Dr. Seuss was supposed to have worn a lucky hat whenever he felt a debilitating bout of writer's block coming on. Beethoven, who relied heavily on caffeine to fuel his creativity, was said to count out exactly 60 beans for each precious cup of inspiration.

It doesn't matter how seemingly silly a ritual is; the mere act of following through with the behavior can drive a positive outcome, as the following wonderfully bizarre experiment demonstrated. Researchers invited participants to perform a karaoke version of the Journey song "Don't Stop Believin'" (see "Don't stop believing: Rituals improve performance," by Alison Wood Brooks, et al., *Harvard Business Review*). To ensure their best efforts, they were informed that their pitch would be judged by karaoke software and they'd be given a bonus of up to $5 for a pitch-perfect version of the song. Before they performed, half the participants were given the following instructions:

> Please do the following ritual: Draw a picture of how you are feeling right now. Sprinkle salt on your drawing. Count to five out loud. Crinkle up your paper. Throw your paper in the trash.

Obviously, following this ritual offered no direct benefit to the participants singing, but those who did it received scores that were on average 13 points out of a 100 higher than those who didn't.

Other experiments have come to the same conclusion: rituals work. As a quick aside, and very coincidentally, I had a "Don't Stop Believin'" ritual myself. Back in college, a good friend of mine had a state-of-the-art (for 1983) car stereo system we would have described as "totally awesome." The unit featured a button labeled "Loudness" that, when pressed, would boost the bass and overall volume to ear-splitting levels. Whenever we drove to a dance or party that year, our ritual was to play "Don't Stop Believin'" as the last song before we arrived, and to always slam the Loudness button at a certain point in the song to crank up the volume and bass. This ritual inevitably seemed to pump us up and put us in the mood to party.

Why are rituals so powerful? There are a couple of explanations, with the first being an assumed belief that you have additional control over a situation by following a standard routine, thereby lowering any anxiety you may feel. Rituals also lead people to have more faith in their mental reserves and ability to maintain concentration and self-discipline. As a result, one can avoid distractions and persist longer. The very good news, as demonstrated by the examples noted previously, is that rituals can work in virtually any domain, including the creation of objectives.

For many organizations, and the teams and individuals that comprise the organization, setting objectives is a new process, one that may benefit from the introduction of rituals. It doesn't have to be wild and bizarre, like the drawing and salt-sprinkling karaoke singers. It can simply be something that signals that it's time to think strategically, get creative, and generate objectives that signal your contribution to success. Your ritual may be as basic as reviewing the company's strategy to frame the discussion, or reiterating your team's mission and why your function in the organization is critical to success.

Or maybe you do want to have some fun: sing a crazy song; draw a picture of what you envision happening in the next period; take a walk outside in the fresh air to generate inspiration. The specific action isn't what matters, necessarily, but the ritual itself does, as well as the fact that it primes you for what comes next: creating objectives. So go ahead, adopt a ritual for the creation of objectives, have some fun, and watch your results improve.

Drawing on the wisdom of crowds

The "wisdom of crowds" is a concept outlined in the book of the same name by author James Surowiecki. He argues persuasively that when working together, a large group of people can prove to be more accurate and show more wisdom than even the most renowned expert. He goes on to suggest that this collective intelligence can be harnessed to make better decisions and solve some of our most complex problems.

One of the reasons the wisdom of crowds is so effective and compelling is that it draws on a diversity of opinions, gathering input from assorted people, all of whom bring to the problem their own unique experience and world view. This variety of input is something you can take advantage of when drafting objectives. Take, for example, the challenge of writing annual company-level objectives. The task naturally falls to your executive leadership team, but you can cast the net a bit wider and draw on other voices that may have a meaningful contribution to make. Obvious choices include your employees, board of directors, and high-value customers.

REMEMBER

Multiple sources of good ideas are available to you when creating objectives. Sometimes going beyond your core team to canvass outside voices will provide insightful suggestions leading to impactful objectives.

When you're creating quarterly or trimester-based objectives for your team or department, you can once again go to the deep well of external wisdom to test your assumptions about what is most important, and gain the perspective of knowledgeable others. You should consider reaching out to your full staff, other teams or units you work with regularly, departments that represent your internal customers in the organization, and external customers if applicable. Canvassing an assortment of opinions can help introduce novel ideas as well as counteract the potentially devastating effects of groupthink, wherein a close-knit group quickly coalesces around a few core ideas and summarily dismisses anything contrary to their insular views.

Considering what's holding you back

For many, many reasons, I'm thrilled to be living now and not in 1841, when disease and poverty ran rampant and the potential for having raw sewage dumped on your unsuspecting head lurked around every street corner. But, believe it or not, those weren't the biggest problems facing painters of the day. Their biggest challenge was keeping oil paints from drying out before they could use them.

For painters such as the American John Goffe Rand, the best solution was to use a pig's bladder sealed with a string. To expose the paint, an artist pricked the bladder with a tack, but of course there was no way to completely seal the plug afterward, which led to the frustrating problem of prematurely dry paint. Additionally, pig bladders weren't the best travel companions, frequently bursting open and wasting what was then an expensive commodity.

Rand studied the problem extensively and devised a solution: the tin paint tube. Although it was slow to catch on, it eventually proved to be exactly what Impressionist artists required to escape their studios and capture inspiration from the natural world around them. Thanks to Rand's portable invention, for the first time in history a painter was able to produce a work onsite, whether in a café, garden, or waterfront. The paint tube also revolutionized the use of color, because it was now practical and affordable to produce and carry dazzling new pigments such as chrome yellow and emerald green, allowing the artist to capture the full majesty of any moment. So important was this invention that Renoir declared, "Without colors in tubes, there would be no Cezanne, no Monet, and no Impressionism."

The moral of this story is the power of recognizing and overcoming problems to improve your situation, and that applies as much to objectives it does to Impressionism paintings. When considering possible objectives, ask yourself what problems are holding you back from executing your strategy. Taking an unvarnished look at the problems that separate you from successful execution is a great way to envision potential objectives.

Incorporating the Characteristics of Effective Objectives

If you'd like to become a more patient, accepting person, I have a few tips for you. Consider trying mindfulness training, suspending all judgment and simply paying attention to the present moment, whatever it brings your way. That's a surefire technique to up your patience game. Or try to foster more empathy, putting yourself in another person's shoes and attempting to understand their perspective on a situation. Finally, may I offer the tried-and-true practice of gratitude, shifting your focus from what you don't have to what you do. Commit to any of those practices and you should be on the path to greater patience in no time. You know what you shouldn't do if you want to become a more patient human being? Build a house.

My wife and I are in the middle of a major, down-to-the studs, renovation project as of this writing, and I'll just say it's not a patience-inducing endeavor. Have you ever done a renovation and lived to tell about it? Admit it — if you're married and have gone through a substantial renovation, you Googled divorce lawyers at least once. The worst part for me is the waiting. I seriously wonder whether planning the first moon landing had as many steps as our home renovation adventure. It never ends. And, apropos to the first paragraph, I'm not the most patient person.

I bring this up because you, too, may be a little impatient, wondering when this chapter will be over and you can get on with the work of rolling up your other sleeve to create key results that go along with your shiny new objectives. Unlike my contractor, whose favorite sentence seems to be, "We're not quite where we were hoping to be," you and I are very close to the finish line on the deep dive into objective setting. There is just one last hurdle to get over, and that is to make certain you're adhering to the characteristics required of a truly effective objective. In the sections that follow, I offer seven attributes against which to gauge your draft objectives to ensure that they provide maximum value.

Making it qualitative

To recap: An *objective* is a statement of a broad qualitative goal designed to propel the organization forward in a desired direction. The word *qualitative* should give you a hint as to whether I think objectives can have numbers. Answer: They shouldn't.

Here, also, is a recap my definition of a *key result,* which is a quantitative statement that measures achievement of the objective. The key result always provides evidence of whether you've met the objective. Therefore, if your objective is, for example, "Increase sales by 20 percent," you've included the key result in the objective. What's left for the key results at that point? You may use them to document how you'll achieve the 20 percent sales increase, but by doing so, you're likely to turn the OKR into a glorified to-do list full of activities that may or may not move the needle on sales, rather than an important tool in the effort to execute your strategy.

Another important issue with including numbers in your objective is that the objectives will lack context, meaning that you don't know why the stated number is important to the business. Consider the earlier example, "Increase sales by 20 percent." Why do you want to increase sales? I know it seems obvious — every company on the planet wants to grow their sales — but what's your particular reason? Are you losing relevance in your markets? Are feisty competitors nipping at your heels? Are you looking to grow market share? By determining your specific rationale, you open yourself to the possibility of numerous key results which, in the end, will prove more meaningful in the execution of your unique strategy.

In the preceding example (increase sales by 20 percent), assume that your biggest challenge is a slew of new competitors entering the market, threatening to steal market share from you. If that's the case, a more strategic objective could be as follows:

Increase sales in order to maintain our competitive position.

This objective provides a much broader range of possible key results that go well beyond a list of sales tactics. With this more encompassing objective in place, you'll likely include key results such as these:

1. Increase sales from *x* to *y*.

2. Increase gross margin percentage from *x* to *y*. (This ensures that you're not growing sales in an unprofitable way through heavy discounting, for example.)

3. Increase market share from *x* to *y*. (This measures the business impact portion of the objective, that of maintaining competitive position.)

Now the OKR is serving its true purpose of helping you overcome a strategic problem, rather than simply replacing a to-do list of actions.

Making it meaningful to you

Meaningful can be a very subjective term; you may find deep meaning in a beautiful sunset, whereas for me it may just signal the end of a busy day. Many people assume that the word *meaningful* implies something that has a profound impact on society or even the world — curing a rare disease or fostering world peace. But something that proves meaningful to you, your department, or your company doesn't have to be so lofty. Anything can be considered meaningful if you perceive it as contributing value, which can come in myriad forms, from solving problems for customers to making your community a better place because of the products or services you provide.

The objectives you choose should always be meaningful to you in some way, representing the value you hope to create for your team, company, or even the world. "Meaningful" of course doesn't mean "easy." In fact, the opposite is usually true. How often have you heard an actor say in an interview that they took on a certain role because it challenged and was meaningful to them in some way? One of my acting heroes, Paul Newman certainly felt that way. I've always felt a bond to the iconic thespian, mostly because I've been called Paul Newman instead of Paul Niven about 44,000 times in my life. Newman, not Niven, was well-known to select roles that required a depth of feeling and nuance that would take him to the emotional brink — and those were the parts he deemed meaningful.

Challenge and meaning go hand in hand in most scenarios, including OKRs. If you've gone through the steps of drafting objectives that I identify earlier, and your final selections don't make you just a bit nervous, they may in fact not be your best choice. If, on the other hand, a little uncertainty, doubt, or even fear has crept into the equation, you're probably on the right path. Success, including with objectives, often lies in a zone of slight discomfort. You know the work is vital, and it's a true representation of the value you hope to deliver, but it's going to be difficult to achieve. When you've found that magical mix, you've most likely discovered the objectives that are right for you.

Ensuring that it's doable in the time period

Whenever possible, you should choose objectives that can be accomplished within the associated time period, meaning that annual objectives should be achieved within the year, quarterly within a quarter, and trimester within a trimester. OKRs are meant to be an agile goal-setting system, allowing you to take action in response to changes in your environment, market conditions, and so on. If you select objectives that are going to take five years to complete, and are committed to seeing them through regardless of what may be taking place in the world around you, then you have little room for agility in your approach and precious few opportunities to make valuable pivots based on what is occurring around you.

Maybe you think that I dangled a bit of an out for you by beginning the previous paragraph with "whenever possible," and you'd be correct if so. It's a fact of organizational life, regardless of whether you're considering annual, quarterly, or trimester-based objectives, that certain of those objectives will be important, meaningful, and challenging enough that they must span more than one period.

As just one example, I've had a number of clients over the years include a company-level objective related to the installation of a new Enterprise Resource Planning (ERP) system. Under the very best of circumstances, depending on the size of the company and the installation, this task can take at least a year, but will often consume even more time. In that case, it's acceptable to include the objective, but you must update your key results frequently to demonstrate progress on the long-term objective.

For lower levels of the organization, meaning anything below the company level, the OKR cadence will most likely be either quarterly or trimesters. My advice is to attempt to limit the majority of your objectives at these levels to a maximum of two periods (two quarters or two trimesters). Departments or teams may have at least one long-term objective that is vital to future success, and therefore will cross over into extended periods; however, to get the most benefit from the OKR process in the form of agility and responsiveness, the vast majority of objectives should be doable in the shorter time frame.

Aligning it vertically and horizontally

An objective is said to be vertically aligned if it contributes to, or is consistent with, a higher-level OKR. "Higher level" in this case refers to anything above the level at which the objective is written. For example, imagine "ABC Company" (hey, give me a break on the name; it's getting late in the chapter and my imagination is running low). Like most organizations, ABC is composed of a number of business units, departments, and teams, including Human Resources (HR). Within

HR are four departments: Rewards, Recruitment, Talent Development, and HR General. When the Rewards department creates objectives, they should attempt to choose something that is consistent with, or aligns to, objectives at the HR and company level. In other words, they should choose something that demonstrates their contribution to overall success.

This process, however, should never result in a forced-fit situation, which involves attempts by the Rewards department to create an objective that clearly has little relevance for their own work but may, if the rationale is stretched enough, link to a company objective. The first and primary task in creating objectives at any level is to determine what is most important to you at this time. Your responsibility at that point is to communicate your choice, noting how it aligns, if in fact it does. If it has no direct alignment to a higher level, the group that wrote the objective must convincingly defend why the chosen objective is vital to their success.

REMEMBER

Horizontal alignment refers to the process of determining whose assistance within the organization you require in order to achieve your own objective. I cover the topic of horizontal alignment in much greater depth in Chapter 10. Feel free to jump ahead for a peek and then come back to complete this chapter.

Keeping it easy to read and understand

If you read this headline in the news tomorrow, would you know what it meant?

WHO & WB establish PPP to Improve HC in EU

To quote one of my favorite movie characters, Wayne Campbell of *Wayne's World*, "Exsqueeze me?" I'd bat about 500 at best in trying to decipher that text. It means "World Health Organization and World Bank establish public-private partnership to improve health care in the European Union." Why not just say that? Because the world loves and is awash in acronyms. One of the biggest problems I face when working with a new client is attempting to quickly master their innumerable list of bizarre sounding corporate abbreviations. It's enough to drive me MAD.

There exists within most organizations an unspoken belief that everyone knows, understands, and is fluent in the entire lexicon of acronyms bandied about in every email, meeting, and town hall since the corporate charter was stamped. But I'm here to tell you a little secret: They don't.

I've been in numerous sessions during which teams are sharing their OKRs with the rest of the organization when some brave soul raises their arm like a white flag of surrender and asks, "I'm sorry — what does AMOTO mean?" Amid some lightly camouflaged condescension, a flurry of apologies typically follows as the speaker clears up the matter by spelling out the bizarre-sounding word animal for the poor knowledge-deprived soul daring to ask the question. But then, inevitably, someone else says, "Thanks for sharing that; I didn't know what it meant, either." A few others follow in those footsteps, acknowledging their ignorance. Soon it's clear that what seemed so obvious is, in fact, not.

One of the great potential benefits of OKRs is transparency, which includes sharing objectives and key results from top to bottom and allowing everyone to get a revealing and insightful glimpse into what their colleagues will be focusing on in the days ahead. This transparency enhances the overall understanding of everyone's role in the corporate universe, and in some cases may even spur spontaneous conversations that drive future collaborations and power product innovations or process breakthroughs. When you write an objective that contains multiple acronyms, or even one, for that matter, you're violating the spirit of clear communication and transparency that OKRs are meant to foster within the organization.

REMEMBER

Never assume that everyone understands your acronyms, and make it a habit to take the extra 15 or so seconds it might require to actually type out the full words comprising your objective.

Controlling the necessary resources

As I relate in Chapter 10, it's not uncommon, and can be very beneficial, for two teams to share OKRs — meaning that they combine forces and work collaboratively on an OKR that provides value to both. Each team contributes effort, know-how, skills, or resources that drive fulfillment of the OKR.

Things get tricky when the word *share* is interpreted by some groups the way a three-year-old may experience the concept when deciding how to distribute toys with a playmate. Most young kids aren't adept at equal distribution and are more likely to scream "Mine!" when grabbing for a toy rather than offering up a civilized, "Here, you can play, too." The OKR equivalent of that behavior is writing an objective despite knowing that another unit or team will be required to do the vast majority of the work to achieve it.

When you draft an objective, it should be with the knowledge that, for the most part, you control the resources necessary to make it a reality. The knowledge or skills necessary to see it through to fruition are within your grasp and available for immediate application, and you control or can access any necessary resources to ensure that the objective is realized.

Providing business value

Based on participating in thousands of meetings over the span of my career, I can say confidently that there is no shortage of ideas circulating in most organizations. The one source of power humanity will never run out of is, of course, brain power, and thus we're fortunate to reap the benefits of that wellspring. But ideas can run on a spectrum, from genius on one hand to outlandish and utterly ridiculous on the other.

Objectives are essentially ideas you're transforming into a methodology for goal setting, and although creativity in their selection is certainly welcome, to execute your strategy effectively, your objectives must reflect solid ideas that are grounded in providing business value to the enterprise. Thursday-morning poker competitions to enhance risk assessment skills, or free yoga classes for everyone in order to increase stamina at the office, may seem like great notions, and I'm sure they would provide some benefits to certain people, but the question is, will they deliver business value aligned with where the company wants to go?

I stress the importance of the objective formula (verb + what you're going to do + in order to / so that) because if you adhere to it, you're forced to carefully consider the true business rationale for delivering on the objective. If you generate the first two components of an objective but are stumped when filling in the business impact portion, the objective you craft is likely not an effective one. The first test of a value-adding objective is its demonstration of business impact or value.

Chapter **9**

Rolling Up Your Sleeves, Part 2: Creating Key Results

S ome things in the world just go better together: peanut butter and jelly; campfires and ghost stories; and my penny-pinching uncle's favorite, buy one, get one free. Two more things that are perfectly suited for one another are objectives and key results. Objectives are aspirational and compelling statements of what you hope to achieve, but on their own, they're really nothing more than wishful thinking. Only by adding a set of key results can you know whether you've made that dent in the universe represented by your chosen objective. You can't have one without the other.

Key results flex their muscles primarily through the use of numbers, and there's nothing like the sheer power of numbers to wash away any confusion or contradiction when it comes to determining whether you've nailed your objective, made it halfway there, or whiffed completely. You either hit your number or you don't — simple as that. Percentages, dollar amounts, raw numbers, or even dates (as in the case of milestone key results) are the ultimate arbiter in this game, letting you know with clarity and precision how well you've done in pursuit of your chosen objective.

In this chapter, I guide you enthusiastically through the wonderful world of key results. First, you examine the types of key results and the most appropriate time to use each. Next comes the process for creating key results that weave together in a story of your successful achievement of objectives. Effective key results consist of a number of characteristics to keep in mind, as you discover in this chapter. Your last stop on the tour will be the gift shop, where you can buy all manner of OKRs swag at our online store — and you won't want to miss the bamboo straws and OKRs sunscreen. Alas, sorry to disappoint you, but there is no "exit through the gift shop" on this tour. I do, however, leave you with the parting gift of some final advice on creating powerful key results.

Looking at the Types of Key Results

In college I possessed a skill prized by all my friends. You may guess that it was admirable interpersonal skills, with the ability to maintain healthy relationships and help to resolve conflicts among others. Such a gift would certainly come in handy at that stage in life, but nope, that wasn't it. The skill I was known for was the art of writing song titles on the inside of cassette tape covers in a long, flowing script, although I tended to write in big letters so that many titles ended in ellipses. To this day, my friends and I refer to a certain Janet Jackson classic as "What have you done dot dot dot."

I was happy to help all my friends, but determining the flow of tunes was by far one of my favorite activities, and before creating a new tape, I got to decide where to place each one in order to optimize the overall effect.

This principle of placement for ideal impact applies to your use of key results as much as it does to my collection of 1980s cassettes. Just as there are many types of songs, so there are different varieties of key results. Metrics and milestones are the most common, and I delve into them in this chapter. Each of them has a place in your OKRs. The trick is determining when and how to use each to guarantee the best outcome — in this case, achieving your objectives. In the sections that follow, I break down each category of key results and supply advice on how to best capitalize on a mix that makes beautiful music for you.

Metric key results

A *metric key result* is anything that contains raw numbers, dollar amounts, or percentages. Because key results are intended to demonstrate achievement of the objective and be quantitative in nature, you should aim to have most of your key results be of the metric variety. This section takes a look at an example of metric key results in action, using a very relevant topic: this book.

As much as I love writing (I've been faithfully chronicling my life, my work, and my adventures since I was about ten years old), my occupation and primary source of revenue is helping organizations effectively execute their strategies with OKRs through my company, OKRsTraining.com. When I accepted the offer to write this book, my client obligations didn't vanish. The organizations I was assisting still expected me to be present and fully engaged with them as they roll out OKRs. And paying clients have strong expectations. If I were to ignore their requirements and spend all my time writing, they would soon be Googling the competition and wishing me well in my future endeavors. Therefore, it has been very important for me to balance the deadline for this book with my client obligations to ensure that everyone is happy, including me. As the deadline for manuscript submission drew nearer, I used the following objective to assist with that desire:

> Finish writing the *OKRs For Dummies* book on time in order to maintain client relationships.

With the objective in place, I next needed to establish key results that would demonstrate its achievement, as follows:

>> Increase the number of pages written per day from three to six.

>> Increase percentage of working hours spent with clients from 50 percent to 100 percent.

>> Maintain client defections at zero.

All three preceding items are metric key results. The first uses raw numbers, as expressed in pages written (and if you think six pages a day is a paltry outcome, try writing a book). The first key result maps to the first portion of the objective related to finishing the book on time. My hypothesis was that if I doubled my current writing output, I'd be able to submit the book to the Dummies team on schedule. This is a particularly helpful key result because I can monitor it every single day to gauge progress.

My second and third key results linked to the final component of the objective: maintaining client relationships. If I increased the number of pages I churned out each day, that would put me ahead of schedule on the submission date and allow me to spend more time with my clients, as represented by the percentage of working hours devoted to their engagements. Finally, to demonstrate achievement of maintaining client relationships, I also needed to ensure that none defected during the writing process, and that goal was captured by my final key result of maintaining client defections at zero.

Notice the last key result isn't written "from *x* to *y*," or from baseline to target. That's because going into the period covered by this OKR, I hadn't had a client defect, so I had no *x*, or baseline, to include, and thus the use of the verb *maintain*.

Numbers provide clean, precise indications of whether the objective was achieved; therefore you should strive, whenever possible, to ensure that the bulk of your key results are metric based.

Terminology matters. It's easy for people to refer to key results as "measures" or "key performance indicators." They're not those things — they're key results, and you should at all times refer to them as such. Sloppy or inconsistent use of terms can lead to confusion and undermine your overall implementation efforts. Make sure that everyone refers to key results as key results.

Milestone key results

A few years ago, I read about a feud that had broken out among members of a Santa Claus guild in California. You read that correctly: a society of Santas. You'd think the Santas would be united on issues of pay, benefits, and working conditions, but it turns out that these portly purveyors of holiday cheer were at each other's beards in disagreement, with some going so far as threatening not to show up for scheduled mall appearances. It seemed so silly at first, but I realized that no matter the domain or field of endeavor, when passionate people unite around a concept or cause, they're going to have differences of opinion.

OKRs are not immune to this phenomenon, and milestone key results are often ground zero for one of the most polarizing debates in the field. That's a pretty good teaser, isn't it? And in the spirit of the nightly news, now that I've got you on the hook I'm going to change the subject in hopes that you'll stick around to learn more about that big debate — after I get through the business of defining a milestone key result.

Milestone key results represent significant activities or processes that are instrumental in the accomplishment of the objective. There are literally innumerable examples of milestone key results, but here are a few to illustrate the concept:

>> Introduce a new employee onboarding process by June 30.

>> Create an executive-approved customer loyalty program by December 31.

>> Produce the new budget submission guidelines by March 31.

With the business of defining milestone key results taken care of, I return to the big debate — the OKR version of the OK Corral. Over the years, I've encountered many OKRs "purists" who insist that the model has no place for milestone key results. According to these pundits, you must focus exclusively on metric key results that indicate business value or impact. Anything less and you risk, in their opinion, turning OKRs into a glorified to-do list.

I agree that you should never have all milestone key results, because in that case the naysayers would be right; you'd be relying on OKRs as a project plan. But milestone key results can play a vital part in forming a strong OKR. Here are reasons you should, when necessary, include milestone key results as part of an OKR:

» **The impact you're striving for is new.** So many people read the book *Measure What Matters* and think, "Oh great, I'll suddenly have all these outcome-based metrics." But they forget that they're often starting from point zero, and milestones have to precede metrics. Organizations become discouraged because of this fact and abandon OKRs altogether, but that's the worst possible, and least rational, reaction.

The fact that you've outlined gaps in your execution is a good thing! These are strategic blind spots that you have to fix, and you frequently can't get to the outcomes without the steps (milestones) to fix them. Virtually all my company's clients who are new to OKRs write milestone key results. Often they're necessary because the business impact key results they'd ultimately like to track have never been measured before. Thus, they need to start with a milestone. For example, some clients are scaling quickly and have never measured employee engagement. To measure (and improve) engagement first requires the identification of an engagement framework, and then administering an initial survey. Both are examples of milestone key results.

» **Milestones demonstrate progress.** Say you have a quarterly objective like this one: "Improve our website to drive inbound leads." Your key result may be "Increase inbound leads from 125 to 200." That's a very sound, value-based metric key result, but here's the problem: Will you sit back and wait for the 90 days of the quarter to pass, hoping you hit your number? Of course not. You can take actions to drive that increase in inbound leads, and those actions are often reflected in milestone key results. For example, in this case, the objective noted improving your website, so a milestone key result could be "Rewrite the Services and About Us pages of our site by February 1st." This is a necessary input to driving inbound leads.

» **Milestones plug gaps.** Earlier in the chapter, I shared my OKR for finishing this book on time to maintain client relationships, which was composed of three metric key results. The set of key results would be made even stronger with the inclusion of a milestone such as "Submit the final manuscript by April 20." That milestone would be a significant event that must occur in order for me to transition my time from writing back to consulting, and ultimately ensuring that no clients defect.

Milestone key results can play an important role in achieving your objectives. Just keep a few things in mind as you use them. One: Always include a date. That's how you'll introduce stretch — in other words, how quickly you can accomplish the milestone without sacrificing quality. Two: Ensure that the milestones you choose predict or drive the business impact key result(s) for which you're ultimately striving. There should a causal connection between the two. Three: Accompany the milestones with a metric key result. The two types of key results should work together to tell the story of your success on the objective.

TIP

To determine the difference between a true milestone key result and a task or activity, use the length of time completing it would take to determine its categorization. Anything you can do in less than a week is most likely a task, whereas anything that will take multiple weeks to achieve represents a milestone.

Following is a quote from a client who, as do many of our clients, includes milestone key results as an important part of the OKRs process:

> "One thing is clear from this effort: We have many gaps in our knowledge, so lots of milestone key results this quarter will help us get to better metrics that we can use going forward."

Fortunately, this executive quickly grasped the power and potential of milestones, something I encourage you to do as well if you hope to derive the maximum benefits from your OKRs investment.

Walking through the Process of Creating Key Results

Creating a set of objectives, whether at the company, team, or even individual level is a significant accomplishment worth celebrating, but of course the work is only half done. Ask anyone who has been through an OKRs implementation, and they'll tell you that although writing objectives is no picnic, coming up with a set of key results that clearly demonstrate achievement of the objective is the challenge that can leave you frustrated, confused, and ultimately demoralized. Put more simply, forming key results is hard.

My feeling, however, is that people make it more difficult than it has to be because they fail to follow any kind of defined process when fashioning their key results. Many teams huddle around a whiteboard or come together on Zoom and begin cranking out potential key results with very little context and no overall plan of attack. Why shouldn't a set of protocols that will greatly increase the likelihood of a successful outcome be in place for the designing of key results? After all, scientists don't make up the rules and procedures of double-blind studies along the way, hoping they might stumble on some breakthrough. Doctors follow precise guidelines in diagnosing illnesses. Following a documented process is a common-sense practice that will markedly improve the quality of your key results.

In Chapter 8, I define *process* like this: A series of actions or steps taken in order to achieve a particular end. The end in this case is a set of key results that prove you've met the objective, and the following sections outline the series of actions to take to create those key results. The path I describe doesn't completely eliminate the difficulty of creating key results — but that's not the point. Designing robust key results should be intellectually stimulating, forcing you to draw deeply from your reservoir of organizational knowledge, but it should never be more difficult than it has to be. By following the path I lay out in this chapter, you can be confident that the key results you establish will be true indicators of accomplishment.

Determining your business impact key result by asking the fundamental question

Here's the formula for writing an objective that I've sprinkled throughout the book:

Verb + What you want/aspire to do + in order to / so that (business impact)

The final component of the formula, the business impact, makes it clear why the objective is important to pursue right now, and why it's strategically relevant for the organization. Therefore, when building out your key results, determining the business impact is the logical place to begin. The fundamental question to ask is, "At the end of the period, how will we know we've achieved the business impact in the objective?"

Here's an example of how determining the business impact works. In Chapter 5, I mention that my family owned a soda factory when I was growing up. It's too bad I wasn't a super precocious kid, like a Doogie Howser (a teenaged physician in a 1990s sitcom) of business so that I could have provided my dad with some OKRs advice. He would have benefited from a guiding hand because his business certainly had its share of challenges. To list just a few, there was increasing competition in his market, global sugar prices were rising, and he had high turnover with his staff. Oh, and a son who was consuming half his profits, but I'll leave that one alone.

Perhaps his biggest problem, however, was old, outdated bottling equipment. I remember going up to the mixing room and being practically lifted off my feet by the heady sugary aroma emanating from the machines. That was heaven to a kid, but I also had some reluctance when gently pulling back the door of that room because the World War II–era equipment belched, heaved, and looked at every moment as if it were about to extend its cold steely arms and squeeze me into a soda bottle. The ancient machinery was constantly breaking down, meaning the line had to stop, no soda was produced, and output was diminished, which later resulted in lower revenues. A logical objective for my dad's company would have been:

Invest in upgraded bottling equipment to increase soda output.

Revisiting the fundamental question, "At the end of the period, how will we know we've achieved the business impact in the objective?" the answer would be increased soda output, as represented by this key result:

Increase the number of cases produced per day from 200 to 300.

It's really that simple. If they increase the number of cases produced from 200 to 300, they're providing clear evidence of achieving increased soda output, the business impact portion of the objective. This is why identifying the "why now?" business impact piece of the objective is so critical. It's like having a free bingo chip. The clearer you state the business impact, the easier it is to answer the fundamental key result question. You know when you write the impact statement that you must measure it with at least one key result.

One further point: If I were reading this book, I'd challenge this so-called expert author (can I challenge myself?) by asking, "If your father had all these problems — increasing competition in his market, rising global sugar prices, and high turnover with staff — how could he afford to invest in upgraded equipment? Would that really be the best objective for him to pursue?" Excellent query!

Remember that OKRs must represent a focus on what matters most in executing strategy and moving the business forward. In this hypothetical situation, my dad had several choices: improve staff training; try new promotions to combat competition; or even reduce the sugar quantity in the recipe. In Chapter 8, I talk about sequencing your objectives in a way that makes them doable (sometimes you have to accomplish one before the next one). If my father did invest in training for his staff, that wouldn't fix the equipment issue and put soda on shelves. Increasing promotions would work only if he had the additional soda to sell, which he wouldn't without investing in equipment upgrades. And finally, reducing the sugar content would only dampen demand, further depressing revenues.

The core problem was the obsolete equipment, so it's the right place to start. Other objectives related to staff training, promotions, or recipe changes could follow at a later date.

Telling the story of success using leading key results

The 2000 film *Memento*, directed by Christopher Nolan, is well known for its unique storytelling structure in which the narrative is shown in reverse order, starting with the ending and then working its way back to the beginning. The movie was praised by critics and received a number of Academy Award nominations, so perhaps the writers were on to something with this "start at the end and work backward" approach. I believe you can use the same technique to great effect when crafting a set of key results.

Your business impact key result represents the ending, in this case, of your strategic story. Now you need to work backward to fill in the missing pieces of the story, and that's where the leading key results enter stage left. A leading key result is one that predicts, drives, or leads to another key result. Here's a very simple example:

Business impact key result: Increase revenue from $50M to $75M.

Leading key result: Increase the number of face-to-face meetings with high-value prospects (those with proposals above $2M) from 25 to 50.

The hypothesis is that having more meetings with high-value prospects will lead to, or drive, the overall business impact key result. Sometimes your leading key results will be milestones, and that's okay, too. Leading key results are important because they act as "early warning systems." In this simple example, if you're not getting any face-to-face meetings with high-value prospects, you're unlikely (based on your hypothesis) to see an increase in revenue, and therefore you need to take action immediately.

Referring to my father's soda factory OKR example (in the previous section) in light of this storytelling and leading key result innovation, hitting the number of cases produced would provide clear evidence that he achieved the business impact portion of his objective (increase soda output). But without the rest of the story in place, the leading key results, he'd be forced to wait until the end of the period and hope he hit the required output, and hope is not a strategy. This OKR is crying out for some leading key results to complete the story and give my dad the ammunition he needs to critically examine his progress.

Telling the story by working backward

There are a couple of ways to illuminate those leading key results. My father could simply work backward from the business impact key result and ask, "What will it take to increase the number of cases produced per day?" Because his equipment was frequently breaking down and forcing the line to stop production, a logical response to that question could be, "Reduce line stoppages," with a corresponding key result of: "Reduce line stoppages from one per day to one per week." With the line running at peak efficiency, output is sure to increase. Now he can ask, "What will it take to reduce line stoppages?" He'd keep asking "What will it take to . . . (drive the subsequent key result)?" until his story is complete with three to five key results.

Telling the story by measuring the objective

A second method of telling the story is going back to the objective and ensuring that you're measuring it in its entirety. In this case, the objective opens with "Invest in upgraded bottling equipment." How would my dad know he's doing that? A very simple key result would be: "Install upgraded bottling equipment by x date." Now he has a gap between that initial key result, the first chapter in his story, and the ending — his business impact of increased output.

To close the gap, he would have to ask, "What happens between buying the equipment and increasing output?" Most likely, he would have to train his staff to ensure that they're taking full advantage of the technological upgrades offered by the shiny new machines. That training could lead to this key result: "Train 100 percent of bottling staff on upgraded equipment by x date." With the new equipment humming along and the staff competently operating it, line stoppages should decrease. The final OKR now looks like this:

Objective: Invest in upgraded bottling equipment to increase soda output.

Key Results:

1. Install upgraded bottling equipment by x date.

2. Train 100 percent of bottling staff on upgraded equipment by x date.

3. Reduce line stoppages from one per day to one per week.

4. Increase the number of cases produced per day from 200 to 300.

TIP

Using the storytelling approach will also aid you in communicating your key results. It's much easier for other teams and stakeholders to understand the relevance and strategic importance of your key results when you frame them in the narrative of a story, showing how they build on one another and ultimately lead to your business impact key result.

Notice how the mix of milestones and metrics weave together into a compelling narrative that tells the story of success and measures the entire objective. I strongly encourage you to adopt this storytelling stance when creating your key results for any and all objectives. It's a far superior technique to simply brainstorming potential key results, which represent nothing more than a discrete list of to-do items and may or may not lead to the accomplishment of your business impact. Plus, you'll be honing your storytelling chops for that second career in screenwriting. (It's never too late: James Ivory was 89 when he took home the gold statue for Best Adapted Screenplay in 2018.)

Don't look for perfect key results

Imagine you're the general manager of an aquarium whose star performers are two adorable and talented dolphins who never fail to leave the crowd thrilled and amazed at their athletic prowess and seemingly human-like intelligence. Things are going along swimmingly until one day you get word from the pool that your two seat-filling attractions are severely ill from nibbling plastic at the edge of their enclosure. What do you do?

This scenario actually played out at an aquarium in Liaoning province of China in 2007. The first thing they did was call in the veterinarians to quickly extract the plastic from the dolphins' tummies. Seems simple enough, but the dolphins had no interest in being poked and prodded with medical instruments, and whenever the vets attempted an intervention, they contracted their stomachs, making any removal impossible.

Now what do you do? You get creative, and I mean really creative. The vets knew that normal procedures weren't going to get the job done, so they improvised by calling in the world's tallest man, 7-foot-9-inch Bao Xishun to lend a hand — or in this case, an arm the length of an airplane wing. Bao was able to reach deep inside the dolphins' stomachs, remove the nasty plastic, and save their lives. All in a day's work for the gentle giant from Inner Mongolia.

Creativity is a prized resource in virtually every field of endeavor, including OKRs. You will undoubtedly face occasions when it seems that finding the perfect key result for your objective is virtually impossible. Those are the moments when you must channel your inner Bao and be creative in designing a key result that, although not perfect, provides insight into your attempt to achieve the objective and gives you something to discuss as a team. This endeavor is particularly relevant when a lag exists between the timing of your objective and the measurement of the business impact key result.

Think, for example, of pharmaceutical companies. In most cases, they're striving toward a business impact key result of breakthrough sales from a new blockbuster drug. However, the drug will likely be in the development pipeline for years, only to be followed by more time navigating the byzantine government approval process. In this case, measuring business impact in the cadence often associated with OKRs (either 90 or 120 days) is virtually impossible.

For another example, a client's Government Relations department was creating OKRs. Their top priority was simple: lobbying the U.S. Congress to pass legislation favorable to their industry and company. The client was attempting to influence the decision-making process in that legislative body in order to ultimately see success in the form of an enacted bill. But bills aren't passed overnight, or in the convenient space of a quarterly cycle. Playing out this situation in the form of an OKR (using a generic objective to protect the identity of the client), here is a possible objective and some key results:

Objective: Lobby Congress in order to have new legislation passed that is favorable to our company.

Key results:

1. Increase the number of hours each member is lobbied from five to eight.
2. Witness the passing of the bill by x date.

The problem with the second key result is the "x date," because it will most likely be many months — well beyond a quarter — into the future. If the company insists on using quarterly OKRs, how can the Government Relations department come up with a suitable key result, one that isn't perfect but provides information they can learn from?

This is where the power of leading key results enters the picture once again. A leading key result holds predictive power and will in fact "lead to" the desired business impact key result. In the preceding example, having the bill passed is the business impact. The question to ask now is, what could lead to, or drive, that key result?

In virtually all cases, the key results you craft are in pursuit of influencing behavior, whether that of a customer, stakeholder, or the members of Congress whom you're actively lobbying. In other words, your quest is to somehow persuade people to do something that's ultimately beneficial to you. For this Government Relations department, that quest is seeing the Congress pass favorable legislation. Because such a quest will take significant time, you must challenge yourself to determine what will lead to, or drive, that behavior, and this is where you exercise visioning and creativity to determine an appropriate leading key result.

There is a space between the action of lobbying and the bill being passed. In that space, the leading key result resides. After the lobbying has been completed, the department must ask the question, "What would indicate that those members of Congress are at least leaning in our direction?" Perhaps it could be "The number of follow-up calls they place for clarification on our position." Any observable behavior you can count that you believe is "driving" or "leading" to the outcome you desire can serve as an effective leading key result.

Follow-up calls from legislators isn't a perfect or overly sophisticated key result, but that's not the aim here. What you want is something that is indicative of success; something easily trackable that you can discuss as a team and act upon if you're not seeing the behaviors you want or need. In this situation, if you've lobbied your targeted members of Congress and haven't heard a peep from those you knew going in were skeptical of your position, you have a problem, one that calls for some intervention. The leading key result serves as a forcing function — that is, it forces assessment (have any Congressional members placed follow up calls?) and action (if they haven't, you'll follow up; if they have, you'll provide the necessary information).

A cliché seemingly as old as time itself is apt here: Don't let the perfect be the enemy of the good. In the absence of a timely business impact key result, lean on the power of leading key results to fill the execution gap.

Using the formulas

All the example key results in this chapter share a pattern. The metric key results are composed this way:

Verb + what you're going to measure / track + from x to y

The milestone key results are penned with this formula:

Verb + what you're going to do + date of completion

For metric key results, starting with a verb is obviously preferable because you want to demonstrate movement in some area of your business. The vast majority of metric-based key results are framed using either negative or positive verbs. On the positive side, you frequently turn to *increase, build, grow, develop,* and so on, whereas on the negative side, you commonly encounter verbs such as *decrease, lower, reduce,* and *eliminate.* The middle portion of the metric key result formula is the place to capture what you'll measure during the period. Going back to the example of my father's soda factory OKR from earlier in the chapter, the business impact key result was measuring the number of cases produced per day.

The final portion of the formula, "from x to y," is so special that it gets its own paragraph (a few, in fact). OKRs are designed to promote visionary thinking, encouraging an individual, team, or the entire company to push beyond the boundaries of the merely possible to the realm of unparalleled breakthroughs. That outer frontier is captured with the y of "x to y." It's the audacious destination you hope to arrive at through ingenuity, grit, and maybe even a little good luck. To give the bold y meaning and context, the key result must contain an x that represents the current baseline or starting point. Imagine that someone on your team presented this key result:

Decrease the time to create a customer proposal to six days.

Does the "six" in this context represent world-class performance that only the best of the best sales teams can accomplish? Or is six a mediocre number that a fly-by-night plumbing outfit from some nondescript business park routinely meets? You don't know, because you don't have any context, and therefore have no idea how much stretch is invested in the number six. Here's a different way to write the key result:

Decrease the time to create a customer proposal from ten days to six days.

Now you're talking, because in this rendition, you have context for the six days and can see that if you hit this key result, it will lead to an almost 40 percent improvement in performance. That's a stretch!

Okay, I can hear you from here admonishing me with this little stinger: "What if we don't have the x, the baseline?" In such a case, you have a couple of options. Number one, you can create a short-term key result to gather baseline data which, once identified, will be plugged into the key result, giving you both parts of the "x to y." Or, if gathering the baseline numbers will prove overly time consuming or costly, you can simply create the target (the y) without an accompanying baseline. This may seem to directly violate the stern warning I just gave about always using "x to y" to show context, but here in the real world, you'll have occasions to discover a powerful key result, likely one you've never previously fathomed, that is ideal in demonstrating achievement of the objective but which has no past data. In that case, if you believe the key result truly indicates success on the objective, go ahead and use it.

WARNING

Metric and milestone key results that fail to follow the formulas outlined here are likely to be composed of vague and nebulous language, making actual scoring and analysis difficult and their ultimate value questionable.

Milestone key results should also follow a formula, which is the following:

Verb + what you're going to do + date of completion

The verb choice is particularly relevant and demanding of precision when identifying milestone key results. Be on the lookout for weasely phrases such as "work with" or "partner with," which are completely open to interpretation depending on who is doing the work. Aim for declarative statements that produce tangible outcomes. For example:

Don't say: Work with Finance on expense reporting.

Do say: Create an executive-approved expense reporting system by June 30.

The date you choose for accomplishing the milestone is also an important consideration because, in this context, it represents the amount of stretch you're putting into the key result. The basic question you must answer when formulating a milestone key result is, how fast can you achieve the milestone without cutting corners or sacrificing quality?

Table 9-1 summarizes the steps in creating key results.

TABLE 9-1   **Steps in the Process of Creating Key Results**

Item	Keep in Mind
Determine your business impact key result by asking the fundamental question.	"At the end of the period, how will we know we've achieved the business impact in the objective?" If you can't answer the question, reexamine your objective to ensure that you've included business impact.
Tell the story of success using leading key results.	Your key results should be linked in a cause-and-effect pattern that ultimately leads to business impact.
Don't look for perfect key results.	Simple, unsophisticated key results that lead or drive business impact are a perfectly acceptable alternative to not providing a key result at all.
Use your formulas.	Whenever possible, include an "x to y" with metric key results and ensure that any milestone key results yield tangible outcomes.

Incorporating the Characteristics of an Effective Key Result

If you combined elements of The Who's "My Generation," a song the Rock and Roll Hall of Fame proclaimed had shaped the genre, with the stomping rhythm of Elvis Costello's "Pump It Up," what popular musical composition may result? According to The Knack lead guitarist Berton Averre, those two numbers served as the inspiration for the band's 1979's smash-hit single, "My Sharona." Searching for an upbeat tune they could close their shows with, Averre and lead vocalist Doug Fieger looked to their own musical heroes for the music, and Fieger drew on his infatuation with a young woman named Sharona Alperin to compose the lyrics. According to Averre, with those simple raw materials in place, they wrote the song in about an hour. About an hour!

I love "My Sharona" and have probably listened to it thousands of times since 1979 (on vinyl, cassette, CD, Sirius, and Apple music). The song has been a standard on FM classic rock stations for decades, has been featured in films, TV, and commercials, and can be heard every day on satellite radio and streaming platforms. If you accept a standard definition of the word effective to be achieving success in producing a desired or intended result, and assume that Averre and Fieger were striving for musical relevance and commercial success, "My Sharona" has been otherworldly in its effectiveness, especially considering the relatively miniscule effort that went into creating it.

Sometimes the stars will align for you and things fall naturally into place with underwhelming effort, as was the case for "My Sharona." However, for most people most of the time, achieving effectiveness in any endeavor requires not just expertise in our chosen fields (Averre and Fieger were expert musicians, of course) but also adhering to a set of core principles that will bring about the outcome we desire.

That is certainly the case with key results. Following the steps outlined in the previous sections is sure to yield many potential key results, but to ensure truly effective key results, they must be faithful to a set of core characteristics that enable them to drive the business value you want and expect from the OKRs process. In the sections that follow, I outline five attributes that should be reflected in each of your key results. Believe it or not, writing these last three paragraphs took me close to an hour. Wouldn't it be wonderful if I could derive "Sharona-sized" royalties from that 60-minute investment.

Making it quantitative

If I were asked to describe or define what a car is, I'd say it's a vehicle with four wheels, powered by either an internal combustion engine or an electric motor that transports a small number of people. Ask a random sample of a hundred people out on any street (trying to avoid being hit by cars), and I'd wager they would offer a similar rendering of the word. Everyone knows what a car is, and despite the fact that the automobile industry has witnessed steady and pioneering innovation since the days of Henry Ford, nobody is going to innovate us into a three-wheeled car anytime soon. (For the record, polymath Buckminster Fuller tried that with his 1933 Dymaxion car which, was so hard to handle that it couldn't be driven in anything other than perfect conditions and later crashed at the entrance to the Chicago's World's Fair.)

Cars, at least within the current boundaries of our knowledge of engineering and physics, have four wheels. Simple as that. In the same vein, key results are always quantitative, meaning that they must include either a raw number, a dollar amount, a percentage, or in the case of milestone key results, a date (which represents a number on the calendar). Numbers serve as pure arbiters of success with key results, settling with precise objectivity the question of whether the desired outcome has been reached. Without a number, you have no discernible way of determining the realization of the key result. Take this example:

Objective: Provide our teams with the tools they need to serve customers faster.

Key result: Teams have the tools they need.

The preceding statement is not a key result; it's more of a proclamation or declaration that at the end of the period will lead to very little insight and learning because, as stated, it doesn't define success. You can't tell whether it refers to every team in the company or only those working in, say, Customer Service. Nor can you tell whether it represents all possible systems and tools an employee could leverage to better care for customers or just a select few that have been proven to improve service and relationships. An enhanced version of this key result would be:

Key result: Increase the percentage of teams reporting (via bi-monthly survey) that they have the software tools they need to serve customers faster from 75 percent to 100 percent.

In the upgraded version, you learn that the current baseline of teams possessing the software tools they need is 75 percent, and you see that the target is stretching it to 100 percent. The extent of improvement is now clear. In defense of this sad "before" key result that I'm mercilessly preying upon, often a poorly written key result is the offspring of a weakly devised objective, which is another reason you must write your objectives with precision and specificity. The old adage "garbage in, garbage out" can easily come into effect in the interplay between objectives and key results.

Shooting for stretch — but ensuring that it's attainable

In Chapter 1, I tell of my goal-setting heroes, the dynamic duo Locke and Latham, who conducted hundreds of studies featuring diverse groups including loggers, truck drivers and of course paper-pushing office workers. After crunching all the numbers, their evidence was unequivocal: Hard or "stretch" goals significantly increase performance in all domains.

The performance difference noted by Locke and Latham wasn't minor, either; in fact, the evidence suggested that those who set difficult-to-achieve stretch goals outperformed people who set easy-to-reach targets by a factor of 250 percent. I could cite reams of scientific jargon they used to support their claims, but, it all boils down to a simple fact: People rise to a challenge and tend to pull back when things are easy.

You may be able to conjure up memories of inspiring and stimulating goals that you knew were hard and placed you in a zone of discomfort but that you fought your way through to ultimately claim victory. One that comes to mind for me is bench pressing 225 pounds. If you ever meet me, you'll discover instantly that I bear no resemblance to a nose tackle for the Green Bay Packers. I've always been tall and on the lean slide. Despite that, weight training has been a habit for me throughout my adult years, but for most of that time, I engaged in a fairly set routine of exercises with consistent weight, never really exceeding my grasp. Then one day I realized I needed to shake things up. At that point, I could bench press probably 180 pounds, so the goal of 225 within six weeks was legitimately audacious. At first, every incremental jump of five pounds felt like sumo wrestlers were squatting on either end of the bar, and I was tempted to revert to the comfort of the status quo. But with time, effort, and sustained enthusiasm, my numbers crept up, and by the sixth week, I grunted my way through a set at 225 pounds. I'm still proud of that achievement.

Higher levels of performance will always result from setting difficult goals, but the million-dollar question is, how do you know what represents stretch for any particular goal? The target you come up with has to inspire grit, persistence, and sustained effort while also remaining within the realm of attainability (more on that shortly). So what's the magic formula? Well, no actual magic formulas exist, but you can apply certain techniques to find motivating targets.

Whenever you're attempting to create a target for something, for example, whether in your personal life or as part of an OKR, look to whoever does it better than anyone else in the world. What do they do? What number represents peak performance for them? Can you climb to that mountain top?

Another way to discover daring targets is to think deeply about what how far you think you can get if you work hard, possess all the necessary resources for success, and happen to have things break your way. You could call that target "X." In that case, you should shoot for "X + 1," just beyond your comfort zone, making it a target that gives you shivers just thinking about it but is a number that, if achieved, will lead to truly outstanding performance and serve as a point of pride for everyone involved. That was the 225 bench press for me.

Here's a fun and easy to remember acronym to draw on when creating stretch targets:

Super **T**errifying **R**eality-bound and **E**nergizing **T**argets that **C**reate **H**igh performance.

I hope the previous paragraphs have you pumped up, ready to reach for the brass ring and go for the gold on stretch targets. However, before you make a public commitment to one that's sure to whip your entire team into a frenzy of wild enthusiasm, step back and make sure you feel it's ultimately attainable. If employees realize that a target isn't attainable but you encourage them to achieve it anyway, the results will not be pretty.

Just look at Wells Fargo, the bank that created a pressure-cooker environment for their salespeople, exemplified by wildly unachievable targets. Attempting to keep pace with these outrageous goals, employees at the once-revered financial institution went on to open millions of unauthorized accounts and credit cards in the names of current customers without their knowledge or consent. The long arm of the law soon caught up with them, slapping them with a jaw-dropping $3 billion penalty to resolve the criminal and civil liability. They could have avoided this King's ransom by simply reining in their outlandish targets, which would have encouraged playing by the rules.

Establish crazy, impossible to reach stretch targets and you're likely to produce malfeasance, misappropriation, malice, and a host of other undesirable words that may or may not start with *m*. As with my advice for concocting a stretch target, no formula exists for how much is too much, but applying some due diligence, conducting conversations with internal and outside experts, and using a little common sense will help you choose targets that find the sweet spot of stretch and attainability.

Limiting the number of key results

Near my home is a little hole-in-the-wall restaurant that sells mostly heart-attack-on-a-plate, instantly guilt-inducing items that I have the good sense to ignore on most occasions but whose donuts get me every time. Soft, moist, baked to perfection; they're irresistible. I've liked donuts ever since I was a little kid watching my grandmother dip her homemade delights in powdered sugar before placing one in my grubby little hand to devour in seconds. Interestingly, this humble snack has a somewhat controversial history because of the numerous accounts about its true provenance.

My favorite donut origin story is the tale of an 1847 Maine boy named Hanson Gregory, who, as related by Leidy Klotz in his book *Subtract*, asked his mother why her fried cakes were soggy in the middle. She had no answer, so young Hanson, ever the experimenter, took out a fork, poked a hole in the middle of a cake, and had his mother try baking it that way. I'm not sure how long the cooking process would have taken in an 1847 cast-iron stove in the forests of Maine, but some time later, what emerged was the delicious treat we've come to know and love. It turns out that removing the dough from the center of the cake allowed the donut to cook more evenly, and would provide later purveyors, like my grandmother and countless global donut shops, more area for sugar, cinnamon, and other high-octane goodies. The moral of this confectionery story is that in this case, and virtually all cases, less is more.

Hanson Gregory isn't the only person to relish the power of subtraction in generating preferential outcomes. Michelangelo described his approach to sculpting like this: "I saw the angel in the marble and carved until I set him free." Pablo Picasso believed that art reached its apex when artists embraced "elimination of the unnecessary." And finally, no less than the quintessential renaissance man himself, Leonardo da Vinci, opined that perfection is achieved when there is nothing left to take away. Do you see where I'm going with this, or should I dip back into my book of quotations? I have yet to mention St. Exupery, William of Ockham, or Lao Tzu, who all sang from the same songbook of subtraction for addition. Your goal when creating a set of key results is not to gather every possible number-based tracking device under the sun, but rather to settle on a small group that demonstrates unequivocal achievement of the objective.

Whenever possible (and it's difficult to think of circumstances when this guideline wouldn't immediately apply), tell the story of success with three to five key results. You shouldn't have just one, and you shouldn't have more than five.

Following is an example to bring this disciplined approach into focus. Nostalgic for my grandmother and hungry over memories of her delicious donuts, I've imagined a little shop called "Mary's Donuts." Although Mary has a good clientele, they mostly tend to buy one item, perhaps just a coffee, or just a donut or two. Mary wants to see the average order size increase, so she decides to launch a loyalty program that earns people points for additional purchases. Here's one version of a possible OKR reflecting her new strategy, which includes just a single key result:

Objective: Create a customer loyalty program in order to increase average order amount.

Key Result: Increase the average order amount from $3 to $5.

On the plus side, Mary's solitary key result clearly links to the business impact portion of the objective and will provide flawless evidence of increasing the average order amount per customer. But if this is a quarterly OKR and Mary goes with this single key result, she'll sit back for 90 days hoping she achieves it. This is not a recipe for success. Key results generate their greatest opportunities for learning and execution when they weave together to tell the story of success and include both leading or driving examples and lagging indicators. Here's a better version of Mary's OKR:

Objective: Create a customer loyalty program in order to increase average order amount.

Key Results:

1. Create a customer loyalty program including benefits, enrollment requirements, and required marketing collateral by April 30.

2. Update the website with program information and sign-up fields by May 15.

3. Increase loyalty program members from 0 to 1,000.

4. Increase average order amount from $3 to $5.

This version of the OKR is much improved because it includes a mix of milestone and metric key results that Mary can simultaneously view as leading and lagging key results. Here's the story Mary is telling with this enhanced OKR: First, she has to create the program. (And notice the specificity here. Great job, Grandma!) Next she'll update her website to ensure that the new program is front and center and that registering is easy and convenient. With the program up and running, her target is 1,000 new members by the end of the quarter. Finally, Mary's hypothesis is that if she can generate 1,000 new fans through the program, they'll spend more per order, which will result in the average order amount climbing from $3 to $5.

In this scenario, because she has a robust set of key results, Mary can take action during the period if things aren't progressing according to plan. For example, if she sets up the program, updates the website, but attracts just five new loyalty-program members, that result is unlikely to drive her business impact key result of increasing average order amount (unless those five people each buy about 5,000 donuts; where is Homer Simpson when you need him?). She then has to decide what to do in response. Maybe she should increase the program's perks in an attempt to spike new registrations? Or does she let the chips fall where they may and use this quarter to learn and reassess? Only by having multiple key results can she engage in this level of strategic analysis and learning.

Finally, consider one additional scenario with multiple key results:

Objective: Create a customer loyalty program in order to increase average order amount.

Key Results:

1. Define goals for the loyalty program.

2. Determine the target audience.

3. Decide on the types of rewards to offer.

4. Determine how to market the program.

5. Create a customer-loyalty program including benefits, enrollment requirements, and required marketing collateral by April 30.

6. Design the sign-.up forms for the webs.

7. Hire a web designer to create the loyalty program page on the website.

8. Update the website with program information and sign-up fields by May 15.

9. Increase loyalty program members from 0 to 1,000.

10. Increase average order amount from $3 to $5.

This time, Mary's mistake is to include a number of tasks or activities as key results, which I talk more about in the section "Ensuring that it's a key result, not a task." She may want to track these tasks as a means of assessing overall progress, but they are too "micro" to be included in the final set of key results, which should be confined to the critical few that will move the needle on the objective.

Making it specific

When you visit the eye doctor for a glasses prescription, the doctor puts you behind a device called a phoropter that looks like something you'd see in an alien movie. You focus on a chart on the wall as the doctor clicks between lenses while asking, "One? Or 2?" Here's a version of that exercise. Without seeing an accompanying objective, which of the following two key results would you pick: one, or two?

1. Increase satisfaction of attendees at our annual user conference from 75 percent to 90 percent.*

   *Satisfaction is measured as a percentage of respondents giving a rating of 4 or 5 out of 5 on speaker quality, networking opportunities provided, and venue amenities.

2. Increase the effectiveness of our core processes by 30 percent.

You don't need a magnifying glass to recognize that option number one is the much better written key result. But consider what word comes to mind concerning the attributes of key result number one that makes it the preferred option. A joke from comedian Lily Tomlin comes to mind: "I vowed to make something of myself when I grew up. I guess I should have been more specific." Thank you, Lily! *Specific* is the word.

Specifity is, along with difficulty, right at the top of goal-setting gurus Locke and Latham's list of effective goal-setting characteristics. (Always remember OKRs are a form of goal setting.) The more specific you make a goal, or in this case a key result, the more likely you are to achieve it.

When you create a very specific key result, you understand what success looks like and immediately know where to direct your actions in pursuit of achieving it. With key result number one in the preceding annual conference example, the definition of satisfaction in this context stands out in high relief. You know exactly what it will take to move from 75 percent to 90 percent so that at the end of the period, there is no confusion or finger-pointing as to what represents success.

Knowing what represents success is not the case with the pitiful number two key result shown above. First, what core processes does that key result refer to? My company, which is relatively small, probably has a dozen or more core processes — training, coaching, consulting, writing, researching, branding, promotions, and so on. A large company can have hundreds of so-called core processes, so without identifying exactly which processes you're referring to, a free-for-all is likely to ensue, ending in confusion and frustration. With the vague, obscure key result number two, people are left scratching their heads, wondering where exactly to find the finish line.

Before you finalize any key result, be sure to take the time to scrutinize every word or phrase it contains and look for any that may be open to interpretation. If a hundred people read your key result, a hundred people should be aligned on the meaning of every single word it contains. If you can't be certain that's true, it's time to reexamine what you've created and add asterisks with more information, link to a supporting document, or spell out in black and white exactly what you mean.

WARNING

Specificity also means to be clear and avoid acronyms, which can confuse even close colleagues. I had a client whose OKRs Champion was engaged to marry a player from the Chicago Cubs. Being a fan of course, she gave Cubs paraphernalia to other members of the staff. After she gave a pen with "CUBS" emblazoned on it to a colleague in the same department, that poor woman, who had no interest in baseball, spent the rest of the day racking her brain. "Center for Unified Business Studies?" "Corporation of United Bus Servicepeople?" Although this isn't an OKRs-specific example, it demonstrates the perils of assuming that everyone will understand your acronyms.

Ensuring that it's a key result, not a task

To make the distinction between these the terms *key result* and *task* as transparent as possible, I start by defining them both:

» **Key result:** A quantitative statement that measures the achievement of a given objective.

» **Task:** A piece of work to be undertaken or done.

The language in the definitions suggests a hierarchical relationship between the two. Key results, especially those of the milestone variety, can be broken down into discrete tasks, but on their own, tasks don't rise to the level of a key result. Revisiting the sprawling empire that is Mary's Donuts, you can see how the difference plays out in the realm of an OKR, and why a task cannot be a key result. One possible version of Mary's OKR listed ten key results (refer to "Limiting the number of key results," earlier in the chapter).

Numbers 1, 2, 3, 4, 6, and 7 in that example are tasks, not true key results. To differentiate the two, it's helpful to estimate the amount of time required to complete it. Number one, "Define goals for the loyalty program," is a considerable undertaking requiring strategic thought, but for a single outlet business like Mary's Donuts, it shouldn't take more than a week to hammer out goals for the program, and anything that can be accomplished in seven days or fewer should be designated a task, not a key result.

Another method of differentiating between tasks and key results is to ask, "If we achieve this, what will happen?" The answer to that question is most likely the key result to include with the final OKR. In the donut shop example, if you ask that of numbers 1, 2, 3, and 4, the logical response is represented by the actual key result, "Create a customer loyalty program including benefits, enrollment requirements, and required marketing collateral by April 30." It encompasses the tasks of which it's composed.

Enumerating every possible task associated with a key result will turn your OKR into a project plan or to-do list, and the detail-heavy minutia will obscure the communication powers of a more compact, narrative-based OKR that makes its strategic relevance immediately apparent to everyone reading the OKRs. Having said all that, identifying the tasks associated with key results is an important part of the process and will pay multiple dividends. Creating associated tasks for each key result helps you

» **Break down the key result:** By outlining the tasks necessary to fulfill the key result, you determine exactly how you'll achieve it.

>> **Plan your work:** Each week, you can use your list of tasks to plan your activities, ensuring that you attend to the items that will drive success on the key result.

>> **Provide a reality check:** Tasks are an excellent reality check on your key results. If you develop a key result and quickly find yourself with a task list that has ballooned to a hundred items, achieving the key result in the allotted time is improbable.

>> **Demonstrate progress:** Task completion allows you to show progress on your path to completing the key result and provides you with material to discuss during check-in meetings.

Table 9-2 summarizes the characteristics of an effective key result.

TABLE 9-2 The Characteristics of an Effective Key Result

Characteristic	Keep in Mind
Quantitative	If it doesn't have a raw number, percentage, dollar amount, or date, it's not a key result.
Stretch but attainable	Your stretch target should make you uncomfortable because of the level of difficulty required, but should also inspire the effort necessary to achieve it.
Limited in number	Tell the story of success with three to five key results, often including a mix of milestones and metric-based key results.
Specific	The more specific you make a key result, the more likely you are to achieve it. Ensure that you have no words that are open to interpretation.
Key results, not tasks	Anything that can be completed in fewer than seven days is a task and not a key result.

Fighting the "You can't measure what we do" syndrome

You're likely to encounter a certain phenomenon in your own implementation, regardless of how well-prepared you are, and even how much executive sponsorship you enjoy. Your rollout may be humming along, with great momentum established on all fronts, when suddenly you run into the brick wall of a team or individual who stubbornly refuses to play along, insisting that their work cannot be measured. To them, it's a hard stop; there is no way they can develop key results because the nature of their work, whether because it's too long term, too dependent on outside forces, or too something else, simply cannot be measured in a systematic way. Phooey, I say. With creativity, ingenuity, and a dose of humility, you can measure anything, so I want to swat that objection aside immediately.

Consider the vexing problem of gang violence in Los Angeles. If L.A. police were to employ OKRs, perhaps they would utilize an objective such as the following:

"Reduce gang violence in order to make our city safer."

With gang-related homicides numbering in the hundreds, it's vital to equip police officers with the very best information in order to prevent future attacks on a population that is almost exclusively young and extremely vulnerable. However, gang violence is an extremely complex problem with many challenging facets, and thus combating it is a monumental task.

An anthropologist at the University of California Los Angeles (UCLA) used a novel measurement approach to combat the problem (see https://www.smithsonianmag.com/innovation/what-can-bees-teach-us-about-gang-warfare-4910299/). His method is something called the Lotka-Volterra equations. In the 1920s, Lotka, an American statistician, and Volterra, an Italian mathematician, discovered that similar-sized rival groups of a species will claim territories whose boundaries form a perpendicular line halfway between each group's home base. The UCLA team took the equations and, using police data on the location of 13 approximately equal-sized gangs in East Los Angeles, mapped their "anchor points," or home base. With the anchor established, they were able to draw corresponding boundaries for each gang's territory and predict where violent clashes were most likely to take place. According to their model, 58.8 percent of violence would occur less than one-fifth of a mile from the border; 87.5 percent would occur within two-fifths of a mile; and 99.8 percent within a full mile. Their predictions turned out to be remarkably accurate. Of the actual 563 gang-related incidents over a three-year period, 58.2 percent were within a fifth of a mile, 83.1 percent within two-fifths, and 97.7 percent within a mile.

The breakthrough in this approach is the accuracy with which the researchers can determine a gang border. Police have sketched gang maps for years but were bound by the conventions of a standard map. That is, they typically draw borders along streets, rivers, and so on. The UCLA team's measurements allow police to pinpoint specific hotspots, and therefore allocate resources with far greater efficiency and effectiveness. In this way, they can ultimately forestall attacks before they occur, reducing gang violence and making the city safer. Objective accomplished! This story should serve as a reminder to you that no problem, no situation, and no team's work is immune to the powerful impact of measurement.

Chapter **10**

Making Your OKRs Even Stronger

B efore the pandemic brought global travel to its knees, I criss-crossed the globe, working with organizations to help them harness the power of OKRs. One day, while unpacking in my hotel room, I noticed a buzzing sound in the room. After a frustrating search for the source of this phantom intruder, I arranged to change rooms. On my way to the front desk for my new key, the buzzing continued down the hallway and elevator. "How could this not be driving everyone mad?" I wondered. At the front desk, the buzzing finally subsided. What a relief! But when I opened the door of my new room and set my things down . . . buzzing! I'm pretty sure that piping in constant buzzing is a torture technique employed with great effectiveness by evildoers far and wide.

After examining the TV, fridge, and air conditioner, the maintenance person sent up to investigate picked up my suitcase, put it on the bed, and said calmly, "It's coming from in there." Somehow the electric beard trimmer in my suitcase had managed to turn itself on. Having assumed that the sound was "out there" in the room, I'd never even considered my own luggage as the source — an enormous mistake that caused stress, wasted time, and most likely downgraded my credibility with the hotel staff.

People constantly make assumptions about many things, and if you've read the previous chapters, you may be assuming that you're ready to go to print with your current set of OKRs. I encourage you to learn from my experience and challenge that assumption by thinking carefully about the topics you'll discover in this chapter, which are sure to make a strong set of OKRs even stronger.

In this chapter, I discuss the importance of alignment to ensure that your OKRs connect to the company's strategy, foster collaboration when necessary, and are consistent with how you want to use OKRs for maximum advantage. The chapter also presents a set of questions that you're sure to get from colleagues around the organization, covering issues like whether to have meeting-based OKRs, when taking shortcuts is possible, and more. This chapter will help you equip yourself with responses to these important and common questions.

Ensuring Alignment among OKRs

Alignment is an important concept that appears in many areas of our lives. If you've just moved to a new house, or want to spice up your current place, you may arrange your furniture so that it aligns with your interior design motif and maximizes the feng shui. Dragging, shoving, and lifting those pieces into just the right position may have triggered a twinge in your back, so it's off to the chiropractor to get your spine back into alignment. Then, if you take some form of transportation, you hope the wheels are in alignment so that you can arrive at home safely and plop onto the sofa that got all this started in the first place. Alignment truly is everywhere, including OKRs.

You need to consider two types of alignment when finalizing your OKRs. The first is the vertical or strategic alignment of your OKRs with the company's overall strategic direction. The other is horizontal alignment, which drives cross-functional collaboration and when applicable, the use of shared OKRs.

Using vertical alignment to drive strategy execution

For any OKRs created below the company level, the team or individual creating them must review and understand the high-level OKRs and then ask themselves, "How can we contribute to the company OKRs?" That's the essence of vertical or strategic alignment in a nutshell: examining your OKRs to determine whether achieving them will help drive success at a higher level of the organization. Naturally, the goal is for your OKRs to signal a clear contribution to the company's chosen goals. Here's an example of vertical alignment using a Marketing department.

Company objective: Increase sales of product *X* to drive overall market share.

Key Results:

1. Launch nationwide promotion campaign by October 15.

2. Increase brand recognition of product *X* from 50 percent to 80 percent of surveyed households.

3. Increase sales of product X from $100M to $160M.

4. Increase company market share in product X's category from 20 percent to 25 percent.

Now imagine I run this company's Marketing division. When creating OKRs, my team and I should look at the company-level OKRs and determine which we can positively influence. After reviewing the OKRs, we determine that although we can't directly control or influence market share, we can help the company increase the recognition of product *X* through enhanced Marketing efforts. In response to that, our OKR might look like this:

Marketing Objective: Provide information on product *X* to drive interest and recognition.

Key Results:

1. Create dedicated social media channels for product *X* by October 7.

2. Increase Twitter followers for product *X* from 0 to 100,000.

3. Publish a bi-weekly newsletter on product X beginning on October 15.

4. Increase product *X* newsletter subscribers from 0 to 50,000.

5. Increase number of downloaded product *X* spec sheets from 10,000 to 20,000.

Looking to the company's overall OKRs and determining your influence gets trickier, however, the lower you descend the corporate hierarchy. Consider a "Community Events" department that is part of the Marketing department. It probably doesn't make sense for them to skip over the Marketing OKRs and jump right to the company-level when drafting their own OKRs. Despite the important role it has to play, a group this deep in the organization isn't likely to draw a direct line of sight from their OKRs to the company's. It's not impossible but, in most cases, it's improbable. What does make sense for Community Events is to look at the OKRs for the department immediately above them (Marketing) and determine whether and how they can influence those OKRs. If the Community Events team concludes that they can contribute to the Marketing OKR, they could create this OKR in response:

Community Events Objective: Deliver information on product X at public events to drive awareness.

Key Results:

1. Obtain necessary permits and permissions to hold pop-up events at seven local malls by October 10.

2. Create information brochures on product X by October 20.

3. Distribute 1,000 brochures at each mall.

4. Increase requests for information on product X from 2,500 to 5,000.

The example OKRs above are different, but they are vertically aligned in support of the company's overall goal of increasing sales of product X to drive market share. Each level clearly signals its unique contribution to the higher-level OKR.

This process of connectivity looks very clean and is a simple concept to grasp, but in reality, certain divisions or departments may scrutinize the company-level OKRs and decide that they can't directly influence any of them. Not to fear: That outcome doesn't preclude those groups from participating in, and benefitting from, the process. If a group can't directly contribute to a company or division level OKR, they simply document (in the form of OKRs) their most critical focus areas in the coming period in order to dramatically improve their own results. It could be a major process change, an experiment of some kind, or a shift in overall direction.

Think connecting, not cascading

I spent some time early in my career working in public accounting. No offense to accountants everywhere, but it wasn't my favorite time, and I've long since retired my calculator. However, one of the comforting aspects of that pursuit was the knowledge that no matter how vexing or complex a problem I faced, I knew there was an answer in the form of Generally Accepted Accounting Principles, or GAAP; the set of rules guiding all accounting actions and decisions.

The OKR world doesn't offer any such guiding principles, but certain "rules" have surfaced that seem to be unbreakable. Among those rules is the notion that when you (the boss) create a key result, it becomes my (the employee's) objective. Known as *cascading*, this is a rule you should avoid because it can be damaging to your OKRs effort.

The problems with cascading

Cascading is problematic for at least two reasons. First, it's simply not practical. Unless you're working in sales, which is perhaps the only function in which the cascading method may prove applicable, your key result may not be a direct fit for my role, function, or responsibilities in a way that enables me to effectively execute it at my level. It's akin to the old "square peg in a round hole" challenge. I may adopt your key result as my objective, but I can actually do little to influence or execute it. Thus the OKR I create, although technically aligned, proves irrelevant and unlikely to motivate performance. The second, and perhaps more important reason, that pure cascading doesn't work is that it robs people of something quite important: intrinsic motivation.

The power of intrinsic motivation

Mountains of research point to the power of intrinsic motivation, which means engaging in an activity because you're internally motivated to do so, rather than being induced by some form of external reward (extrinsic motivation). Even more compelling is that intrinsic motivation can enhance creative results, and that's exactly what you're after when drafting OKRs: visionary and innovative ways of executing your strategy.

REMEMBER

When you cascade, you risk losing the power of intrinsic motivation and the creativity it fosters.

In effect, cascading says, "Make this your objective because I said so." This is the ultimate expression of extrinsic motivation, and it strips away any opportunity for employees to creatively engage with the higher-level OKR and determine a compelling OKR that signals their direct contribution to success.

Focus on connecting, not cascading

Rather than cascading OKRs, you should always focus on *connecting*. Here's how to focus on connecting:

>> Share your OKR with the team below you.

>> Explain your rationale for selecting it.

>> Engage in a conversation with the team on how they might influence it at their level.

This approach facilitates alignment to overall strategic direction but allows for local variations and interpretations that drive creative expression and more meaningful OKRs at all levels.

>> Paul: I made the following a sidebar. Please supply the source where you found this study (book, URL of an article — whatever it is) and authors, if given. –sc

Achieving horizontal alignment by managing dependencies

When my wife and I decided to get a pool in our backyard, we picked a company whose promises were probably too good to be true, but whose bid seemed legitimate. We were dazzled by the renderings the salesman had prepared for us. (Those two attractive people lounging by the shimmering oasis could be us!)

INTRINSIC VERSUS EXTRINSIC MOTIVATION

In one interesting experiment that demonstrates the power of intrinsic motivation, creative writers wrote poems on the topic of snow (see *The Progress Principle: Using Small Wins to Ignite Joy, Engagement, and Creativity at Work,* by Teresa Amabile and Steven Kramer) . Then, one-third of the writers was assigned (without their knowledge) to an extrinsic motivation group. They were given a short "Reasons for Writing" questionnaire that asked them to consider reasons for being a writer; all of the possible options given were, according to previous research, extrinsic — for example, the financial security derived from writing a successful novel.

A second group also filled out a questionnaire that provided only intrinsic reasons, such as "the opportunity for self-expression." The final third of writers, the control group, spent a few minutes reading an irrelevant story. Then the writers wrote a second poem on laughter. At this point, all of the poems were judged for creativity. The results were clear. Although the pre-measure poems (on snow) displayed no differences, those on the topic of laughter written by the group who had contemplated extrinsic motivation were judged to be significantly lower in creativity than the others. Just five minutes spent thinking about extrinsic rewards had lowered their intrinsic motivation, and hence lowered their creativity.

Just days after inking the contract there was a bulldozer in our backyard tearing up everything in sight and digging the massive hole that would eventually be our respite from the blazing heat. But soon came the problems and long delays, and despite our many frustrated e-mails and phone calls, the project continued to spiral downward. Eventually our pool was christened with friends and family, but the experience left a very sour taste and considerable contempt for the company.

This was a clear case of an organization that wasn't in alignment. The salespeople would say pretty much anything you wanted to hear in order to have you commit, thus generating a nice commission for themselves. But the scheduling and installation teams obviously weren't in sync, leading to sub-optimal outcomes for customers who, like us, would inevitably lodge complaints and share the story with others, thus damaging the company's reputation.

If your company has alignment issues, with teams working in silos, at cross-purposes, or not sharing resources when appropriate, the stakes are high and eventually you'll pay the price whether in lost productivity, frustrated customers, declining revenue, or, most regrettably, all of the above.

By following the simple practice I'm about to describe, you can go a long way toward wiping clean the nasty stains of silo-based thinking and lack of alignment, enjoying instead the substantial benefits that arise when cross-functional teams work in harmony toward overall goals.

The practice involves identifying and managing dependencies. As your teams develop OKRs, in addition to ensuring that whenever possible those OKRs vertically align to the company's OKRs, they should take the additional step of determining whose help they need to achieve their OKRs, and document with precision what they mean by "help" in that context.

Here's an example of the process using a fictitious example of a more reputable pool company than the one my wife and I chose. The company's Sales department has the following key result:

Increase number of pools sold and completed from 12 to 20.

Because the company is focusing on growth, this key result is vertically aligned, so "mission accomplished" on that front. But before going into hyper-selling mode and beating the bushes for new customers, this Sales team must pause and ask the all-important question: "Whose help do we need to achieve this key result?" At the top of their list is the Installation department, whose job is to make people's dreams come true in the form of glittering new pools. But it's not enough to make that identification. For the process to be effective, the Sales team now has to determine specifically what form of assistance they require.

The baseline of pools sold and completed in the key result is 12, so that's the number the Installation department likely expects as well. To reach the stretch goal of 20 pools sold and completed, the Sales department will require the Installation team to have available the many materials required to construct eight additional pools, as well as the labor necessary to do the work.

With this information gathered the Sales department can meet with Installation to share their OKR and solicit the requested assistance. You may have read the previous sentence quickly, so I want to redirect your attention to two important words: "meet with." It's not enough for Sales to post a message on Installation's Slack channel, or send the manager an email. For this process to be the most effective, good old-fashioned face-to-face interaction is the best mode of contact.

I've included only one key result with this example, but for clarity, Sales would share the entire OKR with the Installation team. When the two teams connect to discuss the OKR, one of two things may happen:

>> The Installation team will embrace the challenge, and the two teams will go forward with a shared key result. (This is the preferred option.)

>> Alternatively, Installation could draw a line in the sand, note their own priorities, and decide not to participate.

In the latter case, the issue would be escalated to both teams' senior leadership, who then meet (there's that word again) to determine the path forward. That could mean mandating Installation to assist, and of course ensuring they have the resources to do so, or making it clear to Sales that Installation doesn't have the bandwidth in the current period and they (Sales) will have to either downgrade their target or revise the OKR. Regardless of the decision made by senior leaders, everyone benefits from the enhanced transparency of corporate priorities. Table 10-1 summarizes what do to before, during, and after an alignment meeting.

TABLE 10-1

What to Do Before, During, and After an Alignment Meeting

Meeting Phase	What to Do
Before the meeting	Reach out to the team upon whom you're dependent, and schedule a short (30 minute) face-to-face meeting. Before the meeting, you should send them: • A brief note explaining the purpose and importance of the meeting • Your dependent OKRs along with your specific request for assistance. Explain why this OKR is important for both teams.
In the meeting	Share your dependent OKRs. Be specific in your request for assistance. Answer the other team's questions. Document their specific responses (what they do and don't agree to, along with timelines for providing assistance).
After the meeting	Finalize your OKRs: • Meet once again with your boss. • If the team upon which you're dependent has refused to assist (because they're too busy, have other priorities, or have some other reason) share this information with your boss. • They will either accept that and ask that you revise your OKRs accordingly or escalate the matter. Escalation is not a negative; it simply forces a conversation about priorities within the organization, which is exactly what OKRs should do.

Answering Some FAQs about OKRs that You're Sure to Get

Carl Sagan, the celebrated astronomer, astrophysicist, and author, once noted: "There are naïve questions, tedious questions, ill-phrased questions. But every question is a cry to understand the world. There is no such thing as a dumb question." Not so fast on that last one, Carl.

When I was in my senior year of college studying business, one of our classes required that we form groups and create a marketing plan for a new product. My group chose a new type of flame retardant, a product we felt every household and business could use. Unfortunately, one member of our team was vehemently opposed to this practical offering, suggesting that we should go for something more "sexy" (he never did elaborate on that theme, which is probably a good thing). We overruled him, and from that moment on, he completely checked out of the process. Finally, on the day we had to present to the rest of the class, we rehearsed our presentation in front of our professor. We were all fully engaged in the pitch, and I guess our reluctant collaborator felt he had to say something in the presence of our professor, so he offered this question: "Is it flammable?" A flammable flame retardant — now that was a stupid question.

In the sections that follow, I walk you through a number of questions that are definitely not of the ill-advised variety. I've encountered these questions at the vast majority of organizations I've consulted with, and far from being off the mark, they represent curiosity, engagement, and a sincere desire to learn more about, and maximize the effectiveness of, the OKRs process. Being able to answer the queries below will further equip your teams with the knowledge necessary to create strong, strategic, and technically sound OKRs. I'm not sure what my stupid-question-asking college friend would think, but I'm sure Carl Sagan would approve.

What if I can't measure business impact during the quarter?

This may be the question most frequently raised by concerned OKRs creators around the world, people who enthusiastically embrace the notion of including a business impact statement in their objective to promote transparency but are then gripped by a sudden panic when they realize it will be very difficult to actually measure that outcome during the period. It happens to everyone, your humble author included. When I signed on to write this book I was excited to share with you what I've learned over 20 plus years in the trenches of strategy execution, but I also harbored the belief that this book would drive interest in OKRs and lead more organizations to my doorstep, which will result in more training, coaching, and consulting engagements for my company. Here's a draft OKR I created for that purpose.

Objective: Write the *OKRs For Dummies* book in order to drive new client engagements.

Key Results:

1. Write one chapter per week (total of 16 chapters). Note: This is not written "from x to y" because I'm writing the book for the first time, there is no "x."

2. Increase LinkedIn posts generating interest for the book from 20 to 30.

3. Complete the manuscript by March 20.

4. Increase the number of new client engagements from 5 to 10.

Assuming that this is a quarterly OKR, and the manuscript is due a scant 11 days before the end of those 90 days, I'm left with a little over a week to achieve the business impact key result of increasing the number of new client engagements from five to ten. When you then consider the fact that the actual book wouldn't be released for several months after the submission of the manuscript, it becomes almost impossible to hit my impact key result.

You may ask, "In that case, why even bother having the business impact statement in the objective if you can't measure it in a timely way?" The answer for me, and for you when you inevitably encounter this type of situation, is that even though you may not be able to measure the impact, that statement signals the strategic relevance of the objective, so it trumps the fact that it can't immediately be measured. It always needs to be included to drive clarity and transparency.

With that settled, a new question emerges: "If you can't measure the business impact, do you just ignore it for the current period?" Absolutely not, but in the spirit of what I say in Chapter 9, you shouldn't insist on finding a "perfect" key result to replace it. This situation demands that you find something you can count during the period — an indicator that lets you know whether you're on the right track even if it doesn't measure the business impact in a pure sense.

In this situation, you're searching for a key result that is indicative of progress on the business impact key result, one that is quantitative and can be used in discussions with colleagues to determine your trajectory. You can call it an intermediate key result. In my case, an intermediate key result could be:

Reach 2,000 pre-orders for the book.

This key result doesn't map perfectly to the business impact statement in my objective (drive new client engagements), but it is something that I can monitor during the quarterly cycle, and it provides valuable information I can use to assess overall progress. If pre-orders for the book are strong, that's an indication the book will sell well when it's released and at least a portion of those readers will contact me regarding my firm's services, hence driving new client engagements. Conversely, if pre-orders are low, I'll have to intervene quickly, perhaps by mobilizing my marketing team to up the ante on our efforts to promote the book.

And now, yet another question comes up: "What do I do with the original business impact key result?" You can't ignore it, because it represents the ultimate determinant of success of the objective and has to be measured at some point. My advice is to carry forward into the next cycle any OKR for which the business impact key result can't be measured in the current 90 days (or whatever your cadence). The business impact key result will remain the same, and you may determine you need to add new milestones or other quantitative key results as well in your final push to achieving the impact described in the objective.

The business impact portion of your objective will ensure transparency and drive understanding of why you feel it is strategically relevant now. You should always include that impact statement, even if you can't measure it in the current period.

What is the difference between committed and aspirational OKRs?

A *committed key result* is one that, as the name implies, you commit to fully achieving. Anything less than 100 percent success would be considered a failure. In some circles these are also considered "business as usual" key results because they often reflect standard business processes that must be successfully maintained in order to run a thriving business. Hitting revenue targets that appear in the budget approved by your senior leadership could be an example of a committed key result. Because the number appeared in an approved budget, anything less than full realization is not acceptable. Or perhaps customers are eagerly awaiting new features on one of your products, and missing a deadline could spell disaster from both a customer and marketplace standpoint. In that case, releasing the features on time within the period would make sense as a committed OKR.

An *aspirational OKR* is what Google has termed a "moonshot," something that will make a significant difference in your organization and prove very difficult to achieve. This type of OKR is audacious by design, specifically crafted with targets that appear extremely difficult to achieve. Whereas anything less than 100 percent achievement is below par for a committed key result, with the aspirational variety, hitting 60 to 70 percent is considered a win. Aspirational key results require you to think differently and apply creativity and ingenuity to a challenge. In so doing, even if you don't hit the target, your efforts will yield valuable learning you can apply in future periods. Speaking of future periods, given the bold nature of aspirational OKRs, they're likely to span more than one quarter (or trimester depending on your cadence), providing you the time you need to reach such lofty goals.

To be candid, I've wrestled with the use of committed and aspirational OKRs for some time and the challenge still has me pinned to the philosophical mat. On the one hand, I recognize there are some things that simply must get done in order for you to credibly say you had a good period, and those uber priorities can be reflected in committed OKRs. What concerns me is that the popular literature on OKRs, repeatedly declares that OKRs are about stretching yourself beyond what you believe you're capable of, thereby pushing the frontier of the possible ever farther out. If that is the true purpose of OKRs, why would you muddy the water with so-called committed OKRs that, although difficult, are at a decidedly lower altitude than aspirational OKRs? To draw on a previous example, if reaching a revenue target is an necessary committed OKR for the period, why not aim for a much higher target and label it aspirational?

I also worry about the foibles of human nature in this scenario. Imagine that your team is tasked with achieving a stratospherically aspirational OKR, and although the leadership team is saying all the right things about aiming high, and learning along the way, the pressure is immense. How would you feel when you look across the hall and find a team that is focused on a much more achievable, so-called committed OKR? Again, committed doesn't mean easy, but it doesn't imply audacious, either. You may feel that the other team was getting off a little easier, which could lead to hard feelings and a lack of confidence in the legitimacy of the model.

In the end, if you feel that using both types of OKRs can prove helpful, then by all means do so. Just be sure to clearly outline your expectations for both types, and stress how they work together in a synergistic way to enhance overall outcomes.

Is it okay to use meeting-based key results?

If you're like most people, you probably won't have a difficult time recalling at least one fiasco that served as a "meeting" in your organization. I've actually got a list: The time a CEO fell asleep and started snoring like a freight train in the middle of someone's presentation (fortunately I wasn't the one delivering it); and the time when attendees staged a mutiny and walked out of the room (another one when I was fortunate enough to be an innocent bystander, not the leader). Finally, and I did have the displeasure of being part of this sorry affair, there was the time a board member basically held me hostage under the guise of a "strategy meeting" so that he could regale me for hours with tales from his less-than-fascinating life story ("And then there was the time I got my accounting designation . . . let me tell you that was a pretty interesting story . . .") Oy!

No matter the cause, few people truly like meetings or consider them productive. I could fill pages with statistics that bear this out. For example, a 2018 *Wall Street Journal* article cited a survey of senior managers in a range of industries who said the following:

>> Meetings are unproductive and inefficient: 71 percent

>> Meetings keep them from completing their own work: 65 percent

>> Meetings come at the expense of deep thinking: 64 percent

As if meetings themselves aren't bad enough, researchers have now identified a toxic-sounding phenomenon called "meeting recovery syndrome" (see "Why Your Meetings Stink – And What to Do about it," by Steven G. Rogelberg, *Harvard Business Review*). That's right, it turns out the impact of a lousy meeting can linger for hours afterwards, negatively impacting your productivity for at least the rest of the day. This problem seems ripe for a pharmaceutical intervention, don't you think? ("Talk to your doctor to see if Meetinglix is right for you . . . ")

As an OKRs consultant, I find an enormous irony in how often clients create OKRs that call for having not fewer meetings, but more! It seems that when conceiving of OKRs, people think that meetings are not only *not* to be avoided but will serve as a panacea for every conceivable organizational ailment. Are you lacking alignment? Hold more meetings! Seeing a dip in accountability? No problem; let's get together more often to talk things through. Need a jolt of focus? Assemble some slides and gather the troops, pronto!

Here is an example (again from literally dozens I've encountered) of a meetings-based key result submitted by a client:

> Hold structured meetings with my direct reports to support the company's growth objectives.

Regardless of the objective it's associated with, that is not a strong key result. The good news is that you can modify key results like this to make them more effective by following a few simple guidelines:

>> **Make it quantitative:** Remember that the purpose of a key result is to provide quantitative evidence of the achievement of the objective. In other words, you need to be measuring something. What's being measured in the key result above? At present, nothing. If the writer of this key result is convinced that more meeting time is an important indicator of success, create a target and measure it. Perhaps track the number of times they meet, or the number of hours they convene. But really, you're just putting lipstick on a pig with that modest improvement. Better to . . .

>> **Be specific:** Vague language is a key result killer. In the preceding example, the culprit is the word *structured*. What is a structured meeting? Ask 10 people and you're likely to get 10 different answers. Break it down. For you, perhaps a structured meeting goes something like this:

   1. Discuss last month's results.

   2. Examine the sales pipeline.

   3. Determine hiring needs.

   It could be anything. The key is to be specific on your agenda. Then you can measure the percentage of meetings that adhere to your structured agenda. But even with that recommendation, the pig is still a pig. Instead, why not . . .

>> **Pair them up with outcome-based key results:** When I see meeting-based key results, my inclination is to assume good intentions on the part of the writer; they're most likely proposing the idea to have meetings in order to analyze or improve some aspect of performance. With that in mind, and consistent with the advice in the previous bullet, be specific about why you're meeting and what success looks like if you hold a great meeting. If you're suggesting a meeting-based key result to improve (for example) your onboarding process, be sure to also include a key result that actually measures the improvement of onboarding. When you do this, you may find that the meeting-related key result quickly becomes redundant because you've discovered the outcome you're actually striving for.

Using these suggestions, you'll be on your way to improved key results. And that's all I have to say on that because I'm late for . . . wait for it . . . a meeting.

TIP

Be as specific as possible when including meeting-based key results. Don't say this: "Hold regular meetings with my team." Instead say this:

> Hold structured meetings with the four recruiters assigned to my division, to support the growth objectives for the third quarter. We will meet every two weeks to discuss their pipeline of recruits, celebrate the successes, brainstorm solutions for what is not working, determine what we need to do next, and then finish with a division of tasks for the next two weeks.

Can OKRs change during the quarter?

Given the fact that the only certainty in life is change, and everything around us is constantly shifting and evolving, it would seem paradoxical if I were to suggest you can't change OKRs during the quarter, wouldn't it? Fortunately I'm aligned with the conventional thinking on change and am happy to tell you that under the appropriate circumstances, changing OKRs midstream is not only allowable, it's absolutely the correct course of action.

When you create an OKR, you're essentially formulating a hypothesis — one suggesting that if you achieve the designated key results, you will in fact accomplish the objective. Inherent in this hypothesis is a set of assumptions, sometimes stated explicitly and sometimes relegated to the realm of the subconscious. Here's an OKR followed by an explanation of what I mean.

Objective: Hold a nationwide series of OKRs seminars in order to drive new customer acquisition.

Key Results:

1. Determine host cities and venues by April 10.

2. Send an invitation email to all prospects in our sales funnel by April 20.

3. Place follow-up phone calls with 100 percent of email recipients by May 15.

4. Achieve registrations of 100 people per city.

5. Increase new customers acquired from five to ten.

Several major assumptions probably underlie this OKR:

>> They've picked cities with the right target audiences.

>> People will be willing to attend an in-person event.

>> People attending the event are more likely to become new customers.

>> There will be no external disruptions in the way business is conducted around the globe. (This is the biggest one of all.)

Remember the pesky virus called Covid-19? I had actually planned an OKR not unlike what you see above for the summer of 2020, but it was swiftly derailed when the world was essentially shut down by mid-March of that year. In the face of what was happening around me, should I have kept that OKR? Absolutely not. It had zero probability of being achieved given what was taking place in the global economy, and clinging to it would have amounted to little more than wishful thinking, which is rarely a fruitful activity if you hope to stay in business.

It's a good idea to document the assumptions you believe underpin the achievement of your OKR, and to be on the lookout during the early phase of the quarter for information that may bring those assumptions into question.

Valid reasons for changing OKRs mid-quarter

Making a midstream switch doesn't require the earth-shattering implications of a global pandemic or faulty assumptions; several other possible rationales can cause a shuffling of your OKRs mid-quarter. Perhaps, based on market conditions and past results, your company is making a strategic pivot to a new product or target customer group that would surely impact OKRs from top to bottom. Or maybe a high-volume customer took their business to a competitor, leaving you scrambling to regain the missing market share; that situation, too, would ignite changes in OKRs.

Those are very overt indicators that a change is necessary, but there may be subtle cues as well, such as a distinct lack of energy and commitment related to the current OKRs as you review them during weekly or monthly check-ins. If your team has lost all passion for their chosen OKRs, it's a signal that you may have to revise them sooner than later.

Invalid reasons for shifting OKRs midstream

It's probably obvious but worth stating nonetheless that although a multitude of legitimate reasons exist for altering your OKRs during the quarter, one that is not valid is swapping them because they just require too much effort to see through. OKRs should be difficult, forcing you to bring knowledge, creativity, and a healthy serving of grit to bear on a challenging but meaningful goal. That last bit about grit — the passion and perseverance necessary to achieve important goals — is important because research has shown that grit is often a better predictor of success than either IQ or conscientiousness (see "The gritty truth" by Kirsten Weir, *American Psychological Association*).

OKRs are the goal-setting equivalent of going to the gym to improve your fitness. You wouldn't walk into a fitness center on day one, shove aside the steroid-fueled giant who looks like he could lift a Prius with one arm, and attempt to lift what he does. No, you pace yourself, and stick with it when the gains are slower to come than you'd like. You demonstrate some real grit, learning what works along the way because you never lose sight of the ultimate end, which, in the case of OKRs, is the successful achievement of the objective.

REMEMBER

OKRs are not a binding contract. They are always entered into with a sincere desire to succeed, but under certain circumstances, you may need to update them during the quarter.

How do you position your teams for success in creating OKRs?

Job one in preparing your teams to maximize the effectiveness of OKRs and position them for success is to provide the training covered in Chapter 7. Beyond that, however, lies a second lever you can pull to prepare your teams to take the OKRs ball and run with it: Ensure that everyone possesses a deep understanding of the company-level OKRs so that they can determine their own contribution and document it in the form of OKRs.

Most organizations will take the time and effort to craft company-level OKRs that signify their true-north priorities. Those are the priorities that will separate them from their competition and drive execution on a day-to-day basis.

But simply creating OKRs at the leadership level doesn't necessarily lead to employees at every rung of the organizational ladder understanding and, more important, making decisions that will fulfill those OKRs. To create that understanding, the top-level crop of OKRs must be communicated across the company. That communication challenge begins with executives themselves. Communication always starts at the top and filters down. Therefore, ensuring that your executive team is on the same page regarding the company OKRs is paramount to eventually setting your teams up for success.

After your leadership team has developed company-level OKRs, don't pass them off to Corporate Communications and hope for the message encoded in the OKRs to be disseminated and ultimately received by employees. No, you have to realize that each member of your senior team will need to communicate and model the OKRs, and to do that effectively, they need to be consistent in the story they tell.

Telling a consistent story

To ensure a consistent story, before you introduce the company-level OKRs to your employees I recommend a role-playing exercise during which each member of your executive team delivers a short (five to ten minutes) presentation to their peers that outlines company OKRs. The exercise will help you answer these important questions:

1. How does each executive team member sequence the OKRs? Are they telling a coherent story?

2. Do they fully understand what each of the OKRs means? If they simply read what is on the screen behind them, it's clear their knowledge is as deep as a puddle, something change-weary employees are sure to pick up on immediately.

3. Based on the presentations, does anything seem redundant? Or, conversely, is there anything obviously missing in the company's strategic story?

4. How enthusiastic are they about the OKRs? It's difficult to show excitement over something you can't sincerely get behind or support.

5. Is everyone telling a consistent story?

For many members of your leadership team, this exercise will be a new experience, and they may appear somewhat resistant at first. However, after you (the CEO) reiterate the importance of telling a consistent story of the company's success and stress their vital place in the narrative, they should be more than willing to take the stage in an attempt to tell the company's story in a compelling way that will drive understanding and transparency for the teams beneath them.

This exercise is always beneficial, but not because every presentation is as silky smooth as a TED Talk, and every element of the executives' stories is in harmony. Quite the contrary. There will likely be variations in quality, understanding, and commitment. However, if those distinctions aren't discovered and corrected in this forum, the misaligned narratives will be broadcast by each executive to their team, sowing confusion and skepticism when the differences in their stories inevitably pop up in casual conversations throughout the company.

After all the executives take their turns, it's up to the CEO to take the opportunity to discuss the differences in approach and fill in any necessary knowledge gaps. When it comes time for "take two," the stories will be consistent and the rationale for each OKR will be crystal clear.

Working with your team leaders

You don't have to confine the aforementioned role-playing exercise to your executive ranks. If your team or department has created OKRs, try the same approach with your small cadre of leaders. Here are some tips for telling a great OKRs story.

>> Start with a general overview of strategy and why it's critical to the organization and your team.

>> Focus on why change is necessary in your environment.

>> Briefly explain what OKRs are. You've probably already communicated the definition; however, the more you outline what OKRs are, and (and this is vitally important) why you're using them, the greater the likelihood of success.

>> Work through the OKRs and be sure to tell a story of how they link together to drive success. The sequence of OKRs is important.

>> Summarize why this initiative is critical to the company and what's coming next.

>> Take questions.

Maybe you've heard these sayings: "Make sure everyone is singing from the same song sheet" and "Everyone must be rowing in the same direction." In other words, consistency is key! To put your teams in the best place for OKRs glory, ensure that you're telling them a consistent story.

Are there any shortcuts to creating OKRs?

I heard a terrific story recently about the 18th-century mathematician Carl Friedrich Gauss (and who isn't a sucker for a good 18th-century German mathematician story, right?). It goes like this: When Gauss was a schoolboy, a teacher challenged the class to add the numbers from one to one hundred (1 + 2 = 3; 3 +3 = 6; 6 + 4 = 10, and so on). Assuming that this challenge would occupy the students for a considerable time, the teacher was about to leave the room when young Gauss slammed his pencil down and proclaimed "Done!" The teacher, incredulous of course and most likely sour that he couldn't enjoy his version of an 18th-century smoke break, examined the young prodigy's notebook and was astonished to see that he had indeed found the correct answer. (If you want to give it a try, go ahead; I'll wait.)

If you're still crunching numbers after about ten seconds, you're quite a ways behind Gauss, who solved the problem almost instantly. He did it by using a shortcut. Gauss realized that from 1 to 100 there are exactly 50 pairs of matching numbers: 1 + 100 = 101; 2 + 99 = 101; 3 + 98 = 101; and so on. Therefore, he simply multiplied 101 by 50 to determine the correct answer of 5,050. This charming story prompted me to reflect on whether there any possible shortcuts for creating effective OKRs, and the answer is a fence-sitting yes and no.

Shortcuts to effective OKRs

Here are some shortcuts to writing sound OKRs:

>> **Using proven formulas:** Objectives are always composed of three parts: They should begin with a verb, be followed by what you're attempting to achieve, and end with the business impact you're striving toward. Writing objectives can (and probably should be) a difficult assignment, but using a simple formula as a template can help you write OKRs in a consistent fashion, whether you're brand new to the model or a seasoned veteran.

>> **Adhering to a checklist of characteristics:** After you've drafted an OKR, gauge its efficacy by examining it in light of some basic attributes of an effective OKR, such as the following:

- Does the objective contain the three components (verb + what you want to achieve + business impact)?

- Are the key results actually measurable?

- Are the objectives ambitious?

- Can you complete the objectives in 90 days?

>> **Following a regular cadence:** Make the development of OKRs a habit. Your organization should create a cadence for OKRs, typically quarterly, and based on that schedule, you will have predetermined dates by which you should develop, vet, and finalize OKRs. Put those dates in your calendar for the entire year and make them sacrosanct! On the appointed day (or days), ensure that you set aside the time required to assess your situation and create an effective set of OKRs.

Areas that have no shortcuts

Some aspects of the process of creating OKRs don't allow shortcuts. They include:

» **Understanding your company's strategy:** The OKR framework is primarily a strategy execution system, and the key word there is strategy. Your OKRs, whether you're the CEO or a front-line employee, should demonstrate alignment to the company's strategy, and for alignment to occur, you must understand the company's plan.

» **Holding conversations with your manager and direct reports:** You should never create OKRs in a vacuum. By that I mean writing OKRs with no discussion whatsoever, entering them into a template or software system, and then hoping you'll achieve them. Users who employ best practices when creating OKRs hold conversations throughout the organization to ensure that all OKRs have been properly challenged and vetted. When you have a first-draft set of OKRs, sit down with your boss to discuss them. Your boss should give you feedback on items such as the following:

  • Are your OKRs strategically aligned?

  • Do your OKRs introduce enough ambitious stretch?

  • What assistance do you require to achieve them?

If you have direct reports, you should be holding similar conversations with each of them. All this takes time, but the investment will accrue significant benefits in the form of higher-quality OKRs, and improved results.

» **Thinking:** Over the course of my consulting career, I've reviewed literally thousands of OKRs. I've observed many trends over that span, including this one, that I find particularly troubling.

Say a person creates three OKRs. The first is almost always the most technically sound. I can practically see the person huddled over their computer, intellectual steam rising, as they grapple with the ultimately satisfying quest to write a strategically aligned OKR, complete with a strong objective and set of key results that culminate in at least one that measures business impact. The second OKR is okay at best, technically speaking, and the third is typically a short, misaligned brain dump of ideas that don't amount to anything at all resembling an OKR.

Without question, creating high-quality OKRs takes some mental horsepower. And for that, no shortcut is available. However, as is often cited by pundits the world over, the winners over the coming decades will be those who can out-think and out-learn the competition. Taking the time to carefully think about your environment, your unique contribution to success, and how that leads to effective OKRs is one of the most valuable investments you can make.

4

Managing with OKRs

Even after you've written technically sound and strategic OKRs throughout the organization, you're not guaranteed to receive the many benefits the OKRs system has to offer. To maximize your investment in OKRs, it's critical to effectively manage with the framework.

In this part, I give you the lowdown on OKRs meetings: when to hold them and what agenda items are sure to generate the most value for your team. Because "good" meetings are often as elusive as unicorns, I also offer tips for making them informative, engaging, and always valuable. This part also decodes the mechanisms of scoring OKRs, helping you to decipher your results to derive the most possible learning from the process. Finally, you discover how to make OKRs "stick" in your organization so that the framework becomes ingrained in your culture for the long run.

Chapter **11**

Holding OKRs Review Meetings

I n 1860, Prussian Ambassador Otto von Bismarck visited the court of Czar Alexander II, during which they strolled the grounds and came across a sentry standing guard in a very isolated area of the palace lawn. Perplexed, Bismarck asked the czar why the sentry was on duty in such a secluded place. The czar didn't know, so he went to his aide-de-camp and then others until someone finally revealed that it was ancient custom, though no one knew why. More inquiry finally revealed that 80 years earlier, Catherine the Great had dictated that a sentry always be posted on that spot of lawn. It seems that after a long, hard Russian winter, she had looked out her window and gazed upon the first spring flower prodding its way through the frozen soil. The sentry was to stand guard and prevent anyone from picking the beautiful reminder of the change of seasons. Eighty years later, the sentry remained (well, maybe not the same sentry), a memorial to a single flower and to an unchallenged custom that had become sacred for no reason whatsoever.

The idea of accepting things without really challenging them is a problem in many facets of our personal and organizational lives, one that tends to afflict meetings with alarming regularity. Many organizations set standard meetings with fixed agendas and never deviate from them, regardless of what forces may be about to shake the foundations of their business. They fixate on the same old topics and hold the same old rote discussions, which inevitably result in the same old lack of progress. It's the meeting equivalent of Catherine the Great's lonely sentry. Given that there are about 11 million meetings every day in the United States alone, it's safe to say that people aren't getting out of them anytime soon, so your best strategy is to improve them. This chapter offers guidance on how to structure and facilitate OKRs meetings for maximum advantage.

The road to improved OKRs review meetings begins with determining exactly when to hold them — what cadence will position you for the greatest chance of succeeding with the system. Based on hundreds of client experiences, I recommend holding check-in meetings weekly, review meetings monthly, and retrospectives at the end of the period. I profile each of these types of meetings in detail in the pages ahead, as well as share how to make them meaningful and productive. Some of the topics will appear to be common sense, like scheduling them in advance, whereas others may surprise you, such as the value of managing your expectations of the meetings. In the end, this chapter's goal is help you make the most of the time you spend evaluating your OKRs progress.

Determining Your Meeting Cadence

Perhaps you just stumbled dizzily out of what feels like your 11 millionth meeting (or maybe it was so bad that it just felt like 11 million meetings all rolled into one dismal affair), decided to take a short break and do some professional reading to reenergize, and you popped open this book at a page about . . . having more meetings! But if you're still reading, hear me out, because holding productive OKRs review meetings is actually one of the most helpful steps you can take to squeeze the most juice from the framework, and it all boils down to one word: feedback.

As I've noted elsewhere in the book, OKRs are a form of goal setting, and when it comes to goals, the human brain operates on a very simple principle of reducing the discrepancy between where you are now, and where you want to go (the ultimate goal that you've set). When your brain senses that discrepancy, it wants to close it, but without any form of feedback on how you're currently doing, it can't detect any discrepancy, so it doesn't take any action (see *Succeed*, by Heidi Grant Halvorson).

Feedback is foundational to turning your goals into reality because it provides information on your progress, allowing you (and your brain) to process that information and determine next steps. Without feedback, you have no idea what specific actions to take to move closer to your goal. Go faster? Go slower? Blow things up and try a whole new approach? Who knows. But when you add feedback to the mix, context is provided, and you're able to navigate more effectively from your current location to the end state of a fulfilled goal.

The meetings I describe in the sections that follow are intended to ensure timely and relevant feedback is provided on your OKRs, helping you decide what actions are necessary, whether that means kicking things up a notch if you're behind, maintaining progress if you're on track, or ensuring that you stay ahead of the game if things are working well. I recommend that you set up meetings as follows:

» Weekly

» Monthly

» End-of-period (as retrospectives)

I advocate this cadence because I've seen it work, and because (especially at the outset) having more meetings than fewer will work in your favor as you build your OKR muscle. However, my advice isn't binding to each and every organizational context, and you should consider your own culture and current slate of meetings when choosing your cadence for OKRs reviews. My company works with clients who seem completely allergic to the idea of weekly OKRs check-ins, and others who are convinced that a mid-quarter review is the way to go. In the end, as with most things OKRs, the right answer is the answer that's right for your particular organization.

Holding weekly meetings

There are four primary outcomes you're aiming for when holding weekly check-ins, as follows:

» Assessing progress on each OKR.

» Identifying potential issues that could impact achievement.

» Incorporating OKRs into your culture.

» Slowly driving your colleagues insane with the inclusion of yet another meeting on their calendars. (No, scratch this one; it's just a natural side effect of corporate life.)

Assessing progress is the most straightforward of the three and entails the analysis of each OKR to determine whether you're on track or behind. If numbers are available for your key results, you can assess progress quantitatively, but if it's too soon for hard data to be available, you can turn to progress on milestone key results to gauge your efforts.

Regardless of status, it's important to be on the lookout for any issues that could have an effect on the OKRs going forward, such as resources (human, financial, or both), changes in your operating environment, or personnel shifts. You'll want to get out ahead of any potentially harmful issues, so bringing them to light in a weekly meeting is the first line of defense in that battle.

Topics for weekly meetings

To assess progress and be proactive in relation to potential issues, here are some specific topics to include in your weekly meeting, which you should be able to comfortably work through in 30 minutes:

» **Logistics:** This could be as simple as determining who's going to be available in the coming week. If three of your team members plan to be on holiday and a fourth currently has rapidly worsening sniffles, you're going to be seriously depleted in the next seven days, and that will surely impact how much you can accomplish on your OKRs.

» **Priorities:** Where do you need to place your focus and emphasis in the coming week? Are there critical milestones due that are instrumental in driving a metric-based key result? If so, you want to put them high on your list of to-dos. If you've created task lists to accompany your key results, this is an excellent opportunity to review them as well.

» **Status:** As noted previously, checking on the status of your OKRs is a primary reason for holding the session, so be sure to take the time to review progress on each OKR. In addition to reviewing the current status, poll each member of your team as to their confidence regarding the likelihood of achieving each OKR.

You have lots of easy ways to do this, for example by looking at numerical levels. On a scale of one to ten, how confident are you of achieving your OKRs? Or go the old-school traffic light metaphor and use red, yellow, or green to see how your team is moving along. Regardless of the method you employ to gauge confidence, it's important to look for changes week to week. If last week, on a scale of 1 to 10, everyone offered a rousing 10 on each OKR but this week their conviction has cooled to 6, you need to find out what's driving that anchor-like drop and put in place strategies to right the ship.

» **Engagement:** Check with everyone on the team to see whether they're still excited to put forth the discretionary effort necessary to capture the gold on each and every OKR. If you sense significant levels of apathy or indifference surrounding the OKRs, it's time to delve deep and examine why the team no longer feels energized in their pursuit.

Lack of engagement can be particularly troublesome early in your implementation, when creating OKRs is still a new phenomenon and you've yet to hone the skill to a fine point. Lack of engagement can lead to objectives and key results that fail to ignite the team's passion. If you do see engagement trouble on the horizon, remind the team once again why you're embarking on OKRs and review their pivotal role in the company's success.

There are lots of reasons (which is frequently a euphemism for "excuses") for not getting around to these weekly meetings, and I've heard them all: We're too busy! We don't need them. We're agile. We're not beginners, we're seasoned professionals around here, and know what we're doing, and so on. But in fact you do need meetings — not just to address the preceding list of pragmatic items but also to slowly but surely ingrain OKRs into the fabric of your organization, building the goal-setting and execution muscles that will ultimately result in a resilient organization focused on constant learning and flawless execution. Cultures of that ilk aren't built overnight but are constructed brick by brick through constant reinforcement of what matters, and if you truly believe OKRs can be a game changer for your company, you need to commit the considerable time and effort necessary to realize that brilliant future.

Don't be boring!

One final notion to keep in mind as you work through the structure of your weekly meetings is simply this: Regardless of how you plan to spend the time, don't be boring. No one wants to be bored or be forced to endure a bore. I was at a restaurant with friends one evening, and at the next table sat a young man and woman, both in their early 30s, with a man in his mid-50s who was a nonstop, machine-gun "rat tat tat" kind of talker. He literally never stopped talking, and it was glaringly apparent he was boring his two companions to tears. Their heads didn't move; their faces were frozen in fixed, lifeless stares toward the wall. At one point the garrulous fellow said, "And that was the day I came home and found out my wife had left me for her boyfriend." What a shock! My best guess, based on some of the dialog, is that the two younger people worked for him. Can imagine having to deal with a boss like that? Maybe you can, but I sure hope not.

You've got a very captive audience at these weekly meetings, so although I don't suggest using the venue to fine-tune your five-minute set for the local comedy club or attempt to croon the agenda in your best impersonation of Adele, I do recommend the following:

» Keep the discussion spirited and lively
» Encourage participation and vigorous debate

The key word here is *participation,* and I urge you to do whatever it takes to draw in all voices and perspectives to heighten the learning opportunities and enhance the probability of creative breakthroughs. That may take the form of assigning at least one topic to each person to ensure that everyone speaks, or simply calling on people who tend to be quiet in such gatherings.

TIP

If you currently have a weekly meeting scheduled with your team, try to include the OKRs check-in as part of that session, rather than add another meeting to everyone's already overstuffed calendars. You may have to add some time to accommodate a healthy OKRs discussion, but creating the habit of reviewing OKRs will be easier if you build on a meeting already in place.

Holding monthly meetings

Every now and then a dramatic news report emerges about some celebrity, normally one that has been sliding down the alphabet list of popularity and relevance from A to D, who has failed to file income tax returns since the first Bush administration and now, predictably, owes the government millions of dollars. "Insiders" report that the shamed celeb has a cache of unopened bills scattered all over the house that could fill the bed of a small pickup truck and for years has basically pretended their creditors didn't exist. These dramatic stories are mostly designed to boost ratings of newscasts (I can hear the earnest anchor at the top of the broadcast: *Breaking news tonight on that celebrity whose been busted for tax evasion – you won't want to miss this!*"), but they demonstrate the perils of avoiding things we absolutely must do if we expect to avoid costly and negative consequences for ourselves and others.

Obviously, nobody is going to lead the evening news with your picture or throw you in the slammer for neglecting a monthly OKRs review meeting. There are repercussions, though, of missing this opportunity to bring your team together to assess progress, identify issues, and continue to stitch OKRs into the fabric of your culture.

Going monthly to avoid the "set it and forget it" syndrome

The monthly OKRs review meeting tends to be slightly more formal than the weekly session (I recommend using a template to update key results; more on that template later), and provides a great opportunity to analyze each OKR, which will help you continue to emphasize the value of the process and make it an ongoing part of how your business is run. I can't overstate the benefits and importance of driving OKRs deeper into your culture, transitioning it into a core process of strategy execution that everyone accepts and relies on as much as they do budgeting or strategic planning.

Failure to regularly review results brings the dreaded "set it and forget it" syndrome into play and ups the chances considerably that OKRs will eventually be relegated to the scrap yard of abandoned initiatives that people once regarded with great anticipation but are now nothing but a memory or punch line.

Questions to raise during monthly meetings

I hope the preceding warnings have you scared straight and ready to embrace the monthly OKRs meeting. To help you make the most of that event, here are some questions to consider asking during your session, which normally requires 60 to 90 minutes. If you glanced ahead and are doing the math now, I've listed five questions, so that would be 12 minutes each for an hour meeting, or 18 minutes if you're going to stick it out for an hour and a half. But I caution against splitting it up so precisely and instead go with the flow as you get accustomed to the rhythm of these meetings. If a question stimulates a thought-provoking and relevant (big emphasis on *relevant*) conversation, keep it going and embrace the enthusiasm.

>> **What progress have you made with the OKRs so far? What results are you seeing?** It's always important, and encouraging, to start with the success you've seen at this point in the quarter.

>> **What's working and what's not?** As I've mentioned previously, key results represent a hypothesis, or best guess, as to how you will demonstrate achievement of the objective, so considering that aspect, consider whether you have made any assumptions that have proven faulty, or gained information that leads to taking a different path in pursuing success of the key results. Conversely, also consider whether the approaches you've adopted are showing progress and paying dividends.

>> **How confident are you in achieving your OKRs?** Consistent with my advice for the weekly session, it's okay to be informal here. You can ask the team to provide percentages of confidence, ask them to go thumbs up or thumbs down, or draw on the traffic light system. If the team lacks confidence in meeting the OKR, or confidence levels have changed since the last meeting, it's important to delve further and find out why team members feel that way and then brainstorm solutions for turning things around.

>> **What additional assistance do you need to achieve the OKRs?** More assistance could entail enlisting the help of another team or receiving additional resources from the company, but if your backup plan for OKRs glory is having Elon Musk swoop in and buy your company, you've got a problem in more ways than one. Regardless of the source of help, raising all issues with your superior is important so that they can help remove any roadblocks to OKRs success.

>> **Is this still the right OKR to be pursuing this quarter?** As I mention in Chapter 10, you'd never want to abandon an OKR because it's tough to achieve; after all, OKRs should be difficult to attain. That's what makes the system so powerful. But sometimes things happen. Maybe there has been a major issue with a customer or product that demands your immediate attention, or maybe Elon Musk did buy your company! Or perhaps you have two OKRs and it's clear that one just won't be achieved this quarter. In that case, it's better to put your energy into the one you feel confident about achieving and defer the other to the next quarter.

Figure 11-1 provides an example template you can complete for each key result. Obviously, it's important that you complete the templates in advance of the meeting so that attendees can carefully review it when you gather to discuss progress. During the meeting, consider the template to be resources you can draw on for context and additional information as you work through the preceding questions. (You can download a blank version of the example template by going to www.dummies.com/go/okrsfd and scrolling down the page to the Downloads tab. Click that tab to download the Microsoft Word file with the template.)

OKR Updating Template

Objective		
Write the objective here.		
Key Result	**Key Result Type**	
Use this space to write the key result.	Note whether the key result is a metric or milestone.	
Key Result Calculation (for metric KRs)	**KR Target**	**KR Actual**
If a metric key result, describe how it will be calculated.	Include the target here, the y of x to y.	Use this space to note actual performance as of current date.
Progress Update		
Use this space to provide a brief update of progress made on the key result since your last meeting.		
Confidence Level		
Use this space to provide a 1–10 assessment of how confident you are of achieving the key result (1 = low confidence; 10 = high confidence) and provide a brief rationale for your assessment. You could also use "thumbs up" or "thumbs down," or red, yellow, green.		
Assistance Required		
Use this space to note any assistance required (from another team, financial resources, and so on) to ensure that the key result is achieved.		
Upcoming Tasks		
Use this space to list any critical tasks you'll be undertaking between now and the next update meeting (either weekly or monthly)		

FIGURE 11-1: Key result updating template.

TIP

Research suggests that the further you are from a goal, the more effective positive feedback is in helping people achieve that goal. For OKRs, this suggests that in month one, you may want to offer more positive feedback to encourage the effort required to achieve the OKR. For example, feedback such as "You're making great progress, you can do it!" helps people stay on track early on. However, as you inch closer to the end of a period, in this case a quarter or trimester, providing more specific and, when required, negative feedback will focus the team's attention and increase the likelihood of OKR achievement.

Conducting end-of-period retrospectives

In Chapter 10, I briefly regale you with some of the meeting horror stories I've had the displeasure of being part of over the years — the sleeping CEO, the mutiny in Conference room 4A, and the board member who was convinced my life would be improved by hearing his autobiography in painstaking detail. (It wasn't.)

Fortunately, as with most things, the meeting scales tend to at least balance, and I've been in the room for many outstanding (strong word, I know) meetings that showcased creativity and keen insights leading to real "aha" moments for everyone lucky enough to be in attendance.

More than one of those occasions has occurred during an end-of-period (whether quarterly or trimester) retrospective, as teams gather to score OKRs, analyze results, and share objectives and key results for the next period. Generating breakthroughs requires the appropriate raw materials, and this type of meeting has them all: months of results to wade through, actual numbers to assess, and a bevy of questions designed to get the intellectual juices flowing. In this section, I focus primarily on the analysis of results. (I cover scoring OKRs at length in Chapter 12.)

Getting the ball rolling: examining results

As Chapter 12 discusses, when scoring an OKR, most organizations average the scores of the key results to compute the overall tally for the objective. The number that results is a great place to start a discussion — but it's a poor place to end one. To get the conversational ball rolling, you'll of course want a numerical representation of success, which the score will provide, but those aha moments are unlikely to result from merely acknowledging that your final score was a 0.7, a 0.9, or a 0.3. The doors of knowledge are more likely to be opened by going beyond the numbers; asking questions that force you to think deeply about the OKR and priming you for even greater heights of success going forward. (You get major bonus points if you wondered about the reference to the "doors of knowledge," which is my nod to the Aldous Huxley book of that title and which inspired the name one of my favorite bands, The Doors. But I digress . . .)

Following are a number of questions I suggest asking during your retrospective, after you've provided scores for each OKR. And no, I haven't forgotten to mention how long the meeting should last. Most teams, depending on their size and the quantity of OKRs to be reviewed and updated, will devote up to half a day on this very worthwhile gathering. Okay, on to the questions:

>> **Did you choose the right key results given what was happening in your environment?** Remember that every review is an opportunity to conduct a mini environmental or strategic scan of what's happening in your business. Did you focus on the right elements of your environment?

>> **Were the key results ambitious enough? Did they stretch you? Were they too ambitious?** If the OKRs were easy to achieve, you likely left a significant portion of value on the table. Conversely, if the targets were unrealistically high, you could possibly have torpedoed your team's motivation.

» **Were the key results actually measurable?** Consider whether you have the right mix of milestone and metric-based key results (ensuring that you were measuring business impact).

» **Did you "set them and forget them"?** In other words, did you miss any of the check-ins discussed in this chapter. If so, why? This is an important question to answer because, as noted earlier, a primary rationale for these meetings is to incorporate OKRs into your operating rhythm.

» **Did the key results keep you focused on delivering value?** If you ask this question and every head in the room goes down, you've got a problem, and at least one brave soul will probably volunteer that the OKRs seemed like "busy work." If that's the case, you'll have to work diligently in the upcoming period to create OKRs that reflect strategic value and go beyond business as usual.

» **What have you learned this period? How do you raise the bar moving into the upcoming period?** Don't end the meeting until you've surfaced at least one lesson learned for each OKR, and have identified at least three ways to improve going forward.

Exploring deeper questions for a specific OKR

I hope you like questions as much as I do, because in the spirit of western philosophy's founding father Socrates himself, who loved a good query, or a four-year-old who won't stop grabbing a parent's pant leg and peppering them with inquiries, I have even more to offer for use in your end-of-period retrospective. The questions above are designed to provoke discussion when considering results on a larger scale, but sometimes you'll want to plumb the depths on a specific OKR, especially if it's one you fell short on. If that's the case, I recommend taking the time to consider one or all of the following:

» When you created the OKR, you probably had certain assumptions in mind. Were those assumptions validated? If not, what happened and how did that impact the success of the OKR?

» How could senior leaders have assisted you in getting this OKR on track before the end of the period?

» Was there a dependency with another department or group that prevented you from achieving this OKR? If so, had you discussed the dependency with them in advance of the period? What was their response? How can you ensure that critical dependencies don't impede OKR success in the future?

» Conjuring that inquisitive four-year-old, consider using the "5 whys" exercise. Ask: "Why didn't we achieve the OKR?" Keep asking the question for five cycles until you get to the root cause of your shortcoming.

Okay, even Socrates may agree that that's enough of the questions for now. Those should keep you occupied for a while, and, with luck, lead to plenty of wonderful moments when you see someone's face light up because everything just clicked into place for them and it's clear that all the hard work leading to this moment was worth it.

With your OKRs scored and analyzed, your penultimate task in the retrospective is to examine each OKR individually to determine whether you'll be keeping each one for another period (if, for example, you're unable to measure the business impact in this period), deleting it (because you've crushed it), or altering it in some way (changing the wording of the objective to more accurately reflect the business impact for example).

The final piece of business to attend to is finalizing your OKRs for the next period. As noted in the previous paragraph, you may have some holdovers from the current period, but most likely, the OKRs for the next 90 or 120 days reflect your priorities and areas of focus going forward. You may be thinking, "Hang on a minute, what's this about finalizing OKRs for the next period? Finalizing? When do we create them in the first place?" Don't worry; I've got your back: That sequence is covered in Chapter 5.

Getting the Most from Your OKRs Meetings

The preceding sections arm you with a set of provocative questions sure to foster a constructive dialog centered on the analysis of your OKRs. But I have to acknowledge, based on past experience, that meetings of this type — those that require significant focus and concentration on a topic that may be unfamiliar to many people — can be challenging.

Although the range of effectiveness of OKRs review meetings varies widely, many organizations, especially those new to the framework, can struggle to maintain a productive level of dialog and discussion. In one company I worked with that had just adopted the OKRs methodology, a senior leader held a group review session after his teams' first quarter of using the system. Each team in attendance reported their scores, opened the floor for questions from their colleagues, and, then outlined their OKRs for the upcoming quarter.

I wasn't able to attend the meeting, so the client sent me a Zoom recording, and what I heard was telling. Although I had shared many of the questions covered in this chapter, the group clearly found the whole undertaking awkward because they had never followed such a standard procedure in the past. The latter part of the meeting devolved into a rapid-fire reading of OKR scores. Absolutely no questions or requests for clarifications arose from a seemingly otherwise engaged audience (who I'm guessing kept stealing glances at the clock). As the session advanced, the presentations became shorter and shorter. At one point, a presenter said, "Well, the last group took three minutes for their OKRs. We think we can beat that and do it in two." Everyone chuckled, but I believe the sentiment behind the laughs was one of "Yes, please, hurry up."

This was the epitome of a wasted opportunity. You're investing substantial human and financial resources in OKRs, pursuing the promise of improved execution, and the last thing you want to do is let that opportunity slip away in a fog of dreary presentations that raise the possibility of bringing the framework's very potential into question. But, again, the problem is often related to the fact that OKRs, and OKRs meetings, are new to everyone, and overcoming the initial obstacles to anything you're doing for the first time is tricky.

Remember when you learned to ride a bike? You likely didn't hop on the very first time, grab the handlebars tightly, and then soar down the blacktop at 20 miles an hour. You probably wobbled precariously and wouldn't have made it more than a few feet were it not for the guiding and supporting hand of someone helping you. In that same vein, I supply a guiding hand in the sections that follow by offering you a number of tips and techniques to ensure that you get the most from your OKRs meetings.

Scheduling meetings in advance

Back when I worked in a cubicle farm type of office, my immediate neighbor had a poster on her wall that read: "Plan your work. Work your plan. Your plan will work." That 24-x-36-inch declaration made a huge impression on me, introducing me to the power of planning ahead and staying focused on what matters most to help shape the future you envision. Planning and scheduling your OKRs meetings in advance is an absolute must because everyone is busier than ever. Considering the intense competition for your time — other meetings, time for deep thinking, getting at least a few minutes outside of work tasks — if you fail to commit these sessions to the calendar well in advance, they're unlikely to ever take place. Leaving OKRs meetings to chance or trying to squeeze them in between 20 other priorities signals to those reporting to you that you're not taking the process seriously, and they'll hear it loud and clear.

By placing a firm pin in the dates and times you'll hold weekly check-ins, monthly reviews, and end-of-period retrospectives, you'll greatly increase the odds that the sessions will in fact take place and the resulting benefits of enhanced learning will flow your way. I don't base this statement solely on anecdotal evidence; studies support the benefits of scheduling things well in advance.

My favorite example of such a study comes from an experiment conducted by Peter Gollwitzer of New York University (see *Profit from the Positive*, by Margaret H. Greenberg and Senia Maymin). He divided his students into two groups, asking one to write a report about how they spent their Christmas holiday and send it in by December 27th. He gave the second group the same assignment but also asked them to identify exactly where and when they would write the report. For example, a student may declare that they were going to write the report after breakfast on December 26th in their parents' living room. When the due date arrived, the results were telling: 71 percent of the students who specifically outlined where and when they would write the report submitted it on time, whereas just 29 percent of the other set of students turned it in by the designated day. This study on what is known as "implementation intentions" has been replicated many times, and the takeaway is clear: If you want something to happen — an OKRs review meeting, for example — be precise about where and when it will take place.

Of course, everyone has flaws, and even in Gollwitzer's famous study, almost a third of the students who were directed to describe where and when they would write their report failed to do so. Thus, in the spirit of reality, and in recognition of a world in which "stuff happens," not only do you need to schedule your meetings ahead of time, you also need to make them sacrosanct. That's a pretty high-falutin word to apply to a meeting schedule, I know, but the stakes are correspondingly high for me to dig into the thesaurus. If you let a meeting slip, or excuse a team member from attending "just this once," you're sliding down a slippery slope — one that leads to a future in which people don't take your OKRs meetings seriously, putting the entire program in jeopardy.

TAKING OKRs REVIEWS SERIOUSLY

Alan Mulally took the reins as CEO of Ford in 2006 just before the great economic downturn and financial crisis that plagued the globe for most of the following three years. One of his first orders of business was to institute quarterly reviews, and his commitment to the process was tested early on when one of his vice presidents argued that he couldn't attend because the meetings would get in the way of the important work he was conducting on behalf of the company. Recognizing the vital nature of reviewing results in a timely way, Mulally replied with a wry smile, "That's okay — you don't have to come to the meetings . . . I mean, you can't be part of the Ford team if you don't — but it's okay. It doesn't mean you're a bad person." The first person through the door at the next meeting? You got it, a certain vice president who knew his boss was very wedded to the notion of regularly reviewing results (see *American Icon*, by Bryce G. Hoffman).

I'm not suggesting that you resort to the threat of termination to get people to attend your reviews, but I am saying that you need to take the process very seriously, and show that commitment, if you expect others to follow your lead.

Asking simple questions

You may have heard of baseball's legendary Ty Cobb, who reportedly terrorized pitchers, other players, and even a heckler in the stands. Cobb's Hall of Fame career spanned more than two decades, from 1905 to 1928, and to this day he holds a number of records, including the most career batting titles (11). Decades after Cobb retired, a reporter asked him, "Mr. Cobb what sort of batting average do you think you'd have against today's pitchers?" Cobb scratched his chin, thought it over and replied, "I believe I'd bat about 300." The reporter was taken aback, given that Cobb had a lifetime average of 366, so he asked him the obvious question: "Why do you think you'd bat just 300 against today's pitchers?" Cobb, known by all to be surly and no sufferer of fools, barked in reply, "Because I'm 65 years old, you idiot!"

Apparently, asking the simple question can sometimes land you in hot water, especially with legendary baseball curmudgeons. The questions I provide in this section won't incite anyone's ire, and in fact will be welcomed as a means of taking your OKRs-related discussions to a deeper level by going off the standard script and unlocking valuable insights. You can keep this section's cache of questions in your back pocket for when you need to pivot, zoom in or zoom out as applicable, and generally maximize the time spent assessing your OKRs. Here are several categories of simple questions: (see "Relearning the Art of Asking Questions" by Tom Pohlmann and Neethi Mary Thomas, *The Best of HRB*, Spring 2023).

>> **Understanding:** You use these queries to slow things down a notch and ensure that everyone around the table shares an understanding of what's being said, which as everyone knows is not always the case. Unfortunately, in most meetings a topic is put up for discussion, and then everyone waits impatiently for their turn to take a stab at providing input, rarely even acknowledging the previous speaker's point. By asking questions like "What do you mean?" and "How did you come to that conclusion?" or "Can you tell me more about that?" you're putting air back into the conversational balloon and allowing everyone to really think about the issue at hand.

>> **Perspective:** When people gather to discuss items of mutual interest, like the specific OKRs they're pursuing, they commonly descend into the weeds of the issues at hand. This tendency can prove beneficial, to a point, if the descent into minutiae yields meaningful pearls of wisdom, but often the discussions quickly tumble about two miles deep, featuring arcane language understood exclusively by the speaker, and leading to the swift onset of the MEGO effect ("my eyes glaze over") for everyone else. In such situations, it's helpful to zoom out and gain some perspective in order to bring the conversation back to a useful plane. Here you can use questions such as, "Let's bring this up a level; how does what you're saying relate to the issue we were previously discussing?" Or if you feel the speaker has digressed, ask, "Are we asking the right question?"

>> **Unearthing:** OKRs review meetings present abundant opportunities for team members to respectfully challenge one another in pursuit of learning more about the business, and how to improve strategy execution moving forward. For this type of meeting, the key is to ask questions that challenge assumptions and force people to critically encounter the steps they've taken in pursuit of the OKRs. Example questions include, "Tell me specifically what you did in pursuit of that milestone (key result)" or "What did you assume would happen this period that did, and did not occur?" These questions work best when offered in a spirit of sincere inquiry. They should never be weaponized as a veiled attempt to attack or ridicule a colleague.

>> **Reframing:** In the spirit of the adage, "the purest form of flattery is imitation," sometimes it pays to take the knowledge gained from one question or set of questions and apply it to another realm. In the OKR world, that would equate to asking something like this: "How could what we've just discussed and learned about this OKR apply to any of our other OKRs?"

People are typically rewarded and ascend the corporate ladder for answering questions, not asking them. As a result, thinking of and asking rigorous and valuable questions is something of a lost art. Ensure that you take the time in your review meetings to ask as many of the questions presented in this chapter as possible.

Keep focusing on learning

Growing up, I loved watching *The Beverly Hillbillies* on TV (still do occasionally), the story of Jed Clampett and his family who struck it rich by discovering oil and then hightailed it to tony Beverly Hills, where their vast fortune was safeguarded by the miserly banker Milburn Drysdale. Occasionally the Clampett clan would become homesick and ponder the possibility of withdrawing their millions and heading back to the woods, which would spell disaster for the profit-obsessed Drysdale. Whenever such rumblings would surface, Mr. Drysdale would do anything, and I mean anything, to make sure the Clampetts stayed put.

When a departure appeared even remotely possible, he often enlisted his overworked and woefully underappreciated assistant "Miss Jane" Hathaway to intervene in some convoluted and comical plot to keep the Clampetts in California. And if Miss Jane didn't follow his directions to the letter, Mr. Drysdale, smoke rising from his ears, would erupt and let her have it with both barrels. Even as a little kid, I wondered why Miss Jane would tolerate this abuse. She seemed skilled; couldn't she get a job at another bank and be free of her boss's wrath once and for all? Of course, this was a farcical TV comedy with low stakes and thus Miss Jane returned week after week to soak up Mr. Drysdale's rage. But in the real world, anyone treated like Miss Jane would be justifiably frustrated and posting their resume on

Monster.com or Indeed.com within seconds of such tirades, because no one wants, or should be expected, to exist in a culture of blame and ridicule.

Spoiler alert: You're not going to hit 100 percent of every OKR you dream up and pursue, and if you do, you're sandbagging (taking it too easy) and should consider upping your ambition considerably. But I'll assume that you're not of the sandbagging persuasion and accept that knocking every OKR out of the park isn't possible. When it comes time to review your results at the end of the period, and you've inevitably fallen short on at least one OKR, you could adopt a mindset and culture of blaming those who took ownership for key results but missed the mark. You could criticize, belittle, and question their competence like greedy Milburn Drysdale. Or you could instead take the opportunity to critically examine what took place and use it as an opportunity to learn more about your business and apply that wisdom moving forward. If you chose door number one, blaming and criticizing, may I direct you to the nearest anger management center for immediate assistance. The correct choice, of course, is to opt for a stance of questioning and learning in order to grow in the future.

Learning is a wonderful mentality to adopt at any point in the journey of people's personal and professional lives. President Franklin Roosevelt visited the Supreme Court Justice Oliver Wendell Holmes, Jr. in the hospital when the latter was 92 years old and ailing. When Roosevelt entered the room, he found Holmes carefully studying a Greek primer. "Why are you reading that now?" the President asked. The esteemed jurist replied, "Why, Mr. President, to improve my mind." OKRs provide plentiful learning opportunities, starting from your inaugural weekly check-in through, well, until you stop using OKRs, which I hope is never.

Here are some ideas for developing or enhancing a mindset of learning when assessing OKRs results:

>> **Train for it.** If yours is a culture historically polluted by the Mr. Drysdales of the world, but you've seen the light and want to transition from a blaming to learning culture, doing so is not as easy as flicking a light switch. Cultures represent ingrained patterns of thought and action, and you may require professional training and development investments to improve your organization's culture. Countless books, webinars, and professional service firms are available to help you along the way.

>> **Foster the learning culture.** Whether you require some professional help or not, to ingrain the habit of learning you must encourage employees to be curious and ask questions. This chapter provides a lot of material to draw on, and you can build off of that, urging people to adopt the spirt of "yes, and" to come up with even more thought-provoking questions.

Managing your expectations

The sun is out, the sky is painted an endless blue, it's what old timers call a "Chamber of Commerce day," and you're excited about meeting it head on not only because of the splendid weather but because today is your very first weekly OKRs check-in. You get to the meeting room a little early, fire up the electronic white board, distribute some handouts, and wait for rest of the team to make their way in. A few minutes later everyone is seated, small talk has been exchanged, and it's time for the show to begin. You kick things off and turn it over to a team leader to review the first OKR, and they do that. Then . . . crickets. No questions; no discussion. The silence is awkward, and you can palpably sense that everyone is itching to get back to their "real work."

This is not a dream scenario for your first OKRs meeting, and maybe it's not that way at your organization. Perhaps you have a strong culture of stimulating discussions at meetings of all types, during which you encourage vigorous debate, invite all viewpoints, and work in a spirit of constant inquiry. If so, that's wonderful, and you have an enormous leg up on maximizing the benefits of OKRs. However, if your organization is similar to many clients I've worked with over the decades, you may not be fortunate enough to already possess such a positive meeting routine, and the OKRs framework with its associated review process will be entirely novel to the entire employee population. If that's the case, the crickets reaction I described above is not only possible, but sadly also likely.

Your first forays into analyzing OKRs results can present challenges on several fronts. At first, the conversation may be focused on wondering whether you in fact even have the right OKRs. If it's your first go around with the model, that's a legitimate and sensible concern given the ocean of possibilities from which you had to choose. And after you determine that you are comfortable with your batch of OKRs, it can be difficult to avoid plunging ten stories down into operational minutiae and derailing any hope of having a strategic conversation. The whole undertaking can feel burdensome, like a task you have to slog through rather than an inspiring forum for exchanging ideas. The good news is that all these ups and downs are normal, and the really good news is that they're temporary.

It takes time to adjust to any new situation, regardless of the domain. Several years ago, my oldest brother visited me in San Diego and we went on a road trip up to Los Angeles. While we were stopped at a light in Hollywood, a late-model Saab pulled up to next to us, and my brother eagerly shouted through his open window to the driver, "How do you like the Saab?" The driver's face was a mask of pure disbelief, apparently at the notion that some random stranger would actually initiate a conversation at a stop light. The light turned green and we both rolled away, but that didn't stop my brother. He kept up his very solo end of the exchange, yelling across the traffic, "I'm thinking of getting one; is it reliable? How's the service?"

It took a while, but a few blocks later as we were passing the iconic Chateau Marmont hotel, they were like long-lost pals, trading stories about past cars, the merits of buying used versus new, and their overall impression of the Saab brand. That's the power of sticking to it rendered in full L.A. technicolor. In reaction to the Saab driver's initial reticence, my brother could have put up his window, slumped in an embarrassed heap in his seat, and given up, but he didn't. He persevered and in the end was rewarded. The same applies to OKRs review meetings.

Your battle cry in this conflict has to be "trust the process." Keep putting in the effort by ensuring that you assiduously prepare for every meeting, distribute materials in advance, encourage dialog and frank discussion in the sessions, and keep on asking the questions you've found in this chapter. With time, effort, and patience, your meetings will evolve into events that focus everyone on looking forward instead of backward, to the point at which the conversation is organized, strategic, and comfortable. If you don't believe me, ask my brother. Just look for a 2011 Saab 9-3, roll down your window, and start talking. He'll be happy to chat with you.

Keeping the meeting moving

Occasionally when I'm working with a client, and especially if I'm visiting their office, they'll invite me to attend a meeting that doesn't directly relate to OKRs but is potentially valuable to me, such as a session on strategic communications. I remember one such meeting particularly well. After a heavy lunch, we gathered in a warm, practically semitropical, meeting room to hear an update on communication plans relating to the company's strategy.

Given the temperature of the room and the carbohydrate-dense lunch, the conditions weren't exactly ideal for creative discoveries, but they were perfect for sleep. We soldiered on, however, and what was supposed to be a 60-minute update somehow morphed into a two-and-a-half-hour marathon, dominated by one particularly opinionated person who loved to hear themselves talk. (He must have had salad for lunch.) As the session wobbled forward, it was apparent that the woman to my left, who was rocking gently in her chair, was having a very difficult time staying awake. When we entered the room, she was the very essence of youthful energy, but in the span of a couple of hours she had gone from a motivated and vibrant young woman to looking like a drunk celebrity's mugshot. Such is the effect of bad and unnecessarily lengthy meetings.

A meeting at your organization, whether on OKRs or any subject, shouldn't take as long as a medical school education. It's very important to establish momentum and keep things moving to hold everyone's attention and interest. Not that you want to dance from topic to topic, barely scratching the surface of important details, but you must exercise the discipline to know when enough is enough and it's time to move on. In previous sections of the chapter, I provide recommended durations for each type of meeting: weekly check-ins, approximately 30 minutes; monthly reviews, 60 to 90 minutes; and end-of-period retrospectives, up to half a day (depending on the number of teams attending). Whenever possible (meaning almost always, barring unforeseen circumstances), do your best to stick to those limits to ensure that you're providing a fast-paced yet well-organized event.

Here are a few tips to help you adhere to the ticking clock while also fostering an environment that is conducive to robust analysis, candid discussion, and enhanced learning:

>> **Set a clear agenda.** I know, that falls under the category of Captain Obvious meeting advice, but it's one of those caveats that can never be violated and must be constantly reinforced if you hope to have an effective dialog with your team. Failure to put in place a detailed agenda places you at serious risk of succumbing to the disastrous and time-sucking phenomenon of "meeting stew." Not a tasty dish whatsoever, its ingredients consist of random topics that are unrelated and unlikely to produce any strategic insights.

>> **Appoint a facilitator.** Someone has to be the ringmaster of this circus, which is actually a pretty apt metaphor. In a three-ring circus, the Ringmaster introduces each act, provides commentary and background information, and keeps the audience entertained and engaged. The ringmaster is also responsible for the safety of both performers and audience. Likewise, an OKRs meeting facilitator introduces the topics, provides relevant context, and, when necessary, poses the provocative questions required to move the discussion forward. They keep speakers and other attendees safe by following the agenda, encouraging participation, and ensuring a civil discourse throughout.

>> **Stick to the agenda's timing.** Notice that it didn't take long to circle back to the agenda. The fact is, creating a thoughtful agenda is not enough. To benefit from that well-constructed plan, you must steadfastly adhere to the timing allocated for each subject. There are exceptions of course; if you're having a uniquely engaging discussion on a certain subject, one bound to produce

significant wins, then by all means stick with it. But if you're mired in the mud of a topic that won't affect the eventual success of the OKR at hand, move on.

>> **Welcome multiple perspectives.** Or, reverting to the nasty flip side of this one, don't allow one person to dominate the conversation like the voluble robot described at the start of this section. When a single individual holds the floor and refuses to relinquish their white-knuckle grip on the talking stick, it sucks all the oxygen from the room and eliminates any hope of a true group discussion that can yield innovative discoveries. People tune out when one person controls the conversation, escaping to the security of their phones or laptops to distract from the monotony. Your facilitator should put a hasty stop to any grandstanding from a dominant individual, thanking them for their contribution but quickly inviting other points of view.

Keep in mind the "peak-end," rule which suggests that most people judge an experience not on the average of every moment, but based on how they felt at its peak and at its end. For this reason, you want to ensure a strong landing for your meetings. Providing a summary of the valuable insights and learning you've gathered, and thanking everyone for their commitment to OKRs, are two things to consider as you wind down.

Evaluating the meeting

If OKRs meetings are new to your organization, you'll require some patience as you find your footing and begin to make the most of what they have to offer. To help accelerate that learning curve, it will be useful to evaluate the effectiveness of your early sessions on a number of dimensions, honing in on what works and what can be jettisoned in future reviews.

Figure 11-2 provides a meeting evaluation form that you can request all partici-pants to complete at the conclusion of each session. As you can see, it's divided into four parts:

>> **Administrative:** The administrative component focuses on meeting manage-ment 101 elements that have been around as long as meetings themselves, such as starting and ending on time, distributing materials in advance, and ensuring full attendance. These represent the "blocking and tackling," or the basics for conducting an effective meeting, and will prove foundational and essential if you hope to enjoy the benefits of a productive session.

>> **Facilitator:** The next section allows space for judging the work of your facilitator, who is vital to the success of any gathering. A strong facilitator keeps the discussion focused, on point, and moving forward, while also ensuring that all voices are called upon and heard.

>> **Team:** The third portion of the form is used for team members to judge one another and their participation, engagement, and understanding of the overall process. All the elements on the form are important, but early in your implementation, this section may be of particular interest. If initial feedback suggests that team members aren't prepared and don't seem willing to actively participate, you'll need to take immediate action, investigating the root causes of these issues.

>> **Content:** Finally, the content itself is placed under the microscope for evaluation. Were all OKRs reviewed and simple discussion rules followed (what happened, why did it happen, what will we do about it)?

For each specific item within each category, I suggest a very simple rating scale of zero to two, with two representing excellent execution of the attribute, one signifying it was generally well done but could benefit from some improvement, and zero suggesting that you're lacking on that point and improvement is needed. When the scores on each individual item are tallied, you arrive at an overall score for the meeting. For the example in Figure 11-2, the session received 25 of a possible 40 points, resulting in a score of 63 percent, which corresponds to a generally well-done meeting that could be improved moving forward.

Evaluating your meetings using this simple form allows a peek behind the curtain as to how your team perceived the content and overall value of the process. The information will be invaluable as you seek to improve in the future. It also drives accountability because team members know that they're responsible for providing information and actively participating in the meetings. Finally, the assessment process gives you valuable feedback that you can use to refine your efforts and boost the prospects of having people leave the room feeling energized, engaged, and ready to push forward on your OKRs.

Meeting Evaluation

Date: _____
Evaluator: _____
Team Evaluated: _____

Administrative

Meeting started on-time	1
All team members were present	1
Meeting ended on-time	2
Materials distributed at least 24 hours prior to the meeting	2
The OKRs were prepared in compliance with the corporate standards	0

Facilitator

Reviewed the agenda	2
OKRs were used to drive the agenda/conversation	2
Engaged the team	1
Managed the conversation (one topic at a time)	0
Kept the group on-time	2
Kept a list of actions including *Who* does *What* by *When?*	1
Closed the meeting by summarizing the list of actions with confirmation from the owners	2

Team

Active participation (note taking, group discussion, challenging each other...)	1
Provided feedback and support to team members	1
Understand their role and responsibilities	0
Brought provided materials	1

Content

OKRs were reviewed	2
All relevant key results were discussed	2
Discussion included: What happened, why did it happen, what will we do about it?	1
Risks were reviewed	1

Total	25
Total Possible Points	40

Meeting Audit Score	63%

2	Very well executed	>85%
1	Well done, room for some improvement	51%-85%
0	Needs improvement	<50%

Notes:

FIGURE 11-2:
A meeting
evaluation form.

Chapter **12**

Scoring and Analyzing OKRs Results

The "score" of an OKR is the numerical representation of progress you've made, typically recorded on scale of 0.0 to 1.0. OKR scores are vital because they delineate performance, informing you whether you've crushed your goals, achieved just so-so outcomes, or missed the mark entirely.

After you've tabulated scores for your OKRs, you'll want to record them somewhere, and that somewhere could be a Google sheet or doc, an Excel spreadsheet, a PowerPoint document, or a gigantic, triangle-shaped rolling board with numbers affixed to all sides (yes, I've seen it). If those "old school" methods aren't for you, perhaps you'll want to invest in one of the many dedicated OKRs software platforms whose functionality and ease of use never cease to amaze me.

In this chapter, you find out what to score (objectives, key results, or both?) and I dive into the technical process for scoring your OKRs; but don't be alarmed by the word "technical," because whether you're dealing with metric or milestone-based key results, scoring is very easy to master. I then pivot to how to decipher OKRs scores to determine what the numbers are telling you. I also discuss the mechanisms for analyzing OKRs results, looking at the pros and cons of working with dedicated OKRs software versus relatively simple solutions like Microsoft Office or Google products. If you do decide software is the best option for your organization, this chapter can help you select the right tool by outlining a number of elements to consider when making the choice.

Scoring OKRs

Occasionally, when my golf game decides to take an unexpected vacation, I elect to stop keeping score in the middle of a round. This is another pathetic refuge of the exasperated golfer: the misguided belief that playing without the burden of tabulating your sky-high scores will somehow resurrect your swing and get you back on the path to low, or at least respectable, results. Whenever I adopt this nonscoring strategy, something interesting inevitably happens. I wish I could report that the interesting thing is the discovery of a technique or swing thought that elevates my game to PGA-level play, but alas, that's not the case; the more common result is a complete lack of interest in the game and a burning desire to retire to the 19th hole as soon as my golf cart will take me there to drown my sorrows in a cold beverage.

It doesn't matter whether it's golf, OKRs, or parcheesi: If you're not keeping score, you're not playing the game — it's as simple as that. Without the power of numbers to evaluate your OKRs, you're forced to fall back on purely subjective evaluations of performance, likely invoking vague phrases such as "I think we did okay," or "Performance was satisfactory," or, and this is one I use frequently in relation to my golf game, "There's room for improvement." It's difficult to measure actual success, identify areas for improvement, and motivate your team to excel if phrases like those are the best you can come up with when discussing OKRs.

I spill a lot of electronic ink in Chapter 11 on the virtues of asking strong questions when reviewing OKRs results — queries that go well above and beyond a rote review of the numbers associated with an OKR. And although you'll always want to look past the numbers, those dollar amounts, percentages, and raw numbers that comprise your scores are an ideal catalyst to ignite a conversation focused on learning and development that will put the questions I provide in Chapter 11 in the proper context. Only by having scores in the first place are you able to fully harness the power of the questions.

In golf, and all sporting endeavors, practice is of course a critical element to hone your skills, but at the end of the day if you really want to empirical evidence of improvement you've got to get out there on the course, take your lumps, and faithfully record your actual number on each hole. Only then can you rigorously analyze what's taking place and determine where you're succeeding ("Hey, I managed to par two par 5s!") and where you're struggling ("Did I really triple bogey three par 3s???").

The best way to learn more about your business and further your efforts at strategy execution is to score each and every OKR at the end of the period, whether that's a quarter, trimester, or year end. Just as with golf, if you're not tracking your OKR scores, you have no way to measure success and gauge progress. In the sections that follow, I provide guidance on what to score, how to score, and share insights on how to derive meaning from the numbers that make up your OKRs. After I finish all that, I just might head to the golf course — my game may have come back early from vacation!

Understanding What and How to Score

As I say earlier in the chapter, scoring is a necessary and important part of the OKR process. The standard method to score an OKR is to average the scores of the key results (on a scale of 0.0 to 1.0), with the resulting number representing the score for the OKR. In this section, I walk you through a couple of examples of how scoring works in practice.

Scoring example 1: Maximizing the impact of a national sales conference

Imagine a company that relies on a remote sales force across the country to sell their products. In an effort to boost their representatives' success in driving revenue, they hold a national sales conference. Here's a possible OKR, and information on how it would be scored.

Objective: Hold a memorable national conference to increase field sales.

Key Results:

1. Increase the number of sales reps attending the conference from 5,000 to 10,000.

2. Improve attendee satisfaction score on workshops and materials offered from 95 percent to 98 percent.

3. Increase the number of positive social media posts (those containing at least one of these keywords: *exciting, innovative, learning,* and *opportunities*) from 1,000 to 2,000.

4. Increase field sales in the month following the conference from $3,000,000 to $3,500,000.

Here are the results at the end of the period:

1. The number of attendees was 6,000. This translates to a score of 0.2, calculated this way:

   (6,000 – 5,000) / (10,000 – 5,000)

2. Attendee satisfaction score was 99 percent. This represents a score of 1.0 because the target was surpassed. And no, you don't get extra points for exceeding the target.

3. The number of social media posts containing at least one of the keywords was 1,700. The score for this key result is 0.7, which is calculated this way:

   (1,700 – 1,000) / (2,000 – 1,000)

4. Sales were of $3,500,000. Because the target was achieved, this represents a score of 1.0.

Now you compute the average of the four key result scores:

$$0.2 + 1.0 + 0.7 + 1.0 = 2.9$$

2.9/4 (number of key results) = 0.7 (rounded to one decimal place, which is standard)

The final score for this OKR is 0.7.

Interpreting the scores

As I discuss more in the later section "Deciphering your OKRs scores," 0.7 is a good score for an OKR, and some ouch-inducing high-fives would definitely be in order based on this outcome. However, looking beyond the numbers when analyzing your OKRs is always important. In this case, if this were my team, I'd be particularly interested in discussing key result number one, "Increase the number of sales reps attending the conference from 5,000 to 10,000." The team scored just 0.2 on this key result, yet they were successful in achieving the business impact key result of increased sales and scored a healthy 0.7 on the OKR. How is this possible?

When they created this OKR, the team likely hypothesized that to hit their sales key result, they had to get as many sales reps to the conference as possible, hence the goal of doubling attendance. However, because they met the sales target despite having only an additional thousand reps at the conference, perhaps that was a mistaken assumption, and one worth diving into to see what knowledge can be gleaned from it. Further analysis may reveal that, in fact, sales are driven by a small percentage of very high-performing field sales representatives, those most likely to attend conferences hoping to gain early access to the company's latest offerings and sales strategies. That is valuable knowledge that the company can use when thinking about how to leverage the sales reps in the future. Perhaps rather than stage one large, expensive national conference, they instead focus on smaller regional events dedicated to the needs of top-performing sales reps. This is a significant strategic nugget, the variety that can be derived only from taking the time to critically examine your key results, searching for the insights hidden beyond the numbers.

Scoring example 2: Maximizing a rental investment

Imagine you own a property you're listing on a vacation rental site, and although occupancy is acceptable at 80 percent, you'd like to maximize your investment by boosting it to 95 percent. To help you get there, you've decided to renovate the kitchen and main bathroom — two rooms many renters pay particular attention to when deciding to pull the trigger on a booking. Given that scenario, here's a possible OKR.

Objective: Complete kitchen and bath renovation in order to boost occupancy rate.

Key Results:

1. Complete the designs and budgets for both rooms by April 14.

2. Complete renovations of both rooms by May 20.

3. Replace current photos and post updated photos on the website by May 22.

4. Increase weekly views of the property from 100 to 175.

5. Increase occupancy rate for the following four months from 80 percent to 95 percent (compared to the previous year).

At the end of the period the actual results were:

1. The designs and budgets were not completed until April 21, resulting in a score of 0.0.

2. Because the design process was delayed, renovations weren't completed until June 15, leading to another score of 0.0.

3. Pictures were not posted until June 17, hence another 0.0.

4. Weekly views during the quarter increased to 180. That exceeds the target, so it receives a score of 1.0.

5. Occupancy rate for the following four months (compared to the previous year) was 100 percent, once again surpassing the target and resulting in a score of 1.0.

Now you compute the average of the five key result scores:

$$0.0 + 0.0 + 0.0 + 1.0 + 1.0 = 2.0$$

2.0/5 (number of key results) = 0.4

The final score for this OKR is 0.4.

Interpreting the scores

Well, this is very interesting, isn't it? The score for the OKR is a relatively humble 0.4, but the business impact key result of increasing occupancy rate was achieved with flying colors. Does that mean the renovations didn't matter, that perhaps you were enjoying a rising tide in overall vacation rentals and occupancy rates would have increased regardless of what actions you took, if any?

As with the first scoring example, you need to pull back the curtain on the numbers and do some sleuthing to explain these results. In this case, the bump in occupancy could very well be a result of increasing demand for leisure travel, which is happening around the globe as the world emerges from the lockdowns imposed by Covid 19. Or, perhaps the local major league baseball team is looking like a lock to make the playoffs and fans from across the country are excited to catch some games in person. I would argue that the money spent on renovations is still a good investment because favorable circumstances such as the ending of a pandemic or a pennant-winning baseball team may not always grace you with their presence. Plus, the updated rooms will likely give you the opportunity to charge higher nightly rates, increasing that metric as well.

There are numerous potential conclusions to be drawn from the score of your OKRs. You may crush all of your leading/driving key results and fall short on the business impact key result, or you may achieve the impact key result without the aid of the driving key results, as we saw in the previous vacation rental example. As always, your most important task, regardless of the numerical score, is to take the time to don your OKR-anthropologist hat to understand what the results are telling you, what you can learn from them, and how you can apply that knowledge in the days and months ahead.

TIP

If you're concerned about the possibility of low scores despite achieving your business impact key result, you may want to consider weighting the key results and assigning the highest weight to the business impact key result. However, as noted throughout this and the previous chapter, much of the value in the analysis of OKRs is gained from looking beyond the numbers, rendering a weighting process unnecessary.

Scoring milestone key results

All three milestone key results in the vacation rental example in the previous section were scored a zero because they weren't completed by their due dates. In the case of the first key result, "Complete the designs and budgets for both rooms by April 14," the deadline was missed by a scant seven days, so you may wonder, "Can't you give it a score below 1.0 but above 0.0, because after all the milestone was met, just later than planned?" I've had many clients tussle with that question over the years and virtually all, in the end, side with my advice and determine that binary scoring, meaning it is either 0.0 or 1.0, is the right approach for milestone key results.

The challenge of scoring a milestone that misses the mark but is eventually accomplished, is making the judgment call on how late is too late. In some cases, the consequences of being a few days or even a week behind may be minor and have little impact on the prospects of hitting the overall OKR. In other situations, even a one-delay may prove catastrophic and severely jeopardize the chances of hitting the OKR. Imagine the potential magnitude of running a day late in delivering a crucial component or engineering solution on a space mission, for example.

In theory, you could assign arbitrary dates in advance. For example, a week behind schedule represents a score of 0.7; a lag of two weeks equates to a 0.5; being tardy by a month warrants a 0.3; and anything beyond that nets you a goose egg. But I believe that approach violates the spirit of OKRs, which dictates that you stretch to do great things, and that stretch should extend to milestone key results.

When you create a milestone, you should challenge yourself to achieve it as quickly as possible — without sacrificing quality, of course — in order to give the completed milestone time to drive associated metric key results. Telling someone they'll receive a very healthy score of 0.7 for being late opens the door for potential apathy and a lack of urgency, which again is contradictory to the ethos of the OKRs framework. In the end, you hit your milestone or you don't. It's either a 1.0 or a 0.0.

Deciphering your OKRs scores

At the end of the day, what do all these numbers — the 0.3s, 0.7s, 1.0s — really mean, anyway? Earlier in the chapter, I shared example OKRs with accompanying scores, and a 0.7 was labeled "good," whereas a 0.4 in another example was stamped as "humble." Does that mean you need to get out the thesaurus and start searching the synonyms for good, bad, and indifferent when evaluating your OKRs scores? It could lead to some poetic assessments: "Nice job hitting that 0.9 on your OKR, Ferguson; that's transcendent! But you, Tobin — a 0.2 on your OKR, that's impoverished!" Most organizations don't treat the process as a competition of artistic expression, but instead prefer to rely on the conventional traffic light metaphor of red, yellow, and green.

Taking the colorful approach

Regarding what constitutes green, yellow, and red level performance, no set standards exist among all organizations, and you have the discretion to create a scale that works for your culture. However, most organizations I work with adopt a scale that categorizes anything from 0.0 to 0.3 as red, 0.4 to 0.6 as yellow, and 0.7 to 1.0 as green. Figure 12-1 provides a summary.

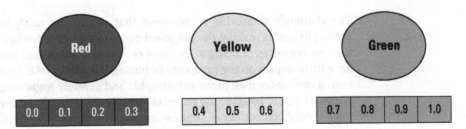

FIGURE 12-1: Color-coded OKRs scores.

Red				Yellow			Green			
0.0	0.1	0.2	0.3	0.4	0.5	0.6	0.7	0.8	0.9	1.0

As I say elsewhere in the chapter, numerical and color-coded scores are effective in serving as the starting point for a lively discussion of results, but the conversation shouldn't end there, and you should not solely judge performance on either the color or number of a score. Consider the earlier example relating to the vacation rental OKR (the Scoring example 2 section) of increasing occupancy rates in the following four months. The numerical score was a 0.4, which would correspond to yellow — not a great rating — yet the business impact key result of occupancy was easily achieved.

Gauging your level of stretch

It may appear from the previous paragraph, and other references in the chapter, that I'm not a fan of numerical scoring, but that's not the case at all, because in addition to providing the impetus for constructive dialogs on performance, OKRs scores are a terrific way to gauge your overall level of ambition and stretch. What that means on the ground is that if you're achieving across-the-board 1.0 scores on all of your OKRs, you're probably being overly conservative in your target setting and have room for more audacious aspirations.

In contrast to not stretching enough, if each of your OKRs limps to the finish line and ends in a score of 0.0, clearly your reach exceeds your current abilities, and it's time to ratchet down the expectations in future periods. Additionally, if you're consistently aiming for the stratosphere and you clearly lack the means to propel yourself there, your team will likely find such impossible targets demotivating and wave the white flag of surrender without even trying. And that's the good news. Those lofty targets may also compel people to act unethically in their pursuit of the mythic green light, leading to corrosive cultures and potentially (at the extreme) illegal activities.

That's what happened at Wells Fargo when they instituted a sales program with unachievable targets. Employees set up unauthorized accounts and duped people into opening unnecessary accounts. These shenanigans cost the bank more than $185 million in fines and made an enormous dent in its reputation.

Establishing the scoring sweet spot

So what's the sweet spot with OKRs scores? If you're playing by the established rules of the OKRs game, creating key results that will stretch you slightly beyond your comfort zone — meaning key results that force creative thinking to see them through to completion — then consistent scores of 0.6 to 0.8 are a reliable indication of strong performance.

That guidance may not sit well with you, especially if your organization's culture finds anything less than 100 percent achievement of goals unacceptable. I've crossed paths with many such companies during my career and am sympathetic to their plight — to a degree. Companies of this type are attempting to build a culture of excellence and distinction, and few would fault them for that.

The worry is about the marginal performance left on the table because everyone knows how things really work and realize that by setting arbitrarily low targets to maintain the shiny veneer of superiority, they'll be rewarded without unleashing the discretionary effort that could lead to true breakthrough performance. If these companies loosened their grip on the concept of exceptionalism, teams would be free to take bigger swings, try innovative approaches, and launch experiments that could vault them to the upper echelons of their markets.

Analyzing OKRs results

I started writing feature length film scripts many years ago and while Hollywood hasn't come calling (yet), it's a hobby I love and find extremely fulfilling. When I got started in the genre I knew very little about the mechanics of writing a screenplay and would often make lengthy notes on plot and potential dialog in long hand on a yellow legal pad. Apparently, and completely unknowingly, I was in good company — video store clerk turned auteur Quentin Tarantino writes all of his first drafts in long hand. Later I graduated to using Word to render my thoughts into something resembling a script. And finally I discovered, and learned to use, dedicated screenwriting software that would automatically format action lines, character names, dialog, and offer a hundred other hacks and shortcuts. I can't say the quality of my writing improved with the use of software but it definitely made things easier and was a huge help in reviewing and editing my work.

A similar choice awaits you when as it relates to analyzing OKRs results. While I wouldn't suggest scrawling OKRs results on a yellow legal pad you could rely on universally accessible tools such as Google sheets, Google docs, Word, Excel, or Powerpoint to capture and review OKRs. Alternatively, you may invest in one of the many sophisticated software tools devoted to OKRs. In the sections that follows I'll provide some of the pros and cons of each approach and, should you be tempted by the many features of software, I'll outline several things to consider before taking the digital plunge.

Considering OKRs software versus "old school" methods

By "old school," I'm not suggesting that you carve out your OKRs on a stone tablet with the office chisel (found in the basement next to the fax machines and piles of disintegrating interoffice memo envelopes). In this context, "old school" refers primarily to Google and Microsoft products that the vast majority of organizations will use if they decide not to invest in an OKRs software application. Those include Google Sheets, Google Docs, Microsoft Word, Excel, and PowerPoint. To a lesser extent, some organizations use other tools such as Trello, Jira, Tableau, or Power BI.

When I refer to OKRs software, I mean programs that are dedicated to capturing, tracking, and analyzing OKRs. Many contain numerous ancillary functions, but their core value proposition is to help you effectively manage with OKRs. The following sections outline some of the pros and cons of each option.

The pros of using Google and Microsoft apps

Here are some of the benefits of using apps like Google Sheets, Google Docs, Microsoft Word, Excel, and PowerPoint to analyze your OKRs:

>> **Accessibility:** Google and Microsoft products are right up there with Rubik's cubes and coffee machines — in other words, they're ubiquitous in most organizations.

>> **Familiarity with the products:** Most people have come up through the ranks with these products — which virtually eliminates any learning curve and adoption issues.

>> **Flexibility:** These tools can be customized to meet the specific needs of teams, allowing for customization in the presentation and analysis of OKRs.

>> **Integration:** Most of these products can integrate at least to some degree with other tools and software systems, allowing for simple imports, exports, tracking, and analysis.

>> **Cost:** These products are typically part of a suite the organization has already paid for, hence they incur no additional expenses.

The cons of using the old-school tools

Now for some of the drawbacks of analyzing OKRs with tools that aren't specifically dedicated to working with OKRs:

>> **Limited functionality:** This is a big drawback. These tools were not specifically designed with OKRs in mind, so they offer far fewer options that you could truly benefit from, such as (to name a few) visualization of OKRs, advanced tracking processes, and alignment functions.

>> **Limited scalability:** If yours is a relatively small organization, you may be able to capture and track OKRs with the Google and Microsoft tools (or, as mentioned earlier, Tableau and a few others). However, for larger organizations, the complex requirements of OKRs across the enterprise can quickly overwhelm the capacity of the old-school tools.

>> **Limited collaboration:** Collaboration is possible with the old-school methods but the degree and ease of working together is limited.

>> **Limited customization:** This is the last of the "limiteds," and may seem out of place because I note flexibility as a "pro" in the previous section. Once again, it's a matter of relative availability of the attribute. Although our old school friends do allow for some degree of customization, it pales in comparison to what you can do with a dedicated software tool.

>> **Security issues:** Although Google and Microsoft products offer some level of security, they aren't as robust as those offered in a dedicated OKRs software package.

The advantages of dedicated OKRs software

Here are some of the upsides of working with software that's dedicated capturing, tracking, and analyzing OKRs:

>> **Enhanced OKR capture, tracking, analysis, and automation:** Software systems devoted to OKRs have been designed to make every aspect of the

process easier, with less room for error. The superior analysis processes improve the potential for making informed data-driven decisions across the enterprise.

>> **Enhanced visibility:** The graphical interface on these systems is outstanding, presenting the data in ways that are sure to stimulate meaningful conversations around OKRs results.

>> **Enhanced collaboration:** OKRs software systems facilitate collaboration among team members, departments, and business units, throughout the organization, making it easier to foster alignment from top to bottom.

The disadvantages of OKRs software

The following issues with OKRs–specific software may or may not pose a problem for your organization, but they're important to take into account:

>> **Cost:** Having to invest in new software is one obvious downside of selecting a solution versus using tools already at your disposal. Most products require an upfront investment plus ongoing maintenance and subscription fees. The good news is that this market has attracted a multitude of players, and the heated competition means that costs are often somewhat negotiable.

>> **Complexity:** *"You want me to learn another new system!"* That is a lament you're likely to hear from at least some change- and software-weary folks in your company if you decide to buy an OKRs software product. Most of these products are "relatively" intuitive, but that statement calls for big air quotes because although they may be touted as easy to use, all will require training.

>> **Security concerns:** I noted security as a concern with the old-school pack of tools as well, and given the age we live in, it appears to be an inescapable potential hazard. Despite the security protocols put in place by software purveyors (and most are very impressive), your confidential data can still be vulnerable to security breaches or cyber attacks.

Choosing the best option for you

When all is said and done, it's in your hands to choose which option best suits your organization, given its level of OKRs maturity and culture. If you can afford to make the investment, my advice is to go for it and buy the software. I suggest doing so for a couple of reasons.

Number one, when you see the list of pros outlined earlier rendered in a real-life scenario, they are truly impressive. I've sat in on countless software demos over the years and am wowed every single time by the capabilities of these tools. You can do so much more, on so many dimensions, with a dedicated software tool than you can with Google or Microsoft products that when you compare the options and remove cost from the equation, choosing to use one is kind of a no-brainer.

My second reason for recommending dedicated software is that its purchase serves as yet another indication to your entire organization that you're very serious about the OKRs implementation. You're indicating that despite the financial cost and the initial lift required by training, you see the value in the OKRs framework and are willing to do whatever is necessary to maximize its potential. That signaling can go a long way to winning over any reluctant or skeptical onlookers.

Knowing What to Look for in Selecting OKRs Software

I once read that the average American spends more time selecting a new TV set than they do in deciding how to allocate the funds in their retirement savings account, if they have one. I could adopt a holier-than-thou stance about that, but picking the right TV is a pretty important decision . . . All joking aside, some people may spend more time on the TV dilemma rather than the retirement account choice because the latter is very difficult, requiring a skillset that not everyone possesses.

The same can be true of selecting the right OKRs software. Most people don't have a PhD in "bits and bytes," sporting circuit-board t-shirts and schmoozing with their buddies at GitHub Universe. The sea of features, functionality, and extras offered by OKRs software providers can be overwhelming, and choosing an OKRs software could turn out to be a crucial decision for the success of your OKRs implementation. In the sections that follow, I break down the features of OKRs software into several categories and outline specific items for you to think about in each one as you test-drive the products. The software you choose should be able to do all the things described in the following sections.

Corporate strategy and strategy execution tools

Your OKRs application should have a dedicated module to help you create and manage your corporate strategy. It should allow you to create strategies of any length of time in combination with the ability to set corporate-level objectives, long-term key results, and short-term key results that business units, departments, teams, and individuals can align to. Although it is a best practice to effectively communicate the strategy to all stakeholders and ask departments and teams to vertically "align-up" to your corporate OKRs, most OKR software includes the ability to "connect-down," allowing all lower-level groups to demonstrate their contribution to overall success.

In addition, the software should allow you to

» Turn activities planned at the corporate level into department or team OKRs with the appropriate OKR naming conventions.

» Drill down into a hierarchical view to see progress at all levels, from corporate, to department, to team, to individual contributor.

» Filter in a variety of ways, such as for specific objectives, cycles or quarters, business units, departments, regions, and perhaps more ways.

» Allow custom categorization of corporate objectives into strategic perspectives, such as Financial, Customer, Internal Processes, and Learning and Growth.

» View high-level strategy maps as well company mission, vision and values statements.

Guidance for team OKRs

For this section, I use the generic term "team," but it can also apply to a business unit, department, region, or some other group.

Ideally, your OKRs software application will provide a step-by-step OKR builder that walks team members through the OKR creation process and includes fields for capturing the team mission, challenges, opportunities, and alignment, both vertical and horizontal.

Vertical alignment should allow teams to directly align with the corporate strategy to automatically calculate progress toward corporate key results, or indirectly align to provide visibility of the team's contribution to the strategy without necessarily calculating progress that doesn't directly impact the corporate key result. For example, a corporate key result may be to increase revenue, and sales teams would directly align their sales OKR that summarizes total revenue at the top, whereas a marketing team may indirectly align with an OKR that counts only sales-qualified leads.

The team OKR capability should also provide you the ability to do the following:

» Align to the strategy at the level of the team objective or specific key results

» Allow key results to have specific due dates within the date range of the full objective

» Allow multiple, specific contributors to be assigned at the key-results level

» Allow each key result to align to separate corporate key results

» Allow teams to post and reply to conversations within a team OKR

» Show the history of team and individual progress over time on graphs and charts

Integration capabilities

Your OKRs software's capability to integrate with a wide variety of other software systems is important because you may need to draw on other platforms when populating an OKR. Following are the types of application that your OKR software should integrate with:

» **Human Resources Information Systems (HRIS) such as Workday or ADP:** You need to be able to synchronize the dynamics of new and separated users, management structures and other employee attributes such as business unit, department, region, roles, etc.

» **Project management tools such as Jira or Azure Dev Ops:** These tools will allow automatic updates for certain key results.

» **Performance management tools such as Success Factors or Cornerstone:** These tools will allow OKRs to be considered in performance assessments and appraisals.

» **Learning Management Systems (LMS) such as TalentLMS or Docebo:** These tools will let you easily integrate and track training related to OKRs.

» **Communications tools such as MS Teams or Slack:** With these tools, users can stay within their flow of work, receive notifications, and easily provide progress updates within the tools they commonly work with.

» **Productivity tools such as MS Office or G-Suite:** These tools integrate activities, tasks, documents, and calendars.

Inspire OKRs software (found at www.inspiresoftware.com and shown in Figure 12-2), is one example of a software system capable of delivering the attributes noted in these sections. Other popular platforms include Quantive, Lattice, Profit, and Workboard.

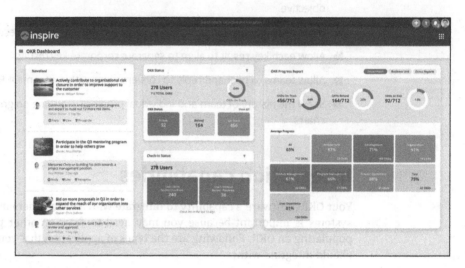

FIGURE 12-2:
OKRs software from Inspire.

Planning and capabilities

To help you achieve your OKRs the OKRs software should include the following:

>> Planning features that allow you to plan activities and tasks against OKRs

>> The ability to plan tasks that synchronize with integrated productivity tools such as MS Outlook calendars, tasks and various to-do lists

>> The ability to prioritize OKRs and tasks for better sorting and visibility

>> The ability to visualize and manage due dates for tasks and activities

>> Check-in capabilities to provide status and progress updates, and that offer other attributes such as confidence-level indicators to help flag leaders on where they need direction or support

>> The ability to check in throughout all areas of the application for easy progress updates

>> A nudging capability to send friendly reminders to users to update their status and progress

>> One-on-one meeting capabilities that allow team leaders and individual contributors to meet and focus their conversations around OKR progress, feedback, recognition and track history of conversations

Reporting capabilities

The ability to readily review OKRs results is one of the primary reasons for investing in OKRs software. To that end, check your preferred software for these attributes:

>> Dashboards to be able to show OKR data side by side with KPI data and other business intelligence views

>> Dashboard configurations at the company level for a variety of shared views such as Monthly Business Reviews, quarterly retrospectives, and focused department views as well as individual dashboards for personalized preferences

>> Reporting at all levels, with an ability to filter by a wide variety of attributes (departmental, region, dates, and so on) and export to a variety of file formats (Excel, PPT, CSV, and others)

>> Custom report building to choose the exact data fields you want to show, group by, and sort

>> Newsfeeds to review status and progress with filters to show insights for specific teams, departments, and alignments to specific corporate OKRs

>> The ability to like, comment on, and recognize OKR achievements through the newsfeeds

Administration capabilities

And of course, don't forget the "fine print" sort of elements a software system needs:

>> A robust administration module for setup, configuration, and group and user management

>> An import capability to pull in work you may already have created in spreadsheets or files

>> Privacy settings for sensitive OKRs

>> Robust notifications to help keep users on track and in the loop

>> Localization for languages in specific regions, such as Spanish in Spain or Spanish in Latin America

>> A standard company home page with widgets including a Quick Start menu to guide new users through the basics

>> The ability to set up custom logos, badges, awards, and other imagery to use throughout the app

Other important software capabilities

Finally, here are some additional things to consider when choosing a software system:

>> The capability for Search, Follow, Tagging Favorites, as well as the ability for users to Like, Recognize, Provide feedback and comments

>> The capability to archive OKRs and allow users to view history at the strategy, team, and individual levels

>> The ability to easily identify owners and contributors with names and photos

>> Multiple KR types such as metric and milestone

>> User profiles for individual settings and preferences

>> A mobile app for updates on the go

>> Robust security and SOC 2 compliance

>> Compliance with the General Data Protection Regulation (GDPR) for data privacy

In the perfectly chosen and wonderfully expressed words of Kevin McCallister in the film *Home Alone*, "You guys give up or are you thirsty for more?" I'm going to make the decision for you and say you've had enough. The lengthy list of attributes shared in the final sections of this chapter should help you earn the respect of your CTO and will certainly keep the OKRs software sales reps on their toes as you work through them during a demo. If you follow the items one by one, I'd be shocked if you don't get at least three "Wow, great question" replies from the software sales rep.

Chapter **13**

Making OKRs Stick

One summer, my dad decided to clad the front of our house in a type of brick called angel stone, a beautiful material that features natural variations producing unique patterns, textures, and colors. Ours was a soft warm hue that shifted from light ivory to sandy brown depending on the light, and we were overwhelmed by the transformation of our home. We enjoyed the stone until one day the unthinkable happened: A piece right in the middle fell off. It looked like a missing tooth, which would have been charming were the front of our house a hockey player, but of course it wasn't. My dad flew into action and refastened the renegade brick immediately, but more followed, and no attempts at finding the right glue succeeded. Repair was no use because of the bigger problem: moisture behind the bricks. Fixing it was like playing whack-a-mole, with the moles winning every time.

My dad's angel stone simply didn't stick and that was, plain and simple, a disaster until the underlying moisture issue was identified and remedied

To give your OKRs the chance to remain in place at your organization for many years, supplying focus, engagement, and alignment from top to bottom, you have to make the framework stick. In this chapter, I outline ways to ensure that your implementation is as sticky as possible, ultimately ingraining OKRs into the culture of the organization.

First, I identify a number of areas you'll want to focus on as you're getting started with your initial rollout efforts of OKRs, such as celebrating early successes, eschewing the idea that OKRs are a project to be completed, ensuring the proper "fit" of OKRs, and using consultants. I then pivot to what you must be cognizant of on an ongoing basis after your OKRs have reached a steady state. These include the provision of ongoing support, the necessity of additional training, the benefits of continuous evaluation, and finally the importance of simply using the framework. Ready to get stuck in a good way? Read on.

Laying the Foundation for OKRs Success

Because I open the chapter with a story about my childhood home, I'll continue the housing theme by starting this section with the topic of foundations. When it comes to building a home, the foundation is essential to ensuring the long-term safety and longevity of the building; it serves as the base upon which the entire structure rests. Without a solid foundation, the house is at risk of seeping moisture, erosion, cracking, and many other undesirable outcomes that could spell dismay and costly repairs for the homeowner.

I know I'm not exactly William Faulkner when it comes to intricate and complex metaphors. If you've ever read (or tried to read) *The Sound and the Fury* you'll know what I mean. Comparing the foundation of a house to the foundation you must set in order to successfully implement an OKRs program is another "hit you over the head" example — obvious, but entirely accurate. You get only one chance at laying the groundwork for an effective OKRs rollout, and the decisions you make and the philosophy you employ at the outset will go a long way in making or breaking the success of the program over the long run.

In the sections that follow, I describe four aspects of your approach that can have an outsized effect on the ultimate impact of your OKRs program:

>> Why it's important to never think of OKRs as a "project"

>> The importance of celebrating successes early and often in your work

>> A sense of how OKRs fit into the broader suite of tools you use

>> The merits of professional help in the form of consultancies to confirm that you're on solid footing as you begin your OKRs adventure

Starting strong is critical if you hope to enjoy the benefits OKRs have to offer. It's not always easy, but as William Faulkner said in the aforementioned *The Sound and the Fury*, "Given the choice between the experience of pain and nothing, I would choose pain." Hey, I think I actually understand that.

Viewing OKRs as a journey, not a project to complete

If you did even a little bit of investigating, I'm sure you would discover that your organization typically engages in a lot of projects. It may have programs and initiatives related to everything from new software installations to modernizing your office's meeting rooms with the latest audio/visual gadgetry, or even launching an employee wellness center complete with a state-of-the-art gym to keep everyone fit and energized (and able to stay at the office longer, but surely that's not the reason for building a gym . . . is it?).

Although every project looks different from the perspective of desired outcomes, most projects share a number of common traits, including careful planning, commitment of human and financial resources, a defined beginning, a finite scope of activity, and a specific end date. At some point, whether they're successfully completed or not, most projects come to an end. But that's not how you want to think about OKRs.

Your OKR implementation resembles a project in that it has to begin on some auspicious day, it requires both human and financial resources, and it's carefully planned according to a well-thought-out scope of activities. Where OKRs differ from a project in a Grand Canyon–sized way is in the definition of an end point. Unless you decide, or are somehow forced, to go out of business and close your doors for the last time, there is never a time when your business and the use of OKRs are finished.

As far as I know, no company has a single point of victory. Amazon could hit a market capitalization of 10 trillion and probably not close up shop, declaring they've done all they can, with Jeff Bezos retiring to his condo on Mars and playing chess with Dwanye "The Rock" Johnson every Tuesday night. Organizations are perpetual-motion machines, with the ground under their feet constantly shifting in the form of changing economic conditions, fluctuating customer preferences, global disruptions like Covid-19, and a thousand other variables. Because your business never ends, your OKRs implementation should likewise carry on, helping you navigate the inevitable challenges and take advantage of the exciting opportunities that come your way. The OKRs you choose will adapt with the changing conditions of your business, and that flexibility is an enormous asset as you remain agile and adaptable in the face of the inevitable whirlwind swirling around you.

WARNING

Referring to OKRs as a project will subtly diminish its ongoing relevance in the minds of your employees, who are accustomed to associating projects with defined end dates.

Projects come and go, with some providing exceptional value to the company and others withering and becoming part of office lore. ("Poor Thompson; he never did recover from the Brownie Bake-off Builds Buddies culture project. I wonder whatever became of all those ovens?") OKRs, on the other hand, help you play the long game, traveling with you every step of the way and helping you remain fluid in your response to the inevitable vicissitudes of modern organizational life and all it entails.

Celebrating success

The OKRs process provides many opportunities to celebrate successes, and I urge you to take advantage of them, perhaps especially as you're learning the ropes and are in the midst of your earliest stages of implementation.

OKRs represent a change, and any disruption to the status quo can be challenging for people to accept, let alone warm up to and embrace. Taking the time to acknowledge even modest wins — achieving significant milestones, hitting an important metric-based key result, uncovering a nugget of insight during an OKRs check-in — can go a long way to reinforcing the value of OKRs, building enthusiasm and momentum, and ingraining OKRs into your culture. Here's a closer look at those benefits:

>> **Reinforcing the value of OKRs:** At several points throughout this book, I mention the importance of communicating the "why" of OKRs; doing so represents a nonnegotiable aspect of any implementation if you hope to win over your teams to the endeavor. Sadly, that "why" can get lost when the flywheel of everyday stresses and operational issues is spinning at warp speed, causing people to possibly lose sight of the value created by OKRs.

Celebrating even small wins can go a long way in helping people remember the reasons for implementing OKRs. It demonstrates that the program is working and, with time and effort. will make an enormous difference in your ability to focus and execute on your most important strategic priorities.

>> **Building enthusiasm and momentum:** OKRs represent a change initiative, and even if they're launched with great fanfare (think balloons, streamers, passionate speeches from the CEO, and maybe even an appearance from your Champion in a velvet cape emblazoned with OKRs spelled out in sequins), sustaining that initial lift of passion can prove to be difficult. But celebrating any and all successes (maybe you completed four weekly check-ins even though some of your team were on PTO and you had to extinguish an operational fire) can demonstrate to everyone that OKRs have a strong place in your ongoing efforts to focus, align, and engage everyone from top to bottom.

>> **Ingraining OKRs into your culture:** Here's a very simple and effective definition of the super-squishy concept of culture: "It's the way we do things around here." Every organization has its own ways of doing things that, when knitted together, form a unique culture.

However, all organizations should aspire to certain attributes of a positive culture, including achievement and recognition. OKRs provide ample opportunities to drive those very desirable aspects of the "way you do things" if you take the time and effort to acknowledge successes. Every time you slow down to celebrate a win, you're planting a seed in the cultural garden; over time, those seeds will blossom in the form of a culture in which everyone, from the C-Suite to the reception desk, is focused on achieving success and recognizing the efforts of those driving that success.

You can leverage numerous forums to celebrate OKRs successes. Many organizations use monthly or quarterly Town Hall meetings to highlight progress at the company level while also taking the opportunity to shine a spotlight of recognition on teams or individuals who were instrumental in generating a win. Within your team, you can use your regularly scheduled check-ins to acknowledge victories and create additional momentum for OKRs. Person-to-person tokens are effective as well. A hand-written note to a colleague for going the extra mile in making a difference on an OKR will always be happily received. And, finally, it never hurts to combine your recognition of wins with a fun social gathering.

Knowing how OKRs fit

My wife and I have a friend who considers himself a master carpenter (note the foreshadowing of "considers himself") who offered his services when we needed a custom-built cabinet in a closet. He arrived at our place clad in the Central Casting garb of bib overalls with just enough paint smears to look authentic, and went to work taking precise measurements of the space and then discussing options with me. A few weeks later, he brought the new cabinet over, and we heaved and maneuvered the wooden behemoth toward the closet. Instead of gliding into the closet effortlessly, however, the cabinet collided violently with the wall on both sides. I can still recall the perplexed look on his face as he reached anxiously for his tape measure and extended it across the cabinet and then the closet space. "It doesn't fit." No kidding, Sherlock. When things don't fit, they don't work, and this cabinet didn't fit.

For your organization to get the most from OKRs, they, too, must "fit" your organization. In this context, I refer to the fit of OKRs with other systems and concepts you employ to keep people informed of what truly matters, and executing those priorities. Specifically, it's vital that your OKRs program, and the OKRs you create, align with the following fundamental building blocks required of any organization (covered in depth in Chapter 6):

>> **Mission:** The mission represents your core purpose — that is, why you exist. OKRs developed across the enterprise should be consistent with this mission if you hope to achieve alignment and engagement. Imagine a used car lot (call it "King's Road Used Cars,") whose mission is this:

- Provide affordable, high-quality used cars to our customers while delivering exceptional customer service.

Given that mission, you could expect to see OKRs focused on innovative ways to find high-quality used cars and methods to enhance customer service, perhaps through simplified credit applications or fresh approaches to the buying process.

>> **Vision:** Think of the vision as a word picture of what the organization ultimately intends to become, whether 5, 10, or 15 years in the future. Your friends at King's Road Used Cars may have the following vision statement:

- By 2030, we will sell 500 cars per year and achieve revenue of $15 million.

The OKRs created must fit with this bold vision for the future, and you would expect them to center on finding clever ways of growing the business to meet those lofty targets. Any OKRs that maintained the status quo would necessarily be rejected because they would not contribute to the vision.

Strategy: The strategy represents the broad priorities adopted by an organization in recognition of its operating environment and in pursuit of its mission and vision. To effectively execute your strategy, the OKRs must drive its eventual execution. At King's Road Used Cars, the strategy to achieve their ambitious vision of growth is centered on broadening their inventory (expanding into foreign cars) and investing heavily in digital marketing to attract the demographic most likely to buy their cars. Both of these strategies lend themselves to OKRs. Expanding into foreign cars, for example, could spawn OKRs related to sourcing the right cars at the right price, finding a wholesale channel partner, and achieving a desired profit margin.

Aligning your OKRs with the company's mission, vision, and strategy drives understanding of those raw materials and promotes transparency and alignment across the enterprise. There is a second use of the word *fit* as it relates to OKRs, and that is in determining how OKRs fit with potentially rival measurement and management systems. For example, in addition to OKRs, some organizations have strategic initiatives, pillars, imperatives, "big rocks," and other easily confused tools. Just a touch of due diligence reveals that many of these systems are very similar and could compete with OKRs for attention from both executives and the larger employee population. I strongly recommend that before you launch OKRs, you conduct an inventory of any and all other systems that could in some way be used to monitor performance and determine whether they're necessary after you begin using OKRs.

Your goal should be a "single version of the truth" as it relates to execution, and OKRs should provide the solitary variety of that truth.

Considering the Use of Consultants I start this section with a couple of important disclosures. Number one, I'm a management consultant. I've been working in this space for almost 25 years, first with two large international firms (you know, the kind with capital letters for names) and for the past 20-plus years as president of my own boutique firm (with letters that actually assemble into a real word). Disclosure number two: If you read this book and are excited about the prospect of using OKRs but would like some additional guidance in the form of professional consulting, I'd be happy to speak with you about my firm's experience and offerings. The second disclosure is primarily one of self-interest because over the years I've had encounters with people who read one of my books but chose another consulting firm because they didn't realize I consulted in the areas I write about. That phenomenon has always mystified me, so let me clear things up. Ladies and gentlemen, please rest assured that I am a proud capitalist and my colleagues and I are open for business should you need our help in any way.

You may be thinking, "Well, shouldn't you put everything I need to know in this book so that I don't need your help?" That's a good point . . . to a point. I've done my best to structure this book in a way that guides you step by step along the path to creating a sustainable OKRs program, complete with tips and techniques I've gathered from thousands of hours training and facilitating in meeting rooms around the globe, and more recently over Zoom and Microsoft Teams. But — oldest cliché in the book coming — like snowflakes and fingerprints, no two organizations are identical, and it would be impossible for me to catalog every possible question, concern, or possibility that may arise as you implement OKRs in your own organization.

Maybe I've got you inching toward my corner with that rationale, but then you're likely to wonder, "Even so, why should I believe anything in this section when you have a personal stake in getting me interested in hiring a consultant?" The simple answer is that for many organizations, the tutelage of an experienced consultant (whoever you choose) can pay outsized dividends when compared with the fees involved in the engagement. Consultants can accelerate your success in a number of ways, including these:

>> Enhancing support by way of expert credibility

>> Shortening the distance from the starting line to tangible results

>> Helping to ingrain OKRs as part of your culture through ongoing support

The following sections take a look at each of these in a bit more detail.

Providing an expert's credibility for the doubters

I've lost count of how many times I've said "I've lost count" in this book, but when you've done something as long as I have, certain themes, questions, and comments come up again and again. One that I've heard on many occasions (yes, I've lost count of how many times), from slightly frustrated but hopeful executives, is: "I could lead this (OKRs) myself, but the message will be so much stronger coming from an outside source." It's true that one of the biggest bangs for your consulting buck is the expert credibility a seasoned professional brings with them and uses to instill buy-in and support for OKRs from an often change-weary and reluctant audience.

Knowledgeable consultants can answer questions from even the crankiest nonbelievers in your company, using their breadth of experience to quell concerns over the framework, demonstrate how it can prove beneficial in virtually any environment, and generally soften what can be formidable resistance to the concept.

Knowing how to fast-track your success

A second benefit of tapping the know-how of a good consultant manifests in a simpler implementation process, one that helps you avoid common barriers frequently befalling enthusiastic but naïve DIYers. Again, every organization is different on some level and requires a unique approach in their application of OKRs, but a veteran consultant with years of experience under their belt likely pulls from a thoughtfully conceived and proven toolkit to accelerate your success.

The skillful consultant can draw on their history of hundreds (or more) engagements to build and execute a plan that significantly fast-tracks your path to results by providing

>> Structured training sessions focusing on precisely what you need to know to succeed

>> Finely tuned facilitation workshops that result in strategic and technically sound OKRs

>> The development of a custom governance process to guide you for the long-term

Supplying ongoing guidance

Finally, a good consultant can provide coaching and guidance over the medium-term to help ensure that you weave OKRs into the fabric of your organization. The longer you use OKRs, the more questions will arise after you've established a solid foothold on the basics and an operating rhythm for the system.

For example, should you link OKRs to performance reviews? What about budgets? And how about the ever-controversial idea of tying OKRs to incentive compensation? You could roll the dice and Google these questions, hoping for meaningful advice, but in keeping with the gambling analogy, doing so would be like pulling the arm of a slot machine and hoping to hit Triple-7s. You'd be much better served by calling on the experience and instincts of the consultant with whom you've forged the path thus far, one who knows your organization and its culture and is attuned to what will and won't work in your unique situation.

Knowing What to Look for in a Consultant

If you agree that an outside perspective would be helpful, here are a number of areas to consider before selecting your consulting partner:

>> **Experience with a capital _E:_** The barriers to entry for calling yourself an OKRs coach or consultant are about as high as a kindergartner's flip-flop. Anyone with even a modicum of time spent at a flip chart writing OKRs, can declare themselves a professional in the field, put up a website, write a couple of blogs, and start canvassing for clients.

However, a consultant you can rely on should bring deep expertise honed through years of practice and supplement that with capabilities in related fields that are sure to enter the conversation in any engagement. For example, every implementation I've been part of over the past two decades has required the application of change-management techniques, the skillful deployment of communications, and the knowledge of strategic planning. If the consultant you're speaking with has no experience in those fields, they may be one chapter ahead of you in the book when you inevitably reach a point that exceeds their experience.

>> **Experience with a small _e:_** My small _e_ focuses on the consultant's experience in your industry or domain. Although some familiarity with your environment is helpful, a deep pool of knowledge can sometimes result in a lack of creativity in approach and a reliance on methods and OKRs that the consultant used with other, similar clients. As I note earlier, the most important aspect of experience is that gained in actual implementations of the framework.

>> **Cultural fit:** The consultant you choose is truly a partner on your journey, and you'll want to ensure that the individual or team can liaise comfortably and

easily in your cultural milieu. Consultants, like the people you meet every day, have different personalities, and based on your culture, some will gel more effectively with your organization than others.

For example you may have a hard-hitting, take-no-prisoners, in-your-face type of culture that would benefit from a very strong facilitator, one only too happy to fight back and engage in strategic combat with you. If, on the other hand, yours is a more genteel culture, that facilitator would likely send people shrieking in horror. During your discovery calls with potential consultants, ensure that your cultural antenna is up and you're on the lookout for signals as to whether the person would work well with your team.

Overall, enlisting the help of a consultant can prove to be a very wise investment of your time and financial resources. However, you may still be reluctant; after all these are consultants I'm talking about. Maybe you'll feel better about engaging with one if I take the opportunity to poke a little fun at the profession first. So here goes, what's the difference between a consultant and a parrot? One squawks endlessly without saying anything useful, and the other is a bird. Feel better now?

Maximizing Your OKRs Success

Early in this chapter, when introducing the topic of what you need to do at the outset of your implementation to ensure that OKRs stick, I use the metaphor of building a foundation for a house. I build on that idea (see what I did there) in this section, which supplies the steps you should take on an ongoing basis to solidify the role of OKRs.

As critical as the foundation is to a home, after the entire structure has been built, there are many things the proactive homeowner must do to ensure the ongoing safety and comfort of the dwelling. Conducting regular inspections of the roof, checking downspouts, maintaining proper ventilation, and many other maintenance boxes must be checked in order to rest assured that the house is able to serve you for decades and beyond.

Once again there is an analogue with OKRs. The items I outline in the preceding sections can help ensure your program rests on solid footing, but to safeguard the long-term viability of OKRs, additional actions are required:

>> Providing ongoing training

>> Offering additional support and resources as required

>> Continuously evaluating and refining the system to meet your evolving needs

>> Using OKRs on a regular basis

I elaborate on each of these requirements in the following sections.

Providing ongoing training

No one likes being ignored. Maybe you've experienced the following type of scenario with a cashier (call him Dave) who answers his phone right when you're ready to check out at a store:

> Dave (on the phone): "Hey . . . uh huh . . . . no way!" (Uproarious laughter.) "Hey, did you show Mike that cartoon I sent you? Uh huh . . . no way!" (More laughter.) On and on the banter goes until Dave glances resentfully at you and says into the phone, "Well, I better get going," as if he had some personal errand to run, not because you've been standing there waiting for him let you check out.

Being ignored is no fun, and if you fail to provide ongoing training related to OKRs, you're the organizational equivalent of Dave, neglecting your employees and depriving them of the skills and knowledge they need to make the most of OKRs. Similar to those waiting at the checkout counter, you have a captive audience with your employees, most of whom will be ready and eager to learn more about OKRs, so don't strand them on an island of ignorance. Following are some areas to consider as you sketch out your ongoing training plan for OKRs.

>> **OKRs fundamentals refreshers:** In Chapter 7, I describe the skills to equip your teams with in order to write technically sound and strategic OKRs. For many people, those skills will be new ones that they must practice quarter after quarter before they become hard-wired into a habit. Forming good habits isn't easy, and over time, some teams and individuals may backslide into writing sloppy OKRs that resemble vague renditions of their business-as-usual responsibilities. You can minimize that risk by offering OKRs fundamental refreshers, which are crisp, 15-to-20-minute sessions that emphasize the techniques for writing strong OKRs that exemplify the essential characteristics of quality. Live sessions are always beneficial, but given the challenges of coordinating calendars, even a recorded session to be watched on demand can pay substantial dividends.

TIP

Include in your OKRs refreshers what I call "Rock Star" OKRs. These are examples of technically well-written and strategically relevant OKRs that are currently in place around the organization. Seeing best-in-class OKRs from their peers often motivates others to ascend to that high bar of achievement.

>> **Managing with OKRs:** As your teams work with OKRs, their requirements evolve. Beyond mastering the fundamentals of writing a technically sound and strategic OKR, they need to come to grips with how best to manage with OKRs and extract the most possible knowledge and insight from each quarter's (or trimester's) numbers. This training equips them with the ability to do just that by supplying a curriculum that focuses on how to run an effective check-in process, what to emphasize during monthly reviews, and how to make the most of end-of-period retrospectives. If your teams are new to the discipline of OKRs, I recommend supplying the questions you expect to be answered in each review cycle (see Chapter 11 for specifics).

>> **Training for new hires:** Your medium-to-long-term goal should be to ingrain OKRs as part of your culture, and you can take a huge step in that direction by introducing the concept to all newbies being onboarded to your organization. Be clear as to why the organization is employing the framework, school them in the fundamentals of writing OKRs, and share your expectations for the newcomer's use of the framework. Most fresh-faced new employees are like sponges wanting to absorb as much of the organization's culture as possible, so don't miss this chance to make them early and effective allies in your cause.

You reap numerous benefits by providing training on an ongoing basis, with perhaps the biggest being its continual reinforcement of the importance of OKRs to your organization. Taking the time to offer refreshers, onboard new employees, and teach the ins and outs of running effective reviews demonstrates your commitment to the framework and provides yet another opportunity to showcase the system's value.

Supplying resources and support

I recall the constant presence of a clock in my childhood home, which sat atop our fridge. I have no idea when my parents first plugged it in — probably around the time Elvis was breaking in — but it was there during my entire tenure at the house, and well beyond. You plugged the clock in and it gave you the time, period. Unfortunately, OKRs aren't like that stalwart clock; you can't "plug in" OKRs via an enthusiastic kickoff and then assume that the system will take root and prosper. To prove valuable and reliable over the long term, OKRs need resources and support.

Resources to consider

One such resource is OKRs software, which I cover in detail in Chapter 12. As noted there, software can prove magical in its rendering of your raw data, bringing OKRs to life in a dynamic way that fosters better analysis and decision making. And just writing the check for the software also signifies your commitment to making OKRs part of your modus operandi.

As impressive as software can be, fortunately we humans are still a necessary part of any successful OKRs implementation. To that end, if yours is a large organization, or you're growing quickly, you may recognize that shepherding the program into the future requires more than the part-time efforts of an already overworked director in HR (or Operations, or Finance, or Strategy). In that case, you may need to step up and recruit an OKRs Champion to take the reins and lead the program logistically and philosophically. (I discuss the Champion's role in Chapter 4.) Without a Champion to identify training needs, pinpoint exactly how OKRs will or won't align with core business processes, and generally assess the best path forward that's consistent with your aims for OKRs, you're gliding in the wind and subject to whatever direction that wind blows, whether or not it's the right path for you. As with software, bringing on a Champion will entail spending some money, but take it from me: The right Champion can absolutely elevate your OKRs program to the next level of effectiveness.

Supportive messaging

Ongoing support of OKRs primarily takes the form of frequent messaging from senior leaders as to the value of the system to your organization. Leaders who are serious about OKRs must take every opportunity to evangelize the system, demonstrating that they stand behind its use and efficacy. There are many ways to do this, including:

>> **Town hall meetings:** Leaders can open every one of these occasions by reiterating why the company is using OKRs and the benefits they deliver.

>> **Emails:** Many senior executives (CEOs, VPs, Directors, Managers) send out regular emails to their staff to keep everyone informed and engaged. OKRs can have a prominent place in these missives.

>> **Walkabouts:** I love the quote, "The map is not the territory," meaning that a model of something is not the same as the thing itself. In the case of OKRs, all may appear well and good, with people attending the requisite training sessions and dutifully inputting OKRs into a system, but is the process really gaining traction? Leaders and managers need to get out of their ivory towers of politics and paper to spend some quality one-on-one time with employees across the company, asking them questions such as, "How is the OKRs program working for you?" and "What OKRs are you working on now, and how are they helping you serve customers better?" Perhaps the most valuable question they can ask is, "What can I do to help you succeed?"

>> **External interviews:** Senior leaders, especially those of larger enterprises, are often quoted in the press. Any chance to squeeze in a mention of the use

of OKRs during one of these interviews is sure to broadcast the executive's support of OKRs.

>> **Hiring a comedian:** Okay, so this one is a little out there, but I have to include it, even if I can recall only one instance of it happening, but it was memorable! A client invited me to give a short OKRs pep talk at an offsite that their entire extended leadership team, probably about a hundred people, attended. The agenda for the day was a tightly guarded secret, and I had no idea who was to follow my brief (but I hoped energizing) address.

After speaking, I took my seat, the lights went down, and a sole spotlight (amazing what they can do in these hotel ballrooms) shone on a door in the corner of the room. As it opened, the signature greeting of one of comedy's most beloved figures boomed over the ceiling speakers, "*Yeah, baby!*" The Austin Powers impersonator, decked out in 1960s mod regalia, was so good that everyone was at first convinced that he was actually Mike Myers. Our Austin went on to hip shake, head bob, and dance about the room for about twenty minutes, miraculously incorporating specific elements of the company's strategy, including OKRs, into the act. I doubt I'm the only one who remembers that wild, cool, and swinging afternoon. And for the record, from that moment on, nobody in the organization ever said I was a tough act to follow.

Continuously evaluating and refining

The ancient Greek philosopher Heraclitus (that's right, I'm pivoting from Austin Powers to Heraclitus) said you can never step in the same river twice. The river is constantly flowing, so the water you stepped in just a second ago has already made its way downstream and been replaced by new water. Thus, the river is always changing and evolving.

Businesses are like Heraclitus's flowing river, constantly evolving, shaping new strategies to fit their environments, and reacting to macro changes in the environment. And because a business never remains static, the mechanisms it uses to gauge progress and success should likewise evolve and change over time.

The imperative to evolve is certainly the case with OKRs. It's important to monitor, evaluate, and refine your program to ensure that it matches the goals of the business and is serving you in the best possible way given the inevitable winds of change you'll face.

Evaluating your OKRs program

Evaluating means determining the condition of something by engaging in careful appraisal and study, so you may wonder how to do that with an OKRs rollout. My advice is to administer surveys (either quarterly or semi-annually) to OKRs users from across the organization to determine how well they feel the system is working for them and the organization as a whole. Basic questions like the following work best:

>> What do you feel is working well with our OKRs implementation?

>> What do you feel is not working well and could be improved?

>> Overall, do you feel that the OKRs program is meeting the goals we set for it?

You could dig in a bit deeper with probing questions on scoring, check-ins, alignment, and favorite background colors for your OKRs software (yes, I've seen debates rage over that life-or-death decision), but given the all-too-real phenomenon of survey fatigue that plagues most organizations, I suggest sticking to the bare minimum of questions. Assuming that you survey users more than once a year, you can always update the questions based on any pressing concerns or feedback you've received informally through the grapevine.

Another way to evaluate the performance of your OKRs implementation is to look externally, drawing information and insights from the wider pool of parties orbiting planet OKRs. This review includes organizations utilizing OKRs who have posted success stories on their website; consulting and training firms that offer best practices and case studies; and software vendors offering tips on how to maximize the use of technology. Thanks to these players and many more, an ever-increasing number of OKRs-related certification programs, blogs, podcasts, and webinars is attempting to push the frontier of knowledge and best practices. By staying current on the latest developments, techniques, and processes, you'll be sure to find at least a few things to tighten the strings on your own implementation.

TIP

Look for colleagues in your network who have implemented OKRs successfully in their own organizations. They can provide insights on what worked for them and what pitfalls to avoid as you deploy OKRs.

Refining your OKRs process

You'll want to put the information gained during the evaluation phase to good use by refining your OKRs program accordingly. The simplest and most effective thing you can do is act on what the survey results are telling you. Say, for example, that in an attempt to quickly embed OKRs into your culture, you've mandated a weekly check-in cadence for all teams using OKRs and asked that they hold at least one 60-minute review every five business days. If 90 percent of survey respondents tell you that's too frequent given other demands, and is not consistent with the company's culture that most people currently thrive in, you'll want to relax the requirement for weekly sessions, perhaps in favor of monthly reviews.

Acting on positive findings is just as important as acting on negative results and can boost overall support for the program. Imagine 60 percent of those completing the survey saying that cross-functional alignment has improved because of the use of OKRs. That result most likely means that several teams are excelling in the process, holding productive conversations with dependent groups and working collaboratively to shape shared OKRs as a result. There is gold in that data! Find those teams and craft company-wide communications based on what they're doing to showcase such a valuable best practice for other teams who haven't yet made the leap. Have those thriving teams speak at the next Town Hall to describe the steps they're taking and the positive outcomes they're seeing. In other words, as the old song goes, accentuate the positive!

You should also refine the program over time to align with any evolution in your OKRs philosophy. As an example, one of the many reasons organizations are attracted to OKRs is the system's emphasis on creating stretch targets, which promotes visionary thinking and jolts a company out of the relative comfort of the status quo. However, that desire to aim for the stars can be at odds with a culture that demands 100 percent achievement of all goals, making it unlikely for teams to go out on a limb that could easily snap and send them crashing to the ground when they don't hit their numbers. In such cases, an organization may launch OKRs with the instruction that teams should strive to meet 100 percent of all OKRs. However, slowly over time, they'll encourage teams to take risks and — importantly — reward that risk taking and experimentation, gradually changing both the culture and their use of OKRs.

Using the system

Maintaining new habits for self-improvement or to accomplish an ambitious task is a hefty challenge. Regardless of the endeavor, whether it's starting an exercise plan, penning the great American novel, or getting the most out of an OKRs implementation, you need to put in the work, day in and day out. No one says that doing so is an easy task. In his book *The War of Art*, Steven Pressfield warns of the concept of resistance, a powerful force that keeps us from doing the work we know we need to do. Resistance can take multiple forms, from procrastination to self-doubt to perfectionism to distraction. All these forms of resistance can manifest in an OKRs implementation.

>> **Procrastination:** "We know OKRs are important, but we just need to get past the next Board meeting, and then we can start really using the system."

>> **Self-doubt:** "Can we do this right now? Do we have the right people in place to lead it? Will our culture support it?"

>> **Perfectionism:** "We need perfect key results for every objective or what's the point?"

>> **Distraction:** "OKRs are a great idea, but we've got so many pressing operational issues to deal with right now."

Phooey, I say. I could think of other words but need to maintain a "G" rating for the book. Pressfield advises that to overcome resistance, people need to foster a mindset of discipline and perseverance, doing the work even when you don't feel like it or it's not convenient. That's the mark of a professional, and you're a professional, right?

With OKRs, all this translates into simply using the system, and more specifically, holding regular check-ins, reviews, and retrospectives. That sounds easy, I know. But like the dieter who says, "Just one cookie," it's easy to rationalize skipping an OKRs check-in because of pressing issues and demands. Unfortunately, the whirlwind of issues never disappears, and soon that one missed meeting can slide to two, maybe three, and before you know it the idea of check-ins is a foggy memory.

The habit of OKRs, like any other, is imprinted with repetition. Through repeated meetings — sessions during which you look beyond the numbers, give tough questions center stage, and allow novel insights to surface — you're laying the tracks that will ultimately lead to the promised land of focus, alignment, and engagement. No excuses. Do the work!

5 The Part of Tens

IN THIS PART . . .

If you're looking for quick and easy-to-implement top ten tips to ensure that you're getting the most from your OKRs implementation, you've come to the right place.

In this part, you uncover a treasure trove of insightful answers to the most commonly raised questions that emerge during the implementation of OKRs. Additionally, I guide you through ten indispensable "musts" for a successful OKRs process, with actionable tips to help you extract the most value from your OKRs implementation. You also discover ten proven tips for crafting effective OKRs, enhancing focus on what truly matters and helping you drive breakthrough outcomes.

Chapter 14

Ten Common Questions about OKRs

To this day I still can't believe she did it, but when I was in college and my sister's house needed painting, she agreed to let a friend and me do the job in return for some much-needed spending money. I had never picked up a brush in my life, but to me painting seemed about as hard as riding a bike (obviously I'd blocked out the painful memories of skinned knees and tears that went along with that learning journey), and I figured that with just a few days of work we'd be up to our ears in cash for the rest of the summer. Turns out painting a house is a lot more complex than we bargained for. There are how many different types of sandpaper? . . . Primer? Wait, there's not just one kind? . . . Hang on, you can't be serious — there's a color called Chantilly Lace white?

The more we learned about what was actually involved in skillfully painting a house, the more questions we had. The good news is that my friend and I both learned a lot that summer — both about painting and about the necessity to get a good education — and my sister's house eventually dazzled in Chantilly Lace white.

Sometimes things that at first glance appear simple are, upon closer inspection and involvement, much more complex. OKRs are one of those things, and as you work with the system, creating OKRs across the enterprise, holding regular reviews and retrospectives, that experience is sure to drive multiple questions as teams grapple with the best ways to take advantage of what this powerful tool has to offer. This chapter offers some "'greatest hits" queries that are sure to bubble up (unlike my sister's paint, thank you very much) during your implementation.

Do OKRs Link to Performance Reviews?

According to research, 95 percent of managers express dissatisfaction with their performance review systems. A plethora (that's a lot!) of statistics all point to the same undeniable conclusion: The process is broken.

Fortunately, a new model of the performance review process is emerging. The evolving view places the focus of this process on more frequent feedback between managers and employees in the form of quarterly or in some cases even monthly conversations. There are no numerical rankings; just open and honest discussions that focus mostly on the future, capitalizing on the employee's strengths to guide enhanced performance.

This recurrent feedback appears to provide benefits. For example, managers who scored in the top quartile for giving frequent recognition and encouragement saw a 42 percent increase in productivity compared with managers who scored in the bottom quartile.

OKRs can play a part in this new and improved approach to performance reviews. Each quarter (for example), a manager can sit with an employee and ask them about their OKRs for the past quarter (what they learned, how they contributed to a shared OKR, and so on) and discuss the next quarter's OKRs to ensure alignment around priorities and expectations. In order to make such a conversation meaningful and productive, however, most organizations will have to provide training to their managers on how to structure the discussion, what questions to ask, and how to assess the employee's psychological safety, among other things.

Should You Link OKRs to Incentive Compensation?

If you go by what most OKRs "experts" and practitioners tell you, the answer to whether to link OKRs to incentive compensation is an ear-shattering no. The primary rationale offered for this stance is the possibility of *sandbagging*, which happens when people or teams set easily achievable targets for their OKRs to ensure that they receive their incentive. At first glance, that concern makes sense; we humans, after all, are self-serving, and who among us wouldn't want to receive an easy reward with little effort invested. But before you write the topic off completely, take a trip back in time to possibly open your mind about this subject.

Twenty-five years, ago the Balanced Scorecard (BSC) was the OKRs of its day — the "hot" performance measurement and management framework. The two systems share a number of attributes, and with the Balanced Scorecard, not only did people forgo debate on the idea of linking it to incentive compensation, but they took that linkage as a given. Robert Kaplan and David Norton, the founders of the Balanced Scorecard, said: "Ultimately, for the Scorecard to create cultural change, incentive compensation must be connected to the achievement of corporate objectives. This issue is not whether, but when and how the connection should be made."

You can step even further back than the BSC to determine whether linking performance to incentive compensation using any framework is a good idea. Entire books have been written on that subject, but here is one compelling argument in favor of the practice: In a study called "What really works" in *Harvard Business Review*, authors Nitin Nohria, William Joyce, and Bruce Robertson bluntly asserted:

It should be obvious that the best way to hold people to high standards is to directly reward achievement. Ninety percent of the winning companies in our study tightly linked pay to performance, while only fifteen percent of the losers did.

"But what about that pesky sandbagging problem?" you say. Well, if you adhere to the true spirit of OKRs and institute a governance process during which managers have regular coaching conversations with their employees, the sandbagging argument is specious at best. OKRs should never be set without negotiation. For example, if Zack reports to Kim, Zack should develop his draft OKRs and then have a conversation with Kim about them to determine whether the level of stretch inherent in the OKRs is appropriate. This conversation fosters understanding of the strategy (which will improve the quality of the OKRs) and drives engagement because Zack is getting direct feedback on what matters most: how he can contribute to the company's strategy execution efforts. Thus, the final OKRs should represent appropriate stretch and be relevant for a potential incentive compensation link.

All this may lead you to think I'm strongly advocating a linkage between incentive compensation and OKRs. That's not the case. I do, however, want you to make an informed decision in light of actual history, and not rely on blogs written by people who have little actual experience in the strategy-execution trenches.

How Many OKRs Should You Have?

The answer to this section's title question is, "As few as possible." I know that's not the most helpful advice, but I do give specific recommendations on the number of OKRs shortly. First, however, let me tell you why fewer is better than many. One of the characteristics of an effective objective (and key result) is that it stretches you beyond your comfort zone, pushing you to think and act creatively in its achievement. Put more simply, OKRs should be hard. If you're taking the exercise seriously and creating OKRs that will require significant effort from the team because they're complex and difficult to achieve, then realistically you don't want an abundant number. Why? Because you have limited resources in the form of attention, cognitive capacity, and hours in the day, and tackling more than even a couple of truly challenging OKRs will overload the system, likely resulting in suboptimal results and potential burnout.

Focusing on a small number of OKRs also forces you to exercise discipline in the selection process. There is an old story, attributed to Mark Twain, in which he tells a friend, "I tried to write you a short letter but it was too hard, so I wrote a long one." It's almost always easier to create a long list of blue-sky, brainstormed, potential OKRs than it is to narrow your focus on what truly matters, isolating the areas that will actually move the needle on executing your strategy. But you can find great value (and satisfaction) in narrowing your perspective, zeroing in on those truly value-creating mechanisms, ranking one over another, and articulating why you made the choices you did. Doing so will give you a richer appreciation for your final selections, and supercharge your motivation to achieve them.

Okay, so what is the magic number of OKRs? For OKRs created by departments or teams operating on a quarterly or trimester-based cadence, I recommend one to two objectives for the period, each accompanied by three to five key results that tell the story of success. Applying that level of intense focus forces you to choose only the most value-adding and impactful OKRs, those most able to fuel a transformation or breakthrough in your business.

TIP

If you can't limit the team to one or two OKRs, and they instead opt to write three, four, or even five, I can virtually guarantee that you've strayed from pursuing truly stretch OKRs and have ventured into business-as-usual territory.

How Do You Overcome Resistance to OKRs?

I've noted throughout the book that OKRs represent a change, and change isn't always embraced by those who have to live with its consequences. Thus, you're likely to have people inside the organization who, for whatever reason, resist adopting OKRs. Fortunately, you have several ways to counteract that reaction:

>> **Determine the root cause of the resistance:** Find out the principal concerns of the people reluctant to jump on the OKRs train. Do they feel that OKRs conflict with other execution systems you're utilizing? Are they concerned that OKRs will be too difficult to implement? Frequently, the source of their discontent is a failed implementation at another organization. If that's the case, you should listen empathetically and note how you'll ensure that the pitfalls they experienced will be avoided in your company.

>> **Know and ceaselessly communicate your "Why OKRs and why now" message:** Communication can defuse any tension around the OKRs framework. After everyone understands why and how OKRs will drive your execution efforts, they'll be more willing to engage. You also want to provide training on OKRs and involve as many people as possible in their development. People are much more likely to understand and support something they help create.

>> **Ensure that senior leaders model the behaviors they expect others to follow:** This high-level leadership is crucial to overcoming resistance to OKRs. Leaders must write technically proficient and strategic OKRs, and then review them frequently to glean insights about the business.

What's in It For Me? Why Should I Care about OKRs?

If you're unfamiliar with the model, or naturally skeptical of any acronym-titled management system, it's easy to write off OKRs as possessing little value to you as an individual cog in the giant wheel that is a modern organization. Here are five reasons you should care about OKRs that demonstrate what's in it for you:

>> To master OKRs you need to become very skilled at the art and science of measurement, and that is a portable skill that you can take with you and use profitably throughout your career.

>> Achieving a challenging OKR — one that truly stretches you and your team — requires creativity, ingenuity, and out-of-the-box thinking. These, too, are skills that will aid you throughout your work life, wherever that takes you.

>> Setting clear OKRs helps you understand what, specifically, is expected of you and what you need to achieve to demonstrate your contribution to overall success. This understanding will help you focus on what matters most and avoid being sidetracked by urgent but unimportant activities.

>> Working collaboratively in a team environment to crush an aspirational OKR is a meaningful and fulfilling activity, sure to enhance your connection to both the team and the organization.

>> To write an effective OKR, you must understand the company's strategy, the company-level OKRs, and any OKRs "above" you in the organizational hierarchy. For some, this may be the first time in their working lives that the organization's purpose and strategy are laid bare in front of them, and the experience can often drive engagement and enhance purpose.

Where Can I Find a Library of Potential OKRs for My Business?

This section's title has an easy answer: Just a few keystrokes on the Google machine and you'll be swimming — nay, drowning — in potential OKRs. "OKRs for sales organizations," "OKRs for Engineering," "OKRs for HR," "OKRs for Operations," "OKRs for Tik Tok videos featuring piano-playing cats." You name the business or function, and you'll find a site, or more likely multiple sites, offering a sea of choices. You may be thinking, "Thanks a lot! Why didn't you put this information on page 1 instead of burying it here? Would have saved me a lot of reading!" And with that, you slam the book shut, head on over to Google, and within minutes, voilà! You've got your OKRs.

Not so fast. A couple of problems (at least) are associated with Googling your way to OKRs glory:

>> **"Your results may vary":** When you do conduct that search for OKRs relating to your business or function, you'll discover a very mixed bag when it comes to the technical quality of what is presented. And by "mixed bag" I mean "generally awful." You'll find objectives that contain numbers (a major no-no), key results that sound more like objectives, and key results that are murky and ambiguous, to note just a few of the shortcomings. Adopting OKRs of this dubious nature is sending a message to your organization that the quality and

technical merits of OKR are of little importance to you, and that's a signal you do not want to convey.

>> **Too generic:** An even bigger reason to generally avoid online libraries is that most of the OKRs you'll find there are so generic that they could apply to virtually any organization on the planet. Your OKRs should be just that: *your* OKRs, reflecting the unique challenges *you* face, the opportunities at *your* doorstep, and the translation of *your* specific strategy. Notice that I say "generally avoid" in the first sentence of this bullet. That's because on the plus side, these online resources can be an effective destination to generate some initial inspiration for your own unique OKRs by helping you start a conversation on what you'll eventually choose to measure after carefully considering your own circumstances. Just be sure to use them for initial inspiration, not final OKRs.

What Do We Do When We Can't Control the Key Results?

This is going to sound a lot like a quote from the film *The Matrix*, but here goes: Control is an illusion. (FYI, there is an actual quote from *The Matrix Reloaded* that is very similar to mine. I'll send a signed book to the first person who emails me at paul@okrstraining.com with the actual quote.) What I mean by "Control is an illusion" is that all measurement is basically a hypothesis — your best guess as to what represents success related to actions you're taking. Here's an example: Imagine a company that wants to transform from being highly transaction focused ("order takers") to fostering deeper bonds with customers in order to drive long-term loyalty and growth. An OKR for that goal may look like this:

Objective: Deliver a customer intimacy strategy to drive loyalty and growth.

Key results:

1. Update all marketing collateral, including our website, by July 21.
2. Train all sales staff on new sales techniques by August 1.
3. Increase inquiries from existing and new customers from 100 to 200 per month.
4. Increase Net Promoter Score (NPS) from 50 to 70.
5. Increase gross revenue from 2,000,000 to 2,700,000.

The company can clearly control key results one and two because both are milestone key results that entail specific actions on their part. They can shepherd the resources and effort necessary to ensure that they do in fact update all marketing materials and train their sales team. Their hypothesis is that by achieving those key results, that success will lead to, or drive, numbers three, four, and five. However, they have no guarantee of meeting the targets set forth in those key results because countless variables could impact the ultimate success on each.

This lack of a guarantee in no way diminishes the value of OKRs or measurement in general. The power of OKRs, as I discuss a number of times in the book, emerges from asking questions and gaining insights into your business based on the numbers you do achieve, whether good or bad. These insights serve as the starting point for discussions on the assumptions you had, any changes in priorities or deficits in resources during the period, and what you've learned that you can harness going forward.

REMEMBER

Although you can't always control the key results, you can always benefit from what they're telling you.

How Do You Balance Stretch OKRs with a High-Achievement Culture?

When writing OKRs, you should create aspirational targets that represent breakthrough performance. Achieving 100 percent of such wildly optimistic goals may not be possible, but hitting even 70 percent may represent a significant uptick in performance. So how do you balance a stretch OKR whose 70 percent achievement is an excellent outcome with a culture that demands 100 percent achievement?

First, recognize the truth — that for many organizations, nothing less than perfection (as in 100 percent achievement) is tolerable. This situation offers a classic good news/bad news scenario. The bad news: It's typically a cultural phenomenon, and cultures are notoriously difficult to change, especially in the short term. The good news: Cultures *can* be changed. The question is how do you successfully navigate this particularly thorny issue? Of course you want your teams to fully achieve their goals, but you also want to encourage the learning, risk-taking, and innovation that are often the by-product of OKRs that exceed their grasp.

As is the case with many organizational dilemmas, senior executive modeling of the desired behavior is key to overcoming this particular challenge. The CEO must create a safe space for teams and individuals, encouraging them to pursue audacious goals, but emphasizing the learning and potential future wins that result from less than perfect actual results. That doesn't mean unquestioned acceptance or tolerance for lackluster efforts. On the contrary, missed targets are diligently analyzed and used as a chance for learning; you can ask, What happened? What did we assume would happen that didn't occur? What can we do differently going forward? Over time, with patience and perseverance, you'll see a shift in your culture, from one that insists on full achievement, regardless of the value you're leaving on the table, to one that values experimentation, innovation, and the risk taking necessary to accelerate results.

How Do You Know Whether OKRs Are Right for Your Organization?

If you are open for business today, your organization can benefit from OKRs. The objectives and key results framework represents a form of goal setting, and goal setting is one of those things — like complying with applicable laws and regulations, assembling the right team, and experiencing at least one annual "reply all" disaster that ends in someone being fired — that all organizations have in common.

Regardless of where you fall on the organizational spectrum, OKRs can add immediate value. If you're a scrappy startup with big ambitions, OKRs will provide much-needed structure and focus as you take your first steps in the big wide world of commerce. Conversely, if yours is an established company that's been around for decades, you can turn to OKRs in an effort to ensure that you're not stuck in the same old measurement routines and missing out on potentially game-changing strategic opportunities. If you've been in business for some time and are fortunate enough to be on a high-growth trajectory, OKRs will provide the compass you need to manage that growth. And if, unfortunately, your organization is struggling, OKRs can serve as a lifeline in the form of focusing on what matters most right now to turn things around.

OKRs will prove to be a valuable addition to your management toolkit regardless of your situation, but to maximize your chances for success, consider the following before making the leap:

>> **Understand why you're embarking on OKRs at this moment.** What is your particular guiding rationale? That mantra will be a crucial ally in your bid to have the entire organization embrace OKRs. See Chapter 3 for details.

>> **Be sure that you're willing to make the resource commitments required to succeed with OKRs.** These resources include the appointment of an OKRs champion and a cadre of ambassadors, and possibly the purchase of OKRs software. Chapter 4 provides detailed information on this topic.

>> **Be willing to approach OKRs with humility and patience.** If you recognize that you will experience bumps in the road but are willing to approach them

with grit and perseverance, OKRs will propel your business to new heights. Many chapters in the book refer to this subject, but in Chapter 10 you find specific guidance relating to OKRs review meetings.

Can Business-as-Usual (BAU) Activities Serve As OKRs?

The easiest way to identify BAU activities is to compile a list of your standard and routine job roles and responsibilities. These are the non-negotiable items you were hired to do and must deliver on week after week, month after month, year after year. Every function has a core list of roles and responsibilities, including mine as president of OKRsTraining.com.

As I sit here at my gilded desk in the corner office on the 50th floor of a Park Avenue skyscraper (okay, I'm actually in a spare bedroom/home office in my basement with one of my cats blocking the monitor), I can think of several core functions I must attend to as part of my job: content creation (blogs, newsletters, social media posts); new product and service development; business development; and marketing. The question is whether these core functions represent candidates to be OKRs. I argue that they do not, for a couple of reasons:

» **These activities are tracked elsewhere and comprise what I consider "health of the business" metrics.** For example, my company monitors and measures business development using the number of inquiries received, the number of new engagements, and revenue. We track content creation using the number of blogs posted, number of downloads, and more. If you consider your own job functions, I'm sure you'll find that most are currently being assessed in some form and manner.

» **These indicators never change.** I'll be tracking these indicators for as long as I'm in business. OKRs, on the other hand, are designed to be agile, reflecting critical areas of focus and strategic relevance right now, which means that by necessity, they will change over time.

Having said all that, I also know that a BAU activity *can* provide the inspiration or rationale for an OKR. Again drawing on my own business, a standard BAU process is business development: attracting new clients. If I notice that my "health" metrics related to that activity aren't as healthy as I'd like, I may create an OKR to boost them. For instance, I could have an OKR dedicated to establishing international field offices or creating a network of affiliated global partners. These are "one off" change-related initiatives that I'm using to respond to current circumstances, and hence are appropriate as OKRs.

Chapter **15**

Ten "Musts" to Ensure OKRs Success

Nothing is quite like returning to a sport you haven't played in more than 35 years to deliver a dose of crushing humility and remind you of just how much you've aged. I dragged my creaky knees back on the tennis court because of the buzz generated by the greats Roger Federer, Novak Djokovic, and Rafael Nadal, who by then had cumulatively racked up an amazing 64 major titles. My plan was to copy at least some of their workout and practice routines to improve my game and increase my overall level of fitness. All three players are legendary in their practice habits, and I was impressed by their commitment to sheer repetition. Among them, they've probably hit enough balls to reach the moon and back a few times over, but they keep getting out there, repeating the same shots and drills in pursuit of perfection.

There is immense power in repetition. Whether it's smashing tennis balls or implementing OKRs, repeating a process can pay great dividends in the long run. This chapter offers the "power sound bite" versions of key concepts covered in depth throughout the book. Keep these ten vital takeaways in mind to share with your teams and ensure a successful OKRs implementation.

Know Why You're Implementing OKRs

Here's a game of "Two lies and a truth." Choose which of the following three statements seems most likely to have been uttered by a typical CEO:

1. To enhance creativity, from now on I'm going to conduct all my meetings via interpretive dance.

2. After three years of beating the market, I think it's only appropriate that going forward I be referred to as "Your Highness."

3. The world is becoming more complicated, and competition in our industry is getting more intense all the time.

I'm secretly pulling for option 1 (I'd love to see that!), but of course it's number 3 by a landslide. The world is becoming more complex all the time, and the need for employees to exercise good judgment and keen decision-making amid uncertainty is increasing right along with that complexity. Everyone is working harder than ever, and if ever there was a need for clarity in purpose and communication, it is now.

When you introduce OKRs to what is most likely a change-fatigued organization fighting on the front lines of volatility and ambiguity, job one is to make it crystal clear why you're engaging in the process and how it will benefit everyone from top to bottom. And (hint), the reason can't be "Because Google does it," or "Because we read *Measure What Matters* and it made sense." Without a guiding rationale in place, you can't expect to win the attention and commitment of a workforce stretched to the limit.

REMEMBER

Taking the time to carefully determine your precise rationale for utilizing OKRs, and communicating that rationale endlessly across the enterprise, will signal to everyone why the investment in time and energy is necessary, as well as increase motivation for both using, and learning from, the OKRs system.

Have an Executive Sponsor, Champion, and Ambassadors in Place

I enjoyed a hot and delicious espresso as I wrote this, courtesy of my old, reliable coffeemaker. What could be simpler: Plug in the trusty machine, add the coffee and water, and moments later, enjoy a tasty beverage. That's what machines do for you: Give them a power source, push the On button, and away you go.

But OKRs are not machines. The system relies heavily on the human element to ensure an effective implementation. The three roles that are most critical to your success with the framework are executive sponsor, OKRs champion, and OKRs ambassador. Chapter 4 takes a deep dive on the purpose and benefits of each of these roles, but here's the in-a-nutshell version:

>> **The executive sponsor:** Supplies the rallying cry for OKRs, making it clear to everyone why the organization is embarking on an OKRs journey, and why now. They give the okay for resources relating to the implementation, which could take the form of software or consultants. Most important, they model the behavior that they hope to see manifested across the enterprise, which means using OKRs to manage the business. Without a vocal and active executive sponsor you can fold up the OKRs tent right now because nobody — repeat, *nobody* — will pay attention.

>> **The OKRs champion:** The champion is the logistical and philosophical heart and soul of your rollout. This individual is the epicenter of all things OKRs in your company. From liaising with external consultants (if you go that route), to organizing training, to participating in software demos, to attending webinars and conferences, to researching OKRs best practices, if it has something to do with OKRs, the champion is at the forefront. A skilled and determined champion, working in unison with a committed executive sponsor, are the two biggest ingredients of OKRs success.

>> **Ambassadors:** These are OKRs "superusers" who are scattered throughout the company and provide first-line support and quality assurance for their designated groups. Simultaneously, they work with the champion to drive buy-in and ongoing support for the process. As critical as the sponsor and champion are to reaching the apex of OKRs potential, they can't be everywhere all at one time. Hence the vital nature of a group of ambassadors who carry the message forward, sharing challenges to be overcome and best practices that can be harnessed company wide.

Provide Training (and Lots of It) to Those Who Will Be Creating OKRs

Here are a few things I know to be true. The human body has 206 bones, the Eiffel Tower in beautiful Paris stretches 330 meters into the sky, and chocolate milk comes from brown cows. What, it doesn't? That's going to come as a pretty big shock to the 42 percent of Americans who think it does. Here's one other thing I know to be absolutely true: Goal setting in the form of OKRs is not a natural muscle for most people, and without proper training, their initial efforts will produce poor OKRs of little value to them or the company, ultimately wasting time and compromising support for the system.

I can attest to the truth of the preceding statement because I've been sent literally thousands of OKRs to review from organizations who attempted to implement the system on their own with no training. Writing a technically sound and strategic OKR is a difficult task at the best of times, but asking someone to do it without the benefit of training on the model's fundamentals is like trying to play pool with both your hands tied behind your back. Writing OKRs is both an art and a science, and if you expect the model to generate positive results, you must provide comprehensive training to ensure that people are equipped with the skills to master both those elements.

After you've decided that OKRs are the right tool at the right time for you, class should be in session. Begin your training with the basics (and see Chapter 7 for lots of additional information):

>> Definitions of an objective and a key result

>> The two types of key results (metric and milestone), and the formulas for writing both objectives and key results

>> The characteristics of effective OKRs, emphasizing the critical importance of specificity in both

>> Exercises for people to draft OKRs, who will discover that this process isn't as easy as it seems

As your implementation progresses, your training curriculum evolves along with it. (See Chapter 7 for many more details on the training curriculum.) After your teams have written their OKRs, it's time to educate them on how to manage with OKRs, detailing expectations for check-ins, and making your scoring mechanism clear. Training is a truly the gift that keeps on giving.

Create an OKRs Playbook

Many organizations are excited about OKRs because of the system's relative simplicity. They also believe that the simplicity means having little need for any form of structure or process. Of course, you don't want to turn OKRs into a bureaucratic red-tape nightmare, but to maximize the system's offerings, you need to put some guidelines in place. The best way to do that is by creating a simple OKRs playbook that lays out the ground rules for OKRs at your organization. A robust

OKRs playbook should be relatively concise, typically under 15 pages, and include the following sections:

>> Why you're using OKRs

>> OKRs "101"

>> Who is in scope for creating OKRs?

>> How to create OKRs and where to put your them

>> Tips for ensuring alignment

>> Recommendations on when to check-in and review OKRs

>> The mechanism for scoring

>> An overall timeline

>> Resources for those requiring additional assistance

The playbook is typically created by your OKRs champion in conjunction with the executive sponsor, OKRs ambassadors, and representative employees from across the organization. A well-constructed playbook makes it clear to everyone how you're employing OKRs and gives them the tools to optimize their use of the framework.

Don't Go Too Far Too Fast

Rummaging through a drawer recently, I stumbled upon not one but two well-worn Blockbuster Video membership cards dating back to the early 2000s. In its heyday, the video behemoth had more than 9,000 stores. Blockbuster enjoyed a great run for a while, constantly expanding the presence of their brick-and-mortar stores to satisfy the demand for home video viewing, but the company neglected to innovate in the digital space, which ultimately led to its demise at the hands of nimble competitors like Netflix.

Hindsight, as they say, is 20/20, but it's clear now that Blockbuster went too far too fast when it came to opening physical stores, while also casting a blind eye on the innovations taking shape in the space. Likewise, you can venture too far too fast with OKRs, which would take the form of creating OKRs at successively lower levels of the organization in rapid fashion, or even dictating that all employees have OKRs from day one of the implementation. Slow and steady is a more prudent mantra to employ with OKRs.

To gain traction for the system and establish all-important momentum, it's imperative to demonstrate benefits at a high level (most likely the company level), ironing out any kinks in your process before expanding the rollout downward. Employees will be looking suspiciously at this new framework and wondering aloud whether it's worth their time and attention. This skepticism makes showing some initial progress crucial in your attempts to win converts and cement OKRs into the organization's culture. Chapter 5 supplies more information on the timing of an OKRs implementation.

TIP

Wherever you choose to begin, whether at the company-level or by piloting with a business unit or department, go through at least a cycle or two to smooth out the wrinkles before expanding the program further.

Ensure Consistency in How Your Teams Write OKRs

Imagine that you're the CEO of a company that has recently launched OKRs with great hopes for the system to drive focus and alignment. You've reached the end of the first quarter, and it's time for your direct reports to share their OKRs results with you. Say that there are three business units, and these are the objectives for each:

Business unit one: Delight our customers.

Business unit two: Decrease supply chain costs by 25 percent in order to boost profitability.

Business unit three: Increase social media presence to drive brand recognition.

Notice how all three are different in terms of the format used. Business unit one's objective is very simple, but it really isn't an objective at all as defined in the OKRs sense of the word. It's more of a slogan or theme.

Business unit two has written an objective that begins with a verb, makes it clear what they're aiming to do (decrease supply chain costs), and why (boost profitability). However, the objective contains a number, which would better serve as a key result.

Finally, business unit three's objective adheres to the formula of a well-written objective:

Verb + what you're going to do + in order to / so that (desired business impact)

If you're the CEO in this scenario, you'll have to change perspectives for each business unit, adjusting your frame of reference based on the way the objective is written, making it difficult to compare apples to apples. OKRs should foster transparency throughout the organization, and Step 1 in making that happen is sticking to the formulas for writing effective objectives and key results.

REMEMBER

Every OKR should be different, in that it will demonstrate the writer's contribution to overall success. However, they should all be formatted in the same way to ensure consistency in approach and improve transparency. Chapters 8 and 9 provide a deep dive into the writing of objectives and key results.

Don't Set Them and Forget Them

When my wife and I moved to California in the late 1990s, I was immediately struck by the beauty of the landscape and particularly taken with the majesty of the many varieties of palm trees we encountered as we settled into our new surroundings. Desiring to learn more about these graceful wonders, I bought a weighty tome that included lavish illustrations captioned with long Latin words. When the book arrived, I dove in, anxious to learn all I could . . . for about two days. Over time, that weighty text migrated from my bedside table to a shelf in my office, to the office closet, to a box in the garage, before finally being donated to a local second-hand bookstore, which I'm sure immediately affixed a "like new" label on it. Although I had great intentions to learn about palm trees, my attention gradually shifted to other things and before I knew it, those intentions had fallen by the wayside.

Whether it's palm trees or successfully implementing OKRs, life can easily get in the way and quickly derail your efforts. The vortex swirling about a modern business can supply endless distractions with the potential to jeopardize your fledgling OKRs program. From pressing business issues, to operational fires that need extinguishing, to preparing for Board meetings, no shortage of urgent calls to action exists. All these issues and many more can tempt you to cancel a weekly OKRs check-in "just this once," but what do you know, a thousand distractions emerge the following week as well, so the meeting gets pushed out once again. Before you know it, four weeks have gone by, and OKRs are a distant memory.

Especially in the early phases of your rollout, sticking to your OKRs review process is absolutely critical. Depending on your chosen cadence, that process will include weekly check-ins and monthly reviews, all leading to end-of-period retrospectives. In addition to slowly and steadily instilling OKRs into your culture, these get-togethers provide exceptional opportunities to generate support for the system, learn what's working, and determine where you can improve in the days ahead. And hey, if it's a nice day, you can even hold your meeting under the shade of a *Phoenix canariensis*. Check out Chapter 11 to learn more about OKRs review meetings.

Go Beyond the Numbers to Learn from OKRs

In my previous book on OKRs (co-written with Ben Lamorte), we define the OKRs concept this way:

A critical thinking framework and ongoing discipline that seeks to ensure employees work together, focusing their efforts to make measurable contributions that drive the company forward.

The reference to an ongoing discipline highlights the importance of not setting and forgetting OKRs, number eight in this chapter's top ten list of must do items to ensure OKRs success. Ensuring that employees work together reflects the importance of horizontal alignment and fostering collaboration among teams when creating OKRs (discussed in Chapter 10 in this book). The next part of the definition, "focusing their efforts to make measurable contributions," shows that OKRs are designed to help you fix your gaze on what truly matters most in achieving quantitative improvements in performance. Finally, the reference to driving the company forward suggests that all of this is in service to helping the company execute its unique strategy.

Now I'll circle back to the words that begin the definition: "A critical thinking framework." The ultimate goal of OKRs is to accelerate your organization's performance, but you won't achieve that goal by simply reading out the key result scores each period and waiting for the magic to happen. The numbers are a terrific place to start a conversation, but you can't end there. I believe this will be my last reference to Peter Drucker in the book (apologies to my wife, who can't get enough Drucker references). One of my favorite lessons from the OG management guru is this pearl: "The most serious mistakes are not being made as a result of wrong answers. The truly dangerous thing is asking the wrong questions" (from "Stress Test Your Strategy," by Robert Simons, *Harvard Business Review*, 2010).

Breakthroughs are rarely generated from raw numbers. If your Net Promoter Score (NPS) is 70, or your brand recognition score is 52, what do those data points really mean in the grand scheme of things? The epiphanies and revelations you seek come not from the numbers, but a deeper investigation into what the numbers are telling you, and that's where Drucker's admonition about questions comes into play. Your job is to lift the veil on the numbers, going beyond and asking questions that stimulate a deeper level of thinking and analysis. The queries I provide in Chapter 11 are a good place to start on that quest.

Learn and Evolve over Time

My favorite tale of humility in action relates to the English writer John Masefield, who served as Poet Laureate of the United Kingdom from 1930 until his death in 1967. Throughout this period, he composed countless poems commemorating royal events or significant public occurrences, all intended to be published in *The Times* on the respective day. Masefield was a revered poet and was awarded many honors during his lifetime, including the Order of Merit in 1935. But he never took publication for granted. Following his death, *The Times* disclosed that he included a stamped, self-addressed envelope with each manuscript so that it could be returned if it were deemed unacceptable (see *The New Oxford Book of Literary Anecdotes*, 2006, John Gross, ed.). Now that was a humble man!

Humility is a positive trait to be revered, whether exhibited in people or organizations, and should be embraced as you embark on the path of OKRs. At the outset, you "don't know what you don't know," and you're likely to make mistakes, whether by enlisting too many people to create OKRs too soon, not having a consistent method of tracking OKRs, failing to recognize the importance of ambassadors, or in other ways. By adopting an attitude of humility and remaining open to the learning opportunities that arise through actual experience, you're conveying a message to your employees that you value the contribution of OKRs to overall success and are committed to getting the process right.

Get Professional Help If You Need It

By "professional help," I don't mean for you to lay on the couch, tell me about your childhood, and we'll work through your issues at $700 an hour, although you may need just that if your OKRs rollout doesn't go to plan. Professional help in this context refers to an outside consultant who will offer guidance and support for your implementation, without ever once asking to hear about your dreams. At least two scenarios would make extending the call for some help a wise decision for you.

Perhaps you're excited by the prospects of adopting OKRs and drooling over the promised benefits of focus, engagement, and alignment, but have modest experience with formal goal setting, and nobody on your senior team has any meaningful experience with OKRs. This is the time to hit the search bar and look for an experienced consultant. OKRs represent a significant lift, and if the concept, and goal setting in general, are novel to your firm, scoping out an appropriate implementation plan on your own will be difficult. An experienced consultant will be able to assess your situation and craft a plan that includes training, coaching, facilitation, and support to ensure that you get the most from your OKRs investment.

Perhaps your organization has been setting goals for years and you're fortunate enough to have members of your senior team who implemented OKRs at prior companies. Unfortunately, that fact still doesn't guarantee a winning implementation. From nonexistent or poor communication of your reason for having OKRs, to insufficient training, to a scattershot rollout plan, an abundance of issues can set you behind the eight ball. If you've started down the OKRs road but see problems emerging — challenges you can't stem quickly and satisfactorily — once again, the prudent decision would be to find external assistance. This is the OKRs equivalent of a 911 call: having someone dispatched ASAP to get your implementation back on track before you lose momentum and, more important, the support and belief of your employees.

Chapter **16**

Ten Tips for Creating Effective OKRs

Chances are, if you're new to OKRs, a few tips on how to write them well will come in handy. You may struggle with aligning your OKRs to the company's strategy, wrestle with how to make them as specific as possible, or wonder who to involve in the effort. This chapter provides you with ten pointers to improve the OKRs you and your teams write.

Know the Organization's Strategy

At the end of the day, you're implementing OKRs to help execute your strategy. Therefore, it's important that all OKRs created, from top to bottom throughout the organization, align with the strategy, and for that to happen, everyone must first know and understand it. When you have a deep working knowledge of the strategy, you have a much greater likelihood of developing OKRs that are focused, relevant, and measurable.

Because virtually every organization on the planet has some sort of strategic plan, it's a good bet yours does as well. Hopefully that plan has been widely communicated by your senior leadership team, and they have taken the time and effort to share the specifics of it, and why they feel it represents the right direction at the right time.

If you're at all unclear about any aspect of the plan, connect with your boss (or your boss's boss, or the CEO if you can get time on their schedule) to work through it in detail. You need to fully comprehend the decisions in the plan regarding

>> The markets and customers you'll serve

>> The specific value proposition your company brings to the table

>> The desired outcomes of the plan

With that knowledge in hand, you're much better equipped to draft OKRs that demonstrate your team's contribution.

REMEMBER

Aligning your OKRs with the company's strategy can also help increase motivation and engagement, as well as provide a sense of purpose and direction. In essence, OKRs that are linked to the organization's strategy create a powerful synergy between team efforts and the broader goals of the organization, resulting in greater success and impact for everyone involved.

Learn How to Write a Technically Sound OKR

Don't let the phrase "technically sound" scare you off. You're not building bridges or assembling aircraft here, but it is important to write an OKR that adheres to some basic principles in order to get the most from the system. My recommendation, whether you're an OKRs rookie using the framework for the first time, or a seasoned veteran who has been writing OKRs for years, is to draft them using the following formulas:

Objective: Verb + what you want to do + in order to / so that

Metric key result: Verb + what you're going to track/count + from x to y

Milestone key result: Verb + what you're going to do + date

Fortunately, these formulas don't reside at the complexity level of a Black-Scholes or Navier-Stokes. What, you don't know the Navier-Stokes equations? Trust me, they're a bit trickier than creating an OKR, or so I've been told.

The first two components of the objective formula are straightforward: Start with a verb because objectives are action oriented, and then follow that verb with a concise description of what you want to do. It's the final piece that requires some extra attention. The "in order to / so that" component forces you to establish the strategic relevance of the objective; why is it important to do this now? Making that determination will help you choose the most vital objectives in executing your strategy.

For metric key results, the most important thing to keep in mind is to write them from "x to y" whenever possible, where x represents the baseline or starting point and y stands in for your desired target. By crafting the key results this way, the degree of stretch becomes apparent to everyone viewing them.

Make Objectives a CRAFT Project

Does a business problem exist that cannot be swiftly overcome with the help of a clever acronym? I don't think so, and to that end I'm going to offer one with five letters, each representing something important to think about as you go through the objective selection process. Because you're developing/building/creating objectives, I use a related word, *craft*, which is an acronym for Challenges, Resources, Advantages, Fire, and Talk:

>> **Challenges:** A good place to begin when brainstorming what objective, or objectives, you'll choose is to determine what can help you overcome any significant challenges you face in your business, things that are currently or have historically held you back from achieving your bolder ambitions.

>> **Resources:** As you compile a list of potential objectives, think carefully about which ones you have the resources or capacity to achieve right now.

>> **Advantages:** This is the flip side of looking at challenges. Here you consider any possible advantages you could exploit to grow your business, enhance your competitive position, or if you're at the department level, dramatically improve your performance.

>> **Fire:** As in, what lights your fire? What are you most passionate about, and why? Look at any trailblazing, exceptionally successful business and you'll discover that they always have a passion for something that pervades every aspect of their operations. What drives you? You're more likely to remain focused on, and motivated by, an objective that reflects a shared passion.

>> **Talk:** Sometimes the most obvious objectives are hiding in plain sight; they're just so obvious you initially overlook them. To that end, as you're considering objectives be sure to canvass the topics you talk about repeatedly in meetings and town halls.

Be Specific

One summer when I was in my early 20s my friends and I decided to go camping at a campground about two hours from where we lived. My buddy Jim was the only one who had been there before and because this was a couple of decades prior to Google Maps, he gave us each verbal directions on how to get there. The pivotal piece of information was this: Turn at the big barn in Margaree. On the appointed day, I hopped in my car, headed out, and when I got to the designated location in Margaree, what did I find? Barns at every corner of the intersection, and they all looked to be the same size to me! Those being the primitive days of no mobile phones, my only recourse was to try different routes, which I did, and as you can imagine, it was pretty dark when I eventually arrived at the campground. As it turns out, "big" clearly wasn't a specific enough adjective to provide accurate directions.

The stakes were relatively low for my camping trip (being a couple of beers behind my pals when I arrived at the campsite was the only consequence) but with OKRs, the implications of not being specific take on much greater significance. Any words or phrases that can be interpreted differently by different people can lead to misunderstandings and confusion as to what qualifies as success with both the objective and the key results. Words like "quality," "efficient," and "sustainable," for example, are open to interpretation based on an individual's unique perspective and can lead to very different expectations of success.

Make sure to carefully review each word and phrase in an OKR before making it final, checking for any potential ambiguity. It's important that every single word has a clear and consistent meaning, so that everyone who reads the OKR, whether it's one person or a hundred, can understand it the same way. If there is any uncertainty or ambiguity, it's time to reconsider and clarify it further. You can do this by providing additional information, linking to supporting documents, or explicitly stating what you mean in detail.

Always Tell the Story of Success with Key Results

Imagine that I asked you to remember the following seven words: lighthouse, broccoli, guitar, cactus, camera, hammock, and fountain. Wait 30 seconds and try to repeat them. Not easy, is it? But what if I told you a story using these words? Let me try:

As I walked down the beach toward the lighthouse, I spotted a patch of broccoli growing among the sand dunes. A man with a guitar was strumming a tune nearby, and I could see a cactus in a pot on his table. I took out my camera to capture the scene and then decided to take a rest in the nearby hammock. As I closed my eyes, I could hear the sound of water trickling from a nearby fountain.

Now, try to remember the seven words again. You likely found it much easier to recall them now that they were used in a story with context and connections. Key results can also benefit from this story effect. When you write an objective, assuming you used the formula of verb + what you want to do + in order to / so that, you know what the business impact is you're striving for (the *in order to*). So you create a key result to measure that business impact. At that point, you write your story by asking a basic question: "What will have to happen to achieve that business impact?" Your answer to that question helps to illuminate potential key results. You continue asking the question until you've created a set of three to five key results that weave together to tell the story of success for your objective.

Telling the story of key results provides two significant benefits:

>> It challenges you to determine the key results that work together to drive business impact. This helps you create relevant key results that measure the achievement of the objective.

>> It greatly enhances your ability to clearly and crisply communicate your key results to colleagues and other parts of the organization.

Don't Look for Perfect Key Results

On that unexpectedly long drive to the campground I describe in the "Be Specific" section, earlier in this chapter, there's a very good chance the electrifying sounds of Van Halen were pumping through my tinny car speakers, keeping me energized as I traveled the back-country roads. I love Van Halen, and here's a great story about the virtuosic band that, yes, relates to OKRs.

According to Dan Heath and Chip Heath in "The Telltale Brown M & M" (*Fast Company*, March 2010), when Van Halen performed live, their massive amount of equipment required technical expertise to set up. As a result, their standard contract with venues was complex and difficult to navigate (David Lee Roth once compared it to the Chinese Yellow Pages). Within the contract, they included a sneaky provision known as Article 126, which stated that no brown pieces of a certain kind of colorful candies could be in the backstage area or the show would be forfeited. This seemingly strange demand was actually a clever way to ensure that the stagehands at each venue were paying attention and following the contract thoroughly. Roth would check the candy bowl upon arrival, and if he found any brown ones, he knew that the venue personnel probably hadn't carefully read the contract, meaning there could be technical errors that would jeopardize the show. This quick assessment was crucial to ensure the success of the concert, because Roth simply didn't have the time or energy to inspect every socket and cable. In essence, it was a shrewd way for Van Halen to prioritize attention to detail and ensure that their performances were always top notch.

Would you consider "Number of brown pieces of candy" to be a complicated, sophisticated, or perfect key result? Not by any stretch of the imagination, but it was an easy metric that Roth could track to determine whether bigger problems may be lurking that could mar the performance. The number of brown candies was a simple yet powerful leading indicator, and many times, that's all you need when creating your own key results. Excuse the cliché here, but if you're struggling to compose a key result, don't let the perfect be the enemy of the good. Look for something simple that you can track with ease — an item that you believe leads or drives the bigger-picture impact you're striving for in the objective.

Balance the Equation

My high school math teachers would get a hearty chuckle out of me invoking a mathematical title to this section, given my less-than-stellar performance in their classes all those years ago. "Balancing the equation" in this context simply means measuring the entire objective with a set of key results in order to tell the full and complete story of success. Following is an example from a direct sales company:

Objective: Equip our field consultants with improved "getting started" training in order to improve their selling performance.

Key Results:

1. Decrease the number of days for first sale from 28 to 20.

2. Increase average consultant sales from 50K to 75K.

The good news here is that the two key results do an excellent job measuring the business impact of improving sales performance. The problem is that what drives sales performance — in this case, equipping the consultants with improved getting started training — has been completely ignored. Without those leading key results, it will be very difficult to take action during the period in an effort to positively influence the business impact. An improved set of key results, which measure the entire objective and therefore "balance the equation," would be the following:

1. Create an executive-endorsed, improved "getting started" training curriculum by July 15.

2. Increase percentage of field consultants completing the training from 60 percent to 100 percent.

3. Decrease the number of days for first sale from 28 to 20.

4. Increase average consultant sales from 50K to 75K.

Now the entire story of success is being documented in the OKR.

Align Vertically and Horizontally

The strongest OKRs are those that align both vertically and horizontally. Vertical alignment, as the name implies, denotes consistency with OKRs that appear "above" those you're creating, and is also known as strategic alignment because you're demonstrating your contribution to higher-level OKRs. In practice, this means that when creating an OKR, you should first look to the company's OKRs, and any OKRs in place for groups north of you in the corporate hierarchy —a business unit OKR, for example.

Your challenge at that point is to create an OKR that distinctly signifies your role in achieving the higher-level OKR. The OKRs you create should be specific to your work, challenges, and opportunities, but whenever possible they should be consistent and align with the higher-level OKRs. An important caveat, however, is that not every OKR you create must show a direct line of sight to a higher-level OKRs. You may face a specific set of circumstances that dictate the creation of an OKR that is specifically centered on your particular situation. What's most important in that case is clearly defending your choice when sharing the OKR with superiors.

TIP

Horizontal alignment comes alive through the process of identifying and managing dependencies. When you create OKRs, it's important to detail whose assistance you need from outside your team to achieve them.

You'll then want to meet with that team (or teams) to discuss your requirements and assess their commitment to assisting you. Should they be on board to work with you, a shared OKR will result. If, they can't provide the help you need, you escalate the situation to leaders who must prioritize and make final judgments on the OKRs. Escalation may appear difficult from a cultural perspective, but when performed objectively, it provides clarity and transparency to all involved.

Make It a Collaborative Effort

I don't consider myself a macho tough-guy sort, but I've sometimes temporarily assumed a version of that persona, especially in front of my wife. A prime example is when moving furniture, say a bulky armchair. She'll say, "Let me help you with that," to which I scoff and reply, "I can do it myself!" Up goes the chair, and the next thing you know I'm Googling chiropractors and buying the drug store out of pain patches.

Many things in life, hoisting furniture and OKRs included, are best done with the aid of other people. If you're a leader and your team is drafting OKRs for the first time, you could take the reins and craft them yourself, but by doing so, you miss out on a number of valuable benefits that derive from involving your team, including these:

>> **Diverse perspectives:** Drawing the entire team into the conversation allows you to tap a broad range of perspectives and ideas, ensuring that the OKRs you write represent different viewpoints and ultimately reflect the best the whole team has to offer.

>> **Alignment:** When creating OKRs as a team, you can get everyone aligned with what you're ultimately trying to achieve and know that each member understands their unique role in driving success. Accountability and ownership are natural and productive offshoots.

>> **Buy-in and support:** Chapter 1, page 1 of any change text will tell you that people are more likely to support something they help create. And speaking of furniture, have you heard of the IKEA effect? It clearly demonstrates that people place a disproportionately high value on products they partially created (he types as he gazes fondly at the IKEA hektogram floor uplighter he put together).

So the next time my wife offers to help me move a piece of furniture, I hope I gladly accept her assistance. And when it comes to crafting OKRs, you should always remember the importance of working with others. By involving your team, you not only create better OKRs but also build a stronger team to rally around their achievement.

Focus on What Really Matters

OKRs have the power to drive alignment, enhance engagement, and offer a host of other benefits, but at the end of the day, perhaps the core purpose of the model is to help your organization execute its unique strategy. To fulfill that purpose, the OKRs created throughout the organization must reflect what truly matters most to each and every team holding a place on the organizational chart.

It's relatively easy to draft a set of OKRs that simply rewrite the team's reason for being — the collective responsibilities embodied by the people that make up the group. But those are just table stakes, meaning the ante required to simply play the great game of business. If you're comfortable with the status quo, maybe languishing behind competitors or recognizing that you're not drawing out anything close to your employees' potential talent, then by all means write OKRs that reflect that status quo. But don't expect positive change or growth to occur anytime soon, or any time at all for that matter.

REMEMBER

To execute effectively, you must move beyond the core functions of your team and isolate the actions — likely the new, innovative, and experimental ones — that will move the needle on execution. Sure, it's hard work, but finding those things and representing them in the form of strategic OKRs is where the magic really happens and the fun begins.

Index

A

The ABCs of OKRs (e-book), 117
accountability, 32
acronyms, 158
administrative assistants, 39–40
ADP, 249
advantages, in CRAFT project, 295
Alexander II, 213
alignment of OKRs
  benefits, 27–28
  connecting *vs.* cascading, 192–194
  horizontal alignment, 194–196, 299–300
  meeting phases and activities, 197
  overview, 189–190
  vertical alignment, 190–192, 299–300
Amabile, Teresa, 194
Amazon, 94
ambassadors
  as coach on OKRs creation and review, 64
  distinguishing between business-as-usual work and OKRs, 64
  as internal expert and system evangelist, 62
  as liaison with other ambassadors and the champion, 64
  maximizing OKRs success with other ambassadors, 66
  meetings, 58
  OKRs success and, 285
  overview, 60
  as point of contact for OKR-related issues, 63
  profile of, 64–65
  roles of, 61–64
American Icon (Hoffman), 225
annual cadence, 82–83
annual objectives, 138–140
Armstrong, Neil, 97
artificial intelligence, 143–144
The Art of War (Pressfield), 268

aspirational OKR, 200–201
assumptions, in this book, 3
autonomy, 134
Averre, Berton, 177
Azure Dev Ops, 249

B

Babes in Arms (Broadway production), 67
Bailey, George (fictional character), 92
Balanced Scorecard (BSC), 17–18, 275
benefits of OKRs
  accountability and, 32
  DECK acronym, 34
  dependencies, identifying and managing, 29–30
  ease of use, 33–34
  employee engagement, 30–31
  focusing on what matters most, 26–27
  organizational challenges, overcoming, 20–25
  overview, 19
  to people in your organization, 26–34
  silos and, 29
  vertical and horizontal alignment, 27–28
  visionary thinking, 32–33
The Beverly Hillbillies (TV show), 227
Beyond Performance 2.0 (Keller and Schaninger), 41, 51, 113
Bismarck, Otto von, 213
Blockbuster, 287
Bock, Laszlo, 93
book, about, 2–3
bootlegged OKRs, 77
Bossidy, Larry, 20
brainstorming, 101–102
Brenn, Erich, 37
Brin, Sergey, 11
Brooks, Alison Wood, 152
BSC (Balanced Scorecard), 17–18

software *(continued)*
  security concerns in, 246
  selecting, 247–252
  team OKRs capability, 248–249
Sony Corporation, 94
spiritual goals, 8
sponsors
  belief in OKRs, 50
  defining success, 50
  determining playbook with champion and executive team, 51
  educating executives, 54
  as final escalation point for OKRs issues, 51–52
  funding approval, 50–51
  gaining, 53–55
  knowledge of OKRs, 50
  linking OKRs to challenges, 54
  OKRs success and, 285
  piloting OKRs in own unit, 54
  for pilot programs, 78
  responsibilities, 49–54
  sponsorship in action, 52–53
  training inclusion, 119–120
  use of OKRs at senior leadership level, 50
status, 216
Stewart, Jimmy, 92
Stillness Is the Key (Holiday), 26
Stolen Focus (Hari), 117
strategy. *See also* mission(s); vision
  acknowledging difficulty of executing, 20–23
  creating effective OKRs and, 293–294
  customers and, 105, 107–108
  definition, 90, 103
  execution failure, causes of, 21–22
  getting started with, 104–105
  importance to OKRs success, 103–104
  measuring elements of, 22–23
  OKR shortcuts and, 209
  OKRs success and, 258
  overview, 89, 102–103
  products or services to sell, 105, 107
  subquestions, 106–108
  value proposition, 105, 108
Strategy That Works (Leinward and Mainardi), 21

stretch OKRs, 78, 87, 280–281
stretch targets, 179–181, 242–243
Succeed (Halvorson), 214
success factors
  consistency in writing OKRs, 288–289
  getting professional help, 291–292
  going beyond the numbers, 290–291
  having sponsor, champion, and ambassadors, 284–285
  knowing reasons for implementing OKRs, 284
  learning and evolving over time, 291
  not going too far and too fast, 287–288
  overview, 283
  playbook, creating, 286–287
  review meetings, 289–290
  training, 285–286
Success Factors (performance management tool), 249
success of OKRs
  celebrating, 256–257
  consultants and, 261–262
  enthusiasm and momentum building in, 256
  evaluating OKRs program, 266–267
  expert credibility and, 260
  fast-tracking, 260
  knowing how OKRs fit, 257–259
  laying foundation for, 253–262
  maximizing, 262–269
  mission and, 258
  organizational culture and, 257
  overview, 253–254
  refining OKRs process, 267–268
  resources, 264–265
  strategy and, 258
  supportive messaging, 264–265
  ten "musts" for, 283–292
  training for, 263–264
  using the system, 268–269
  value and, 256
  viewing OKRs as a journey, 255–256
  vision and, 258
support groups
  definition, 80
  OKRs for, 80–81
supportive messaging, 264–265
Surowiecki, James, 153

About the Author

Paul R. Niven is a management consultant, author, and noted speaker on the subjects of Strategy, Strategy Execution, Objectives and Key Results (OKRs), and Balanced Scorecard. As the founder of OKRsTraining.com, he has developed successful strategy execution systems for clients large and small in a wide variety of organizations, including Fortune 1000 companies, public sector, and nonprofit agencies. Since 2001, the company has assisted more than 500 organizations around across the globe to effectively execute their strategy. A small sample of clients includes Mercedes-Benz, Humana, Walmart Canada, and The Michael J. Fox Foundation.

Paul is the author of six previous books on strategy and strategy execution, which have been translated into more than 15 languages around the world.

Dedication

To my wife Lois for her unwavering support and encouragement in my writing adventures.

Author's Acknowledgments

This book was written to serve as a comprehensive and easily accessible guide for organizations venturing into, or currently navigating, an OKRs implementation. My role as author was to offer actionable and, as important, credible advice to assist readers on their path to success. If I succeeded in that task, it's primarily due to the invaluable experience I've gained from engaging with hundreds of organizations over the past two-plus decades as a consultant. I extend my sincere gratitude to each and every one of these organizations for their trust, generosity, and commitment to improvement through better strategy execution using OKRs. I'd also like to extend a special thank you to my colleagues at OKRsTraining.com, Kevin Baum and Zack Ross, for their many valuable contributions, both to our firm's success and the field of OKRs. Finally, my sincere thanks to Susan Christophersen, Tracy Boggier, Vicki Adang, and the entire Dummies team for skillfully guiding me through the very specific requirements of writing a *For Dummies* book.

Publisher's Acknowledgments

Senior Acquisitions Editor: Tracy Boggier

Senior Managing Editor: Kristie Pyles

Project Manager and Copy Editor:
Susan Christophersen

Technical Editor: Zachary Ross

Production Editor: Pradesh Kumar

Cover Image: © jamesteohart/Shutterstock

Leverage the power

Dummies is the global leader in the reference category and one of the most trusted and highly regarded brands in the world. No longer just focused on books, customers now have access to the dummies content they need in the format they want. Together we'll craft a solution that engages your customers, stands out from the competition, and helps you meet your goals.

Advertising & Sponsorships

Connect with an engaged audience on a powerful multimedia site, and position your message alongside expert how-to content. Dummies.com is a one-stop shop for free, online information and know-how curated by a team of experts.

- Targeted ads
- Video
- Email Marketing
- Microsites
- Sweepstakes sponsorship

20 MILLION PAGE VIEWS EVERY SINGLE MONTH

15 MILLION UNIQUE VISITORS PER MONTH

43% OF ALL VISITORS ACCESS THE SITE VIA THEIR MOBILE DEVICES

700,000 NEWSLETTER SUBSCRIPTIONS TO THE INBOXES OF *300,000* UNIQUE INDIVIDUALS EVERY WEEK

# of dummies

Custom Publishing

Reach a global audience in any language by creating a solution that will differentiate you from competitors, amplify your message, and encourage customers to make a buying decision.

- Apps
- Books
- eBooks
- Video
- Audio
- Webinars

Brand Licensing & Content

Leverage the strength of the world's most popular reference brand to reach new audiences and channels of distribution.

For more information, visit dummies.com/biz

PERSONAL ENRICHMENT

Staying Sharp dummies

9781119187790
USA $26.00
CAN $31.99
UK £19.99

Facebook dummies

9781119179030
USA $21.99
CAN $25.99
UK £16.99

Guitar dummies

9781119293354
USA $24.99
CAN $29.99
UK £17.99

Investing dummies

9781119293347
USA $22.99
CAN $27.99
UK £16.99

Beekeeping dummies

9781119310068
USA $22.99
CAN $27.99
UK £16.99

Digital Photography dummies

9781119235606
USA $24.99
CAN $29.99
UK £17.99

Meditation dummies

9781119251163
USA $24.99
CAN $29.99
UK £17.99

Pregnancy ALL-IN-ONE dummies

9781119235491
USA $26.99
CAN $31.99
UK £19.99

Samsung Galaxy S7 dummies

9781119279952
USA $24.99
CAN $29.99
UK £17.99

iPhone dummies

9781119283133
USA $24.99
CAN $29.99
UK £17.99

Crocheting dummies

9781119287117
USA $24.99
CAN $29.99
UK £16.99

Nutrition dummies

9781119130246
USA $22.99
CAN $27.99
UK £16.99

PROFESSIONAL DEVELOPMENT

Windows 10 dummies

9781119311041
USA $24.99
CAN $29.99
UK £17.99

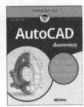

AutoCAD dummies

9781119255796
USA $39.99
CAN $47.99
UK £27.99

Excel 2016 dummies

9781119293439
USA $26.99
CAN $31.99
UK £19.99

QuickBooks 2017 dummies

9781119281467
USA $26.99
CAN $31.99
UK £19.99

macOS Sierra dummies

9781119280651
USA $29.99
CAN $35.99
UK £21.99

LinkedIn dummies

9781119251132
USA $24.99
CAN $29.99
UK £17.99

Windows 10 ALL-IN-ONE dummies

9781119310563
USA $34.00
CAN $41.99
UK £24.99

SharePoint 2016 dummies

9781119181705
USA $29.99
CAN $35.99
UK £21.99

Fundamental Analysis dummies

9781119263593
USA $26.99
CAN $31.99
UK £19.99

Networking dummies

9781119257769
USA $29.99
CAN $35.99
UK £21.99

Office 2016 dummies

9781119293477
USA $26.99
CAN $31.99
UK £19.99

Office 365 dummies

9781119265313
USA $24.99
CAN $29.99
UK £17.99

Salesforce.com dummies

9781119239314
USA $29.99
CAN $35.99
UK £21.99

Coding dummies

9781119293323
USA $29.99
CAN $35.99
UK £21.99